Beyond the Cornucopia Kids

A DIRECTION DYNAMICS BOOK

BEYOND THE CORNUCOPIA KIDS

Bruce A. Baldwin, Ph.D.

DIRECTION DYNAMICS
Wilmington, NC
1988

Cover Design: Kaye Davis, Greensboro, NC

Printed by Carter Printing Company, Richmond, VA

Library of Congress Catalog Card Number: 88-070117

ISBN 0-933583-07-9

Published and distributed by: DIRECTION DYNAMICS
                               309 Honeycutt Drive
                               Wilmington, NC 28412

Bulk order discounts on DIRECTION DYNAMICS books are available when ordered in quantities of six or more. Please contact DIRECTION DYNAMICS for details.

Manufactured in the United States of America

DEDICATION

To Joyce's parents and mine for the healthy values we learned from them. To Travis and Elissa, our children, who will receive the same from us.

ACKNOWLEDGEMENTS

It is most difficult to write any book, much less a book on parenting, without the time, patience, and expertise of others. First, I will always be indebted to the Editors and staff of Piedmont Airlines' superb inflight magazine PACE in which much of the material in this book has appeared. To Mary Kay Dodson, a great big thank you for editorial services that pinpointed all those "invisible" manuscript errors. Kaye Davis is certainly appreciated for her ability to bring a cover design from concept to hard-hitting reality. The staff of Carter Printing Company also deserves many thanks for their endless patience in working out the large and small details of publication. Perhaps most deeply felt of all, I want to acknowledge Joyce, my wife, for her true partnership in working on this book with me. It simply would not have been possible without her encouragement, insights, and plain hard work. Finally, the true heroes of this book must be recognized. They are the many parents who have shared their hopes and their fears and their frustrations attempting to raise healthy achieving children in the midst of the sometimes confusing and often superficial social environment in which we all must live.

CONTENTS

Introduction

Known Basics, New Realities, and You!

Recently, in an adult Sunday School class, there was a most animated discussion. In fact, there hadn't been so many opinions expressed so openly for months. Class members, for the most part parents, had been talking about the pressures that had evolved from contemporary lifestyles. With a deep faith within, virtually all of these men and women agreed that there was in fact life after death. However, the issue that provoked intense discussion was whether there was *life after birth!* And, of course, they were talking about the birth of their children.

These men and women were, in fact, acknowledging not only the good times, but also the many stresses and strains that good parenting these days brings to families. Along with life in general, effective parenting is becoming more complex in a rapidly changing world. On the other hand, these parents were also well aware that the liabilities of not parenting well are also increasing. This book, BEYOND THE CORNUCOPIA KIDS: HOW TO RAISE HEALTHY ACHIEVING CHILDREN, had its origins in these kinds of concerns.

During years of conducting seminars on lifestyle issues across the country, geared to involved parents and achieving men and women, I was afforded a wonderful opportunity to talk informally with parents about their hopes and feelings and fears. Two areas of concern were consistently mentioned by these men and women, most of whom were attempting to balance the demands of raising families with busy careers. The first was the intense daily pressure they were experiencing. They lamented the increasing responsibilities at work, the requirements of maintaining a home, and the time needed for involvement in community affairs, while at the same time trying to remain caring parents and loving spouses.

The second major issue expressed by these men and women was an apprehension about their children's ability to "make it" in the real world. Almost across the board, these mainstream middle-class American parents shared three qualities.

1. THEY WERE COMMITTED TO DOING THEIR BEST. That is, these parents had a value system that emphasized personal responsibility and doing well in every part of their lives, including being good parents. Their well-developed work ethic was obvious from what they had accomplished in life. They lived in reasonably nice homes in reasonably nice neighborhoods. They had stable incomes and successful careers. Although not rich by any means, these parents worked hard and were certainly "making it."

2. THEY WERE CONCERNED ABOUT THEIR CHILDREN. To a one, these parents wanted to do the very best they could for their children to help them "make it" as they themselves did. However, in spite of this commitment to help, they began to doubt that the kids were learning the values and the skills necessary for personal maturity and career success. These parents knew what the score was and what the expectations of the marketplace were. And, they wanted their children to be achievers just like they were. But they didn't see it happening.

3. THEY WERE CONFUSED ABOUT WHAT WAS CAUSING THE PROBLEM. These parents were providing for their children in the best way they knew how. The kids lived in a nice home, attended good schools, were given plenty of spending money, and had many of the extras in life that just weren't available when their parents were growing up. The problem was that with all this giving, the kids just seemed to want more. And, they didn't seem to appreciate what they did have. The kids just weren't exhibiting the kinds of behaviors that inspired confidence in parents that their children were going to succeed.

To be more specific, these parents' complaints about their children's growth toward maturity focused on three fundamentals that just didn't seem to be developing. Further, these parental concerns were in areas that were absolutely critical to success in a career, in good relationships, and in competent adulthood.

COMPLAINT #1: "OUR KIDS' VALUES SEEM VERY SHALLOW AND SELF-SERVING." These children, many of them reaching biological adulthood, seemed to be interested only in pleasure-seeking activities. And, their behavior was often completely irresponsible. They demanded all the "right things" to keep up with their friends or what was "in" at the time, but they weren't willing to put forth much personal effort to earn them. Parents' perceptions were that the kids' life values were remaining immature and quite shallow. They were right.

COMPLAINT #2: "WE DON'T SEE OUR CHILDREN MOTIVATED TO BECOME SELF-SUFFICIENT." The kids didn't seem to share the same achievement motivation that characterized their parents. Their laid-back, present-oriented attitude reflected a basically uncaring attitude about the future. They just didn't seem to have what it takes to meet difficult challenges successfully. Nor did they possess the willingness to sacrifice to attain long-term personal goals. They wanted it all right now and without effort.

COMPLAINT #3: "WE DON'T SEE THE CHILDREN DEVELOP-ING A SENSE OF RESPONSIBILITY AS THEY SHOULD." This deficit was most noticeable in terms of basic work habits and personal accountability. Many of the children were highly manipulative and consistently put great energy into evading their commitments at school and at home. Parents expressed extreme levels of frustration resulting from the need to always "hound" their children into accepting even minimal responsibility for the consequences of their actions.

From these frequently expressed parental concerns evolved the concept of the Cornucopia Kids. By and large, the vast majority of these children were raised in good homes with interested parents. *However, during the course of their development, their experiences at home were antithetical to what is required to develop emotional maturity, achievement motivation, and personal accountability.* The source of this problem, now endemic in this country, lies in the quality of the family environment created by well-intentioned, but misguided parents who attempt to give their children a competitive edge by providing them with every material advantage.

These parents were missing a very significant reality. They failed to examine the quality of life at home from the perspective of a child. The fact is that children raised in these kinds of indulgent home environments were developing a value system and a way of relating to the world at large that directly reflected their personal experiences in the family. Defined, a Cornucopia Kid is *"a child who develops an expectation, based on years of experience in the home, that the good life will always be available for the asking and without the need to develop personal accountability or achievement motivation."* And, of course, it is parents who are expected to continue providing the good life indefinitely as they have been doing all along!

In May, 1985, these initial ideas about Cornucopia Kids were discussed in an article published in PACE, the inflight magazine of Piedmont Airlines. Its title was simple and direct: "The Cornucopia Kids: Giving Children Too Much May Be Giving Too Little." The results of that article stirred a virtual firestorm of public interest. Across the length and breadth of the country, it seemed to touch a nerve in parents and educators concerned with child development. Requests to reprint the article came continually (and still do) as did telephone calls asking for more information. Feedback indicated that the article helped parents to define more clearly how to raise healthy achieving children. These parents intuitively knew that something was happening at home that was not good for their children, but they had been unable to clearly conceptualize the problem before reading the article.

The theme of the article is quite basic. The bottom line is that giving too much too easily to children does not provide them with an advantage. In fact, the net effect of too much giving is to short-circuit what parents want to see develop in their children. In a nutshell, giving too much materially to children actually blocks the development of achievement motivation, personal responsibility, and emotional maturity. These are exactly the same things that parents had been complaining about most vociferously!

From this wellspring of interest from concerned parents and educators, this book evolved. It is an expanded and more detailed account of the family environment and parental behavior that promotes healthy achievement motivation, emotional maturity, and personal responsibility in children. Its purpose is to systematically examine the issues and to provide helpful strategies to parents as they seek to give their children more of what they really need to grow toward competent adulthood rather than lavishing them materially. As a starting point for you to understand this growing problem, three myths about Cornucopia Kids must be removed immediately.

MYTH #1: RAISING CORNUCOPIA KIDS IS ONLY A PROBLEM OF THE VERY RICH. The fact is that the great majority of Cornucopia Kids these days are raised in solidly middle-class homes. In addition, this destructive parenting pattern of giving too much is also commonly found in households struggling to make ends meet financially. Further, vulnerability to raising Cornucopia Kids also seems quite independent of the educational level of parents.

MYTH #2: CORNUCOPIA KIDS ARE ONLY FOUND IN SUB-URBIA. While these children are frequently found in suburbs and bedroom communities, this phenomenon is by no means confined to these areas. Cornucopia Kids these days are found from the smallest of rural villages to the largest cities and in every size community in between. Increased mobility, vastly improved communications, and the homogenization of American culture have all aided in the spread of this now rapidly growing social problem.

MYTH #3: CONTEMPORARY SOCIETY IS TO BLAME FOR ALL THE CORNUCOPIA KIDS AROUND. The unspoken corollary of this myth is that parents cannot do anything about this problem. Superficially, this myth may seem valid, but it is not. There is no question that a myriad of shallow and materialistic social values do abound these days. And, they are picked up by the kids through school and television and seeing what friends possess. However, make no mistake about it. It is entirely possible these days for economically successful parents to create a home environment that *prevents* the development of Cornucopia Kids! That's the point of this book.

About This Book

For those parents about to read this book, a few points of clarification about its structure are in order. Some readers may start with page one and read from beginning to end. Others may focus only on specific chapters that relate to parenting issues of concern at a particular time. Still others will use it as a basic reference book on positive parenting to refer to from time to time. While each chapter is more or less self-contained, a number of themes tie together all the ideas presented in the book. As you read, keep these five objectives in mind. Together, they define the goals of this book.

READING OBJECTIVE #1: TO INTEGRATE AN UNDERSTANDING OF CURRENT SOCIAL REALITIES WITH BASIC PARENTING SKILLS TO BETTER MEET THE NEEDS OF CHILDREN. These days, parents' lifestyles have become immensely more complex and pressured than ever before. And, children are exposed to more outside influences than in the past. One result is that parents find themselves confused because old guidelines for parenting seem to have disappeared. However, the fact is that what children need to grow up to be healthy achievers and emotionally mature adults has *not* changed. The major objective of this book is to help parents understand the sociocultural environment in which their children are growing and at the same time to apply enduring and unchanging parenting skills effectively within that environment.

READING OBJECTIVE #2: TO HELP PARENTS UNDERSTAND THEMSELVES AND NOURISH THEIR OWN RELATIONSHIP WHILE THEY ARE RAISING CHILDREN. There can be little doubt that the parenting years are some of the most hectic and pressure-packed of the entire lifespan. And, childhood experiences, dormant for many years, often resurface to create problems in raising children when that individual becomes a parent. All of these pressures can put unbearable strains on the key relationship in a family, the marriage. Another important objective of this book is to provide a context for parents to better understand themselves and how their parents affected them. Then they can do what is required to maintain an emotionally healthy and growing relationship with one another. And, while remaining close to one another, they can consistently work together toward better parenting by overcoming negative influences from the past.

READING OBJECTIVE #3: TO HELP PARENTS DEVELOP SPE-CIFIC, EFFECTIVE STRATEGIES FOR POSITIVE PARENTING. If the problems of too much giving (and giving in) to children are understood by parents, then specific guidelines to help them become more effective in raising healthy achieving children are required. To meet this need, another major objective of this book lies in providing concepts and ideas that help parents do what is right for their children, not what is easy. It is extremely important for parents first to see beyond the superficial social values that are rampant these days and then to parent in ways that transform this deeper understanding into actual practice.

READING OBJECTIVE #4: TO CREATE AN AWARENESS OF AN INTEGRATED WHOLE. Those reading this book will notice similar concepts being discussed in different contexts in different chapters. There are several reasons for this. First, many of the suggestions serve several positive parenting purposes. For example, in several chapters parents are strongly encouraged to limit television viewing time for children. Following this guideline impacts on children in several ways: 1) it provides more quality time for the family to be together, 2) it fosters creativity and trial-and-error learning, and 3) it reduces dependence on external stimulation to occupy time. The overall goal of this kind of repetition is to emphasize the multiple impacts of specific parenting guidelines and by so doing to create in the reader a Gestalt: that is, an overall sense of effective parenting bound together by reasonable internal consistency of its constituent parts.

READING OBJECTIVE #5: TO MAKE THE USE OF COMMON SENSE A HIGH PRIORITY FOR PARENTS. A basic reality is that no book on raising children, including this one, can provide parents with all the answers. Nor should any one book. The emphasis in any good self-help book is to aid in clarifying issues and then to provide useful guidelines for change. However, *it is then up to parents to use their own good common sense in applying new understandings to present circumstances.* With this in mind, the intent of this book is not to provide cut-and-dried answers. Further, it is *not* the objective of this book to convince parents of the rightness of every concept contained herein. Rather, it is to provide a backdrop of clearly stated ideas that will enable men and women to more clearly define *themselves* as parents and then to use common sense and their own defined values to more effectively guide their children toward competent and responsible adulthood.

A Vignette Before Beginning

It's true that parenting a child to adulthood is at once one of the most important tasks of parents and one for which there is virtually no advance preparation. You learn as you go, and there is no doubt that parenting is a challenge. It is often stressful and is, not infrequently, quite frustrating. For parents in the midst of the hectic parenting years, it is sometimes difficult to accept that the ultimate rewards of all your efforts may not come until your children have become adults themselves, but in the end it is well worth it to see your child take his or her place in the world as a responsible and competent adult. But, it doesn't happen automatically. And, it doesn't have to happen at all unless you understand the issues and translate personal resolve into effective parenting. A short but true story about one Cornucopia Kid underscores this point.

Two parents on a vacation flight had come across the original article on the Cornucopia Kids and had kept it. After reading it thoroughly, they realized they were well on their way to creating Cornucopia Kids in their home through indiscriminate giving. Frustrated by the immature behavior of their adolescent son in particular, they handed him their copy of the article. "Read this," they said, "and then tell us what you think!" He left and returned shortly. His parents asked him for his reaction. "Mom, Dad, I agree with everything it says," he replied, "but it's *your* problem, not mine!"

No one will ever know whether this answer was sincerely thought out or whether it was the kind of flip response that adolescents are so prone to give to their parents these days. Regardless of the intent, this young man's answer was absolutely correct. It *was* his parents' problem. And, so it could easily be for you. But, helping your children to become healthy achievers instead of Cornucopia Kids is entirely possible; however, you've got to know how to do it. Doing it right and doing it well is what BEYOND THE CORNUCOPIA KIDS is all about.

Chapter 1

The Cornucopia Kids: Giving Children Too Much May Be Giving Too Little

Listening in on households in suburbs all across America, solid middle-class parents are talking. They are frustrated, and the focus of their distress is their children. Their concerned remarks are telling.

"Those kids have everything. I don't understand why their grades are so poor."

"Johnny's work habits are atrocious. We give him every advantage, and he still goofs up."

"Jane did it again! She just isn't responsible and doesn't seem to care about anything."

"It seems that the more we give the kids, the more they want. And, they don't appreciate what they do have."

"I've tried and tried to get Andy to do some work around the yard. I'll even pay him. He isn't interested."

Heading each of these homes are hardworking parents who have finally achieved a comfortable standard of living. They are achievers. They are accountants, engineers, businessmen and women, managers, and teachers. Their work is stable, their salaries are adequate, and they are involved in their communities. To a one, they want to be the best parents possible. They understand the rules of the success game, and they want to see their children "make it" as they did. But, they are also fearful because they don't see a strong work ethic emerging in their children. The kids just want to spend all their time having a good time. When with passing years, the children don't seem to grow beyond this immature orientation, the parents become more worried. These concerned parents are not sure what is wrong. And, they're not sure what to do.

Although not rich by any means, these families are successful by middle-class standards. Their rising incomes even leave some discretionary money for the "good things in life." Their homes are filled with electronic marvels: home computers, video games, stereos, VCR's. There are recreational "toys" for everyone, including Mom and Dad. With the help of parental largesse, children eagerly keep up with the latest fads. On the surface, it seems that all is well in mainstream middle-class America. It is not. Beneath the veneer of affluence, there is a serious problem: healthy work habits in the children are being steadily weakened. Without realizing it, well-meaning parents are helping their children become Cornucopia Kids.

The cornucopia is the mythical horn of plenty always full to overflowing, the traditional symbol of a good harvest, a fitting sign of the good life these families are living. In children raised in this most comfortable environment, a serious liability is emerging that, unfortunately, is becoming ever more common. These are the Cornucopia Kids. Basically, a Cornucopia Kid is "a child who grows up with the expectation, based on years of direct experience in the home, that the good life will always be available for the asking without the need to develop personal accountability or achievement motivation."

In a nutshell, such children grow up with unrealistic expectations of the world of work they will have to face on their own later in life. Little experience in the home leads to learning the direct relationship between effort and reward. Aided and abetted by unknowing parental conspirators, the work ethic in these children is slow to germinate and sometimes does not blossom at all. It is certainly not suggested that parents apologize for their hard-won affluence. This lifestyle is the reward for years of dedicated effort and self-sacrifice. Yet, in subtle ways, the parents' material well-being can be extremely detrimental to the children's maturation into emotionally healthy and responsible adults.

Under the guise of being "advantaged," Cornucopia Kids lead lives of easy leisure. Well-meaning parents provide them with plenty of "things" to occupy them. What is less obvious is that with this parental philosophy, the children do not emotionally mature. Values and skills necessary for success in life are not learned. In fact, parents these days, to help their children grow up to be healthy achievers, must systematically address three rapidly growing areas of social and family concern.

CORNUCOPIA CONCERN #1: THE DEVELOPMENT OF A

"SPLIT-ETHIC" FAMILY. It's a given that most parents who have made it to middle-class comfort are achievers. They know the rules of the marketplace and have the skills that reflect achievement motivation. Then, with a pattern of materialistic indulgence in the home, these same parents raise children who are underachievers! This "split-ethic," seen in so many families these days, is cause for great disappointment by parents.

CORNUCOPIA CONCERN #2: CREATING AN "UNREAL" WORLD FOR THE KIDS. These days, it is entirely possible for parents to create a home environment for the kids that is far removed from the real world. Children who grow up in such family environments, the Cornucopia Cocoon, must then face harsh realities when they leave home "cold turkey." In fact, the artificial home environment may be so far removed from the expectations of the marketplace and the requirements for mature adult functioning that "culture shock" is a mild term for the kids' rude awakening when they must face it.

CONCERN #3: THE INCREASING NEED FOR "CHARACTER STRENGTH" IN PARENTS. As little as one generation ago, middle-class parents simply did not have as much to give to their children. Then, the kids knew they weren't going to get much unless they earned it because it wasn't there to give. Now, with more affluence and more goods available to buy, the question for parents is tougher by far: "If you have it to give, and the kids know it, are you strong enough *not* to give materially except under conditions that foster personal maturity and accountability?" Sadly, for too many parents, the answer is no.

It is entirely possible to both remain an affluent, achieving parent and avoid raising Cornucopia Kids, but it takes a little know-how. To do so requires rediscovering some basic values that are often forgotten amidst the good life as it is lived in most middle-class communities. It may also require that you be a bit different than your neighbors up and down the street. However, the payoff is that your children will learn some basic values that will help them follow you to success instead of remaining immature, marginal achievers.

The Indulged Child

Children certainly do not "catch" this problem accidentally, nor are they born with it. Instead, patterns of unhealthy parental giving directly teach unhealthy attitudes about life and living that become progressively dysfunctional with age. For good reasons and bad, parents continue to give excessively, and the resulting inappropriate expectations of the children are affirmed again and again. Paradoxically, the parents' *words* may reflect their strong work ethic. However, the words are hollow because they are so inconsistent with the broad pattern of parental indulgence. Even to a child, when there is inconsistency between words and behavior, the behavior is perceived as reality.

Here are listed a number of highly questionable parental behaviors that help create Cornucopia Kids. Use them as a way to examine your responses to your children. You may find that you are giving (and giving in) too much.

_____ 1. Your child's room is filled virtually to overflowing with toys and other fun things because you know neighbors' children have the same.

_____ 2. You consistently give in to your child's demands for more things after only token resistance.

_____ 3. Your child starts many new projects or hobbies, but then loses interest and never follows through to completion.

_____ 4. You help your child excessively with homework and other school projects.

_____ 5. Your child gets all the latest "fad" items shortly after they hit the market.

_____ 6. With your help, your child always has unearned money available for spending.

_____ 7. You threaten your child with punishment for breaking rules or other infractions, but you hardly ever follow through.

_____ 8. You often jump in to protect your child from directly experiencing the consequences of inappropriate behavior.

_____ 9. Your child frequently responds to you with rude disrespect, and good manners are not demanded at all times.

_____ 10. You permit your children to watch a great deal of television daily, even on school days, because then the kids do not bother you.

As you examine this partial list of indulgent parental behaviors, perhaps you see yourself and your neighbors. To further your awareness, you might benefit from looking at your behavior patterns from a child's point of view: Life is secure. Life is good. Little is demanded. What is demanded can usually be avoided. Little personal account-ability is necessary. There is an electronic babysitter in the living room. There is always lots to eat in the refrigerator, and you get pretty much what you want for the asking. Can you as a parent see the trend? The development of the Cornucopia Kids begins here. The cushy environment you have created is the Cornucopia Cocoon. The results are predictable.

Why Parents Give Too Much

Parents who give or give in too much to their children inadvertently communicate a powerful and destructive perception to the kids that is consistently reinforced over the years: "I am in control. I can get whatever I want from my parents. I do not have to listen to anybody. Good things will come if I just demand them or make a scene." This message is not lost on the children, and it is internalized as a way of relating to the world in general and to other people in particular. When this belief becomes ingrained, the stage is set for the resulting Cornucopia Kid to remain immature and to encounter difficulty later in life both in work and in other relationships.

The parents of such children also lose. Parental indulgence trans-mits to the child an inappropriate sense of grandiosity and power. This power, once given, is quickly mobilized and used to control parents. Visiting this country, the Duke of Windsor with some wry humor remarked: "The thing that impresses me most about America is the way parents obey their children." In many homes, there is just a bit too much truth in this comment for comfort.

The obvious question is why this sad state of affairs occurs so frequently. In fact, a number of unresolved issues within parents lead to this major parenting weakness. Here are a dozen of the most commonly encountered parental vulnerabilities that lead to loss of power and ultimately to the inability to parent effectively.

INDULGENCE DYNAMIC #1: GIVING IN AS A WAY TO AVOID CONFRONTATION OR REJECTION. Far too many parents fear a child's anger or the pouting withdrawal that results if they don't give the children everything they want! Once a child senses this vulner-ability, it is seized upon as a way to apply pressure and to demand more and more. Parents are punished if they do not give in, so they do. As time passes, more power shifts to the child.

INDULGENCE DYNAMIC #2: GIVING "THINGS" AS A SUBSTITUTE FOR TIME. Parents may try to reduce their guilt for not spending quality time with their children by indulging them with too many "things" or too much money. This same guilt may also motivate permissive parenting and lax discipline. The child takes all that is given, but ultimately resents the parent because inverted priorities are clear.

INDULGENCE DYNAMIC #3: GIVING AS A RESPONSE TO MARITAL DIFFERENCES. The classic pattern here is one strict parent and one indulgent parent. Usually, this combination is a prescription for trouble. The permissive parent, wanting always to be the "good guy," finds ways to covertly "undo" or otherwise thwart reasonable discipline imposed by the other. The result is marital discord and an immature, indulged child.

INDULGENCE DYNAMIC #4: GIVING BY A NONCUSTODIAL PARENT. Here a divorced parent indulges a child during visitation, usually as a naive attempt to "buy" a relationship with a child. As a result, discipline and the development of positive values in the home of the parent with primary custody is compromised. In many instances, this pattern contains within it an element of hostility directed to an estranged spouse.

INDULGENCE DYNAMIC #5: GIVING TO COMPENSATE FOR CHILDHOOD DEPRIVATION. "My child is going to have everything I didn't have growing up" is the byword here. The result is untempered material giving. A parent, often poor and painfully deprived during childhood, goes overboard to make sure that a child does not have similar experiences. The overdone result is an undisciplined Cornucopia Kid.

INDULGENCE DYNAMIC #6: GIVING AS A RESPONSE TO COMMUNITY IMAGE NEEDS. Keeping up with the Joneses beautifully dovetails with your child's growing needs to have all the "in" things. You give too much in order to conform to the status quo in the neighborhood, but that doesn't make it right. It only reflects your naivete about sound parenting values and a need to reassure yourself that you're as successful as anyone else.

INDULGENCE DYNAMIC #7: GIVING TO COMPENSATE FOR PURITANICAL PARENTING. Adults whose parents were excessively strict often turn out to be highly permissive parents who give too much materially to their children. Then, to make matters worse, they also compensate by failing to enforce reasonable discipline as well.

"I'm never going to do to my children what my parents did to me" is their theme. The kids are delighted.

INDULGENCE DYNAMIC #8: TO GIVE IS EASIER THAN TO DENY. Tired, harried, and overworked parents often find that it just takes too much energy to deny their children whatever it is they want. With all their many responsibilities, they just don't have the energy to hold the line. As a result, the kids learn to nag and to pester until emotionally fatigued parents lose their resolve. Everybody loses.

INDULGENCE DYNAMIC #9: GIVING AS THE RESULT OF MANIPULATION BY CHILDREN. Over their short lifetimes, children learn how to get what they want by trial and error learning. When certain responses are made, the kids learn that parents give in and the manipulative behavior is reinforced. Even a child of about two years is perfectly capable of detecting and using emotional leverage to meet personal needs.

INDULGENCE DYNAMICS #10: GIVING BY GRANDPARENTS WHO DON'T SHARE PARENTAL VALUES. This can be a particular problem when grandparents live close by, especially if they babysit the children while parents work. Despite the stated wishes and admonitions of parents, these grandparents sometimes materially indulge, fail to discipline, and otherwise thwart the development of positive values in children who frequently spend time with them.

INDULGENCE DYNAMIC #11: GIVING TO "THE BABY" OF THE FAMILY. In many families, older children tend to be achievers. However, the youngest child, the baby, is in fact babied! This child is often indulged, is not as effectively disciplined, and is automatically granted unearned privileges at an earlier age than older brothers and sisters. The result? "The baby" becomes a Cornucopia Kid.

INDULGENCE DYNAMIC #12: GIVING BECAUSE PARENTS ARE "CORNUCOPIA KIDS" THEMSELVES. Make no mistake about it, at this point in time, there are plenty of adults around who have been raised as Cornucopia Kids themselves. As parents, they characteristically model immature behaviors for their children and indulge their children as an extension of themselves. The result is predictable: the pattern is passed on.

Characteristics of Cornucopia Kids

Certainly not all children who grow up in middle-class homes will become Cornucopia Kids. In fact, effective parenting combined with the opportunity afforded by relative affluence can have a very positive effect on children's life skills. It is when strong parenting skills are absent and more and more things are given to the children just to satisfy them that this emotionally destructive problem occurs. At all ages, Cornucopia Kids exhibit a consistent pattern of behavioral characteristics that together define this very maladaptive style of relating to work, to others, and to life in general. Here are ten signs to look for. You may even know some adult Cornucopia Kids who exhibit them!

CORNUCOPIA CHARACTERISTIC #1: YOUR CHILD DEMANDS ONLY THE BEST. In clothes, in toys, and in other things, "top of the line" is the bottom line here. No second-hand, second-rate goods are accepted. Even if the cost is outrageous, if it is not the best, it just is not acceptable and this child will tell you so in no uncertain terms.

CORNUCOPIA CHARACTERISTIC #2: A HIGH NEED FOR CON-STANT STIMULATION IS PRESENT. This child wants action all the time. The stimulation must come from external sources because the capacity for creatively occupying oneself is undeveloped. When external stimulation is not present, you will quickly hear two words loud and clear: "I'm bored."

CORNUCOPIA CHARACTERISTIC #3: THERE IS A CONSIS-TENT PATTERN OF INCOMPLETION. Cornucopia Kids rarely follow through to completion on a project or hobby once the novelty and the fun wear off. Then it becomes too much work to continue. It is easier to move on to something new and exciting. As a result, there is little capacity to gain depth in any area of endeavor.

CORNUCOPIA CHARACTERISTIC #4: THERE IS A DEEP NEED FOR ACCEPTANCE BY OTHERS. These children often seem quite social, but their relationships tend to be superficial. It is not uncommon to find "friendships" purchased by giving gifts, buying things for others, or providing opportunities for fun times. This relationship pattern is a signal of the deep, personal insecurity that lies within.

CORNUCOPIA CHARACTERISTIC #5: THE CAPACITY FOR COMPASSION IS UNDEVELOPED. These immature "children" of whatever age are so used to responding only to *their* needs that there is no sensitivity to the needs and feelings of other people. By extension, good manners and other social graces are often lacking because they have not been demanded by parents.

CORNUCOPIA CHARACTERISTIC #6: A CLEAR CONTEMPT FOR MATERIAL THINGS. It should not be surprising that a child who gets too many things so easily has little respect for possessions. Taking mature responsibility for personal property does not develop because when things are lost or broken, they are quickly fixed or replaced by compliant parents. This cavalier attitude extends to others' property as well.

CORNUCOPIA CHARACTERISTIC #7: SELF-INDULGENCE AND EXCESS ARE BEHAVIOR THEMES. A Cornucopia Kid is prone to self-indulgent excess because internal limits and self-discipline have not developed. The reason is obvious: no external limits have been enforced through consistent parental discipline. Procrastination and clever work avoidance techniques are also part of this pattern.

CORNUCOPIA CHARACTERISTIC #8: YOU SEE AN ALL-TOO-EASY DECEITFULNESS. Because there is so little accountability demanded, finding ways "to get away with it" soon becomes an integral part of the Cornucopia Kids' style. The reason? Because errors of omission, half-truths, blaming others, excuses, manipulation, and outright lies work so well with gullible parents who do not want to deal with the facts.

CORNUCOPIA CHARACTERISTIC #9: PROBLEMS WITH PERFORMANCE. When it comes to really "putting out" in situations where high levels of performance are expected, Cornucopia Kids cop out instead. Inside they are very insecure because, with parental help, they have never had to face tough situations and experience the sense of mastery that comes from successfully meeting difficult challenges.

CORNUCOPIA CHARACTERISTIC #10: THERE IS A STRONG PRESENT ORIENTATION. "Preparing for *my* future? Are you kidding? There's too much fun to have right now!" Extremely pleasure-prone and present-oriented, the Cornucopia Kids consider the future irrelevant. If there is a choice between experiencing pleasure right now and working for long-term goals, you know what the decision will always be.

Easy Erroneous Assumptions

You are probably already beginning to realize how destructive parental indulgence promotes the development of Cornucopia Kids along with the personal immaturity, the lack of character strength, and the undeveloped achievement motivation that characterizes them. This problem is frequently compounded by parents who, over the years, drift away from their own experiences attaining success. Consequently, they fail to promote in their children the necessary values and skills which led to the good life they are now living. These days, shallow and highly questionable social values abound. And, the kids are quick to adopt them because of their own immature ways of perceiving the world. It's all too easy for parents to pick them up, too.

The net result is that there are a number of widespread, but erroneous beliefs about "making it," popularly held and often reinforced among unaware adults, that lead parents to widely miss the mark in their attempts to provide the ingredients necessary for success in their children. Although middle-class lifestyles have changed over the years, the basic expectations of the marketplace and the skills necessary to live the good life have changed remarkably little. However, these values and skills are often clouded by the popular, but superficial and less enduring ways of relating to life experience. As a result, core values and skills are more difficult to clearly conceptualize and integrate into positive parenting than ever before. But, that's exactly what effective parents must do.

To pave the way for you to actively parent in ways that will reduce the probability of raising Cornucopia Kids, the first step is to eliminate a number of easy and erroneous beliefs about attaining success. Here are nine faulty premises on which many well-meaning, but short-sighted men and women base their parenting. Although so popularly reinforced that they are quite easy to accept, each one is actually invalid. And, to the extent that parents live by these faulty premises themselves, their ability to live the good life is compromised. Think carefully about each fallacious assumption. Then eliminate all that you find from the way you live and how you parent.

FAULTY PREMISE #1: PARENTS' PRIMARY ROLE IN EDU-CATING THEIR CHILDREN IS ONLY TO BACK UP THE SCHOOLS. No question about it—helping with homework, communicating with teachers, and reinforcing values taught at school are important. However, this easy parental stance completely neglects critical training for success that can only occur at home. These days, it is necessary for parents not only to back up the formal curriculum being learned at school, but also to actively teach a second, informal, but extremely important curriculum of success at home.

FAULTY PREMISE #2: ALL THE INGREDIENTS FOR SUCCESS ARE AVAILABLE FOR PURCHASE BY PARENTS. A spinoff from a very materialistically-oriented society, this common attitude reflects the idea that parents can buy anything, even success for the kids. Naive parents try to buy relationships with their children or attempt to insure success by purchasing opportunities to learn. However, the hard reality is that the real price of success for the kids is in-depth understanding, clear and healthy family values, a modicum of common sense, hard work, and persistence by parents.

FAULTY PREMISE #3: IF AN ACTIVITY ISN'T STRUCTURED AND EVALUATED BY ADULTS, THEN IT ISN'T IMPORTANT TO SUCCESS. These days, anxious parents begin "hothousing" children by pushing them into academically-oriented activities virtually from birth. The feeling is that if an activity isn't carefully designed by adults and then evaluated by experts, then it can't be worth much. This sad mistake by parents often robs children of childhood by not allowing them free time just to be kids, to play, and to have fun. The fallout comes later in the form of unhappy and stressed students who "turn off" to learning.

FAULTY PREMISE #4: A CHILD'S IQ SCORE IS A GOOD PREDICTOR OF SUCCESS. Insecure parents often use a child's IQ score to "one-up" neighbors and reassure themselves of a child's ultimate success. Research has shown a reasonably consistent positive correlation between grades in school and IQ. What is less known, however, is that the relationship between economic success and IQ is virtually nil if one begins the correlation with the normal IQ range and above. *Raw intellectual potential as measured by an IQ test is just not a good predictor of career success once a child is out of school.*

FAULTY PREMISE #5: TO GET TO THE TOP, ALL YOU NEED IS TECHNICAL EXPERTISE. Career ladders do initially depend highly on the direct application of technical knowledge and related skills. However, with advancement, management expertise, leadership capability, and relationship skills become even more important. Short-sighted individuals who rely solely on technical expertise without sound people-skills often find it most difficult to keep advancing. And, when relationship skills are lacking, marital and family problems are often the result.

FAULTY PREMISE #6: ALL WORTHWHILE ACTIVITIES MUST BE HIGHLY GOAL-ORIENTED AND COMPETITIVE. Achievement-oriented parents, often highly competitive themselves, pass this orientation on to their children. Always pushing to meet goals, to be the best, and to win every time may be positive within limits. However, cooperation and teamwork are at least as important as competitive skills these days. And, don't forget that to really relax and enjoy life requires that excessive goal-orientation and competitiveness be put aside.

FAULTY PREMISE #7: GRADES WILL EITHER MAKE YOU OR BREAK YOU. With considerable validity, an educator once commented that the best thing grades predict is future grades, but not necessarily success! Without question students should be encouraged to obtain the best grades possible and to work to potential in school. However, history is replete with examples of accomplished men and women who were not good students in school, but who blossomed later. While grades *are* required to obtain necessary credentials for many careers, they become virtually meaningless as a criterion of success once on the job.

FAULTY PREMISE #8: A COLLEGE EDUCATION IS AN ABSOLUTE MUST FOR MAKING A GOOD LIVING. While a college degree is definitely a prerequisite for some careers, it is certainly not true for all. There are many high-quality, non-collegiate training opportunities for careers that provide an excellent living. Technical schools, short-term courses, apprenticeship programs, and training in the armed services are just a few. While basic training and an interest in ongoing learning are absolutely crucial to success, there are definitely viable alternatives to college these days.

FAULTY PREMISE #9: HAPPINESS ALWAYS FOLLOWS ECONOMIC SUCCESS. Two points about this assumption are important. First, most successful men and women recall with fond memories earlier years when they were less economically successful, but happier and more carefree. Second, there is an implication in this myth that you can't be happy along the way. An unintended but prevalent social message is that you must wait until you've "made it" for contentment to come. Savvy parents see through this common misperception and teach their children deeper values that bring personal fulfillment all along life's path.

From Affluence to Achievement

"I can do it even if it's tough" is the essence of mastery motivation. It is a necessary quality for success in the difficult and competitive work world that eventually all children must face as they grow to adult-hood. Healthy mastery motivation requires trust in personal capabili-ties, persistence, a history of success, the capacity to work toward long-term goals, and self-discipline. All of these qualities remain undeveloped in Cornucopia Kids who are kept emotionally immature within their comfortable, middle-class Cornucopia Cocoons—that is, until they must face the world on their own to become self-sufficient and responsible adults. Then they encounter extreme difficulty be-cause they have not learned the values and the skills necessary to deal successfully with the real world. It certainly would not be going too far to say that these children have been inadvertently trained all their lives by misguided parents to be incompetent!

No matter what your children's ages, now is the time to begin parenting in ways that will promote the development of achievement motivation in all of your children. Healthy parenting values are perhaps the strongest possible way to do that. The key question is, "How do you train a child who has everything to be tough and accountable?" The answer is to give less and more. That is, to give fewer "things," but more personal involvement in directly training your children in values that will permit them to succeed later in life. The consequences of neglecting critical home-based training for success can be catastrophic to the development of adult competency. Perhaps a short story will nicely underscore this point.

"Once upon a time there were two butterflies who were delighted when their own baby caterpillar came into the world. As most parents do, they looked forward to seeing their young one turn into a beautiful butterfly just like they were. Because they cared so much, they gave their child everything a young caterpillar could possibly want. When the time came, they even helped build the protective cocoon within which the metamorphosis would take place. Then they waited with eager anticipation for a beautiful young butterfly to make a grand entrance into the adult world.

At long last, they saw the cocoon breaking away. To their shock and dismay, their young caterpillar emerged without changing at all! Their still immature youngster greeted them with an explana-tion: 'It's too tough to be a butterfly these days. You have to fly on your own and find your own food. And, there's no one around to take care of you. I've decided to stay just the way I am and keep you company.' To the parent butterflies' distress, that is just what that apprehensive young caterpillar did."

As you now realize, the crisis of confidence in Cornucopia Kids has its roots in parental behaviors that keep children immature. When it comes time to fly on their own, they find the culture shock of the demanding real world frightening and severe. Again, there is no necessary antithesis between a lifestyle of relative affluence and raising healthy, achieving children. To make sure that mastery motivation is being learned, however, you must closely examine the values that you are transmitting to your children through your parenting responses. When you look closely, you may find that you are teaching your children values that are the polar opposite of those that brought success and the good life to you.

In a nutshell, Cornucopia Kids suffer from *your* success. Their extravagant lives of easy living will cause you to suffer as well, long after they have reached the age of majority. Although biology is not destiny, as Heraclitus (540–475 B.C.) stated, "Character *is* destiny." As a responsible parent, it is your mandate to instill integrity instead of indulgence; to create character, not conformity; to build motivation rather than materialism; to demand sensitivity in lieu of selfishness. Through that process, you will grow in wisdom and your children will grow toward responsible maturity. If you do not accept this challenge, you may find that you have an immature caterpillar (or several of them), unable to make it in the real world, hanging around eating you out of house and home indefinitely . . . literally . . . figuratively . . . disappointingly.

Chapter 2

The Hidden Curriculum
of Success
(or Why Dick and Jane
Didn't Succeed
Despite Every Advantage!)

The scene opens. It's dawn. Two small children hungrily wolf down a few scraps of food. In the sparsely furnished home, a dim bulb barely lights the kitchen. It's not quite warm inside and bitter outside, but it's time for school. Dad's been gone for hours putting in a typical twelve-hour day at hard labor. With a mother's love, the two children are readied. Their ragged, patched jackets worn thin, shoes falling apart.

With a piece of day-old bread and a smidgeon of cheese for lunch, the kids leave. They slowly trudge the five miles to school through swirling drifts of snow. They return late in the afternoon to work until dusk so the family can survive. Then it's homework long into the night before a bone-tiring day finally ends. At six and eight years, the kids are exhausted. Only after long years of struggle against painful deprivation and hardship do they finally make it to success.

This is the story that Dick and Jane's parents would love to tell, inspiring their children to toughen up, to overcome life's problems, and, thus, to ultimately succeed. The problem is that it just isn't true. However, neither parent did have it particularly easy growing up. Both from modest backgrounds, they had the basics at home, but little else. If they wanted something extra, hard work was the only way to get it. After they met and married, their struggle for success continued through more education, sacrifice, hard work, and doing without. Gradually, things got easier.

When Dick and Jane arrived, the family was economically comfortable. Living in a reasonably nice house in a reasonably nice neighborhood, the family had a stable income and was well-liked by neighbors. Dick and Jane were provided with every affordable advantage as their parents continued to sacrifice to help their children become successful. The kids went to a good school, were involved in many extracurricular activities, had the latest clothes, and were provided quite adequate spending money. Dick and Jane and their parents had become part of the Great American Middle-Class.

There was only one catch. Despite obvious advantages, neither Dick nor Jane ever really "made it" as adults. The kids (now grown) had problems at work and at home in their marriages. Their parents were not only disappointed, but confused. They had done all the right things, hadn't they? What *was* the problem? In retrospect, it seemed that all the benefits they provided for the kids had had no real effect. Parental sacrifices seemed to count for nil. And, the children weren't even grateful! Their current attitudes revealed their immaturity. They had never really grown up.

Dick and Jane had become part of a contemporary American tragedy, although neither they nor their parents realized it until too late. What happened here? What went wrong? In a nutshell, what Dick and Jane's now-successful parents failed to understand is that there are *two* complementary curricula of success that must be learned during the growing years. At school, one was well-taught to Dick and Jane (although not necessarily well-learned). At home, the other was almost completely neglected. Without a solid foundation of both, the kids' later success was sorely compromised.

THE FIRST CURRICULUM: FORMAL EDUCATION TAUGHT PRIMARILY AT SCHOOL. The core of the school experience focuses primarily on cognitive development. The primary task of the schools is to prepare young people to take their place in an extremely complex society where high levels of knowledge, related work skills, and understanding of a changing world are absolutely required.

THE SECOND CURRICULUM: BASIC LIFE SKILLS TAUGHT PRIMARILY AT HOME. This subject matter is composed of a constellation of values, skills, and behaviors that must be actively taught by parents. These life skills, complemented by intellectual knowledge, powerfully influence career success, the quality of relationships, and the capacity for healthy living.

Although it may initially sound absurd, it's a fact that parental neglect of the home-based Hidden Curriculum of Success can easily create a family environment where the kids are unknowingly taught to fail! While many parents have an intuitive sense of the Hidden Curriculum, too often their intuitive wisdom is put aside because no one else seems to be reinforcing the same values. Their rationale is erroneous: "If no one else is doing it, then it can't be right. Can it?" The answer, of course, is a resounding YES!

Here's the bottom line. *Unless well-intentioned parents can clearly conceptualize the Hidden Curriculum and actively teach it despite the fact that it makes them a bit different from neighbors, children may grow up educationally disadvantaged despite living in a good home with successful parents who have a quite adequate income.* Now let's pursue this most provocative statement. Let's explore the issues more thoroughly and take a closer look at why Dick and Jane didn't succeed despite every advantage!

The Hidden Keys to Success

If the Hidden Curriculum of Success is primarily the responsibility of parents, then just what is it all about? The answer is as easily missed as it is easy to understand once clearly conceptualized. Its core lies in seven highly interrelated areas of skill that simply cannot be learned through school attendance alone. To teach the Second Curriculum well, parents must first accept the importance of these skills and understand how each one fits with success later in life. Then they must make needed changes at home so as to make each one of them an integral part of the family's values, thereby helping the children learn them.

Here are these seven Keys to Success defined with a rationale and an explanation of what was missed in Dick and Jane's home environment. Included with each is a Home Values Assessment consisting of several questions for parents to use as focal points for evaluating their parenting.

THE FIRST HIDDEN KEY: PARENTS MUST HELP THEIR CHILDREN DEVELOP INTERNAL SECURITY AND PERSONAL SELF-ACCEPTANCE.

Rationale: Living in a constantly changing and unpredictable world, it is necessary for a child to base self-esteem and personal security within himself rather than relying on external factors to define personal adequacy.

The only emotionally healthy kind of personal security stems from acceptance and love provided by parents complemented by a stable home environment. Although growing up within a successful family, Dick and Jane were actually disadvantaged in this regard. If self-esteem is based on externals (clothes, spending money, fad items, and possessions), then that self-esteem is vulnerable because these externals can be taken away or may quickly go out of style. Parents are the keys to helping their children build internal security. To do this, they must transcend an easy emphasis on "things" and provide instead time, care, and love. Security carried within as self-trust and self-acceptance is the only buffer against an unstable world and the vicissitudes of life.

At home, Dick and Jane were provided with just about everything they desired. At school, they wore the right clothes and had all the "in" things. As far as home life was concerned, there was little because they were never there! And, parents didn't insist on it because they were so busy themselves. Because of this, communication among family members was limited, thus producing no real sense of close-ness. Home was basically a place to eat and sleep. Feeling guilty for not spending time with the kids, parents compensated by giving material things instead. Internally, the family was fragmented, but no one realized it until much later.

HOME VALUES ASSESSMENT

1. As parents, do you affectionately touch your children regularly with hugs, pats on the back, and a caring shoulder to cry on when necessary?

2. Do you insist on adequate time during the week for all family members to be together, share experiences, and just talk?

3. In your relationship with each of your children, do you regularly and spontaneously tell them they are loved, no matter what?

4. As parents, do you model emotional closeness and intimacy in your marriage for the kids to observe and imitate?

5. Can and do you say "no" to requests for fad items by the kids who want them just because everyone else has them?

THE SECOND HIDDEN KEY: THE CHILDREN MUST LEARN A SENSE OF PERSONAL ACCOUNTABILITY.

Rationale: To succeed in a career and to have healthy relation-ships, it is necessary to accept personal responsibility for actions and their consequences.

A stark reality is that the expectations of the world demand personal accountability—that is, accepting the direct relationship between behavior and consequences. Through *external* limits initially set by parents, a child gradually learns to control responses and to live by *internal* limits later in life. From this perspective, parental discipline is the road to learning self-discipline and personal control. Conversely, when parents neglect discipline or when they help children avoid the consequences of their behavior, the youngsters experience a rude awakening later in the adult world where personal accountability is an absolute must.

During their growing years, Dick and Jane didn't experience much in the way of discipline. It wasn't that their parents didn't try. The fact was that both parents were vulnerable, and the kids from an early age learned to manipulate them. The problem was compounded by parental denial. They just didn't want to believe *their* kids were misbehaving even when the evidence was clear. And, Dick and Jane always had such convincing excuses: A coincidence. A case of mistaken identity. It was someone else's fault. An accident. Somebody's trying to get me into trouble. To make matters worse, Dick and Jane's parents wanted their kids to be successful so badly that they routinely "fixed" problems for them. And, they weren't averse to telling a little white lie on their offsprings' behalf when they were in trouble.

HOME VALUES ASSESSMENT

1. As parents, do you agree on reasonable limits for the kids and support one another in demanding that they be respected?

2. Do you consistently respond positively and reward the kids when they stay within set limits?

3. When there is a problem, do you get all the facts and then decide what to do instead of automatically believing the kids' excuses?

4. Have you identified your personal vulnerabilities so the kids can't manipulate you to escape discipline?

5. When your child is in the wrong, do you insist that the consequences be faced with follow-through as necessary?

THE THIRD HIDDEN KEY: PARENTS MUST HELP THEIR CHILDREN LEARN HEALTHY ACHIEVEMENT MOTIVATION.

Rationale: Meeting challenges and reaching personal goals require a base of personal experience with success—success attained by overcoming hardships, obstacles, and setbacks.

Many naive parents easily succeed in providing their children with myriad opportunities to sample new experiences. However, as quantity is inadvertently chosen over quality, the kids don't follow through on anything. The children move from activity to activity, staying with each one only as long as it is fun and new. When it becomes difficult or routine, it's off to something else. With this hopscotching, children don't learn healthy achievement motivation that depends on making things happen through persistence, hard work, acceptance of adversity, and the successful surmounting of obstacles.

Throughout their development, Dick and Jane had fun to a fault. They were provided with a smorgasbord of extracurricular involvements (some of them quite expensive). The parental rationale was that such activities were not only opportunities to learn, but would give their children an edge over others. However, parents didn't spot the telltale pattern. The kids never really stayed with anything for long. Furthermore, parents didn't insist that they do so. The children whined and wheedled, claiming boredom. Soon they were off to something else. Over the years, neither child developed commitment to an activity or high levels of skill at anything. And, neither coped well with hardship, failure, and problems. They escaped instead. Not surprisingly, Dick and Jane's "fun and games" development seriously compromised successfully meeting challenges later in life.

HOME VALUES ASSESSMENT

1. Do you insist that your children limit their activities and do fewer things well instead of many things superficially?

2. Do you support persistence in what your children do, with lots of encouragement and positive feedback when there are difficulties?

3. Is there within the family an insistence that children follow through to completion projects or activities once started?

4. As parents, do you help your children to accept failure as part of success and to use setbacks as learning experiences?

5. Even though it's painful, do you avoid taking over when a child is experiencing a problem, instead helping that child assume personal control of the situation?

THE FOURTH HIDDEN KEY: YOUR CHILDREN MUST DEVELOP A POSITIVE RELATIONSHIP TO THE WORK WORLD.

Rationale: There is a direct relationship between work skills and attitudes that are primarily learned through home-based work responsibilities and one's success as an adult.

As youngsters, Dick and Jane's parents had to work for any extras. They did odd jobs around the neighborhood and eventually clerked part-time at local stores. Both also worked to help pay their way through college. It was difficult but rewarding. After years of dedication and hard work, they finally moved over the hump economically. Now, as part of the benefits of their parents' success, Dick and Jane were spared the same kinds of experiences. From day one, the kids were provided with plenty of spending money and were assigned no responsibilities for chores at home. Further, they had little incentive to do odd jobs because they already had everything they needed in the way of cash and purchasing power.

As you may have already guessed, because of their parents' misguided motives, Dick and Jane had very poor attitudes about work because they had not experienced much of it during their development. They did homework only if pushed by parents and, correspondingly, their work habits were atrocious. They did only what they had to do to get by and no more. Thus, when they later faced the work world and its expectations for punctuality, initiative, acceptance of responsibility, and respect for authority, they were ill-prepared. Well-meaning parents had spared them critical learning experiences. Despite being bright, Dick and Jane as adults adjusted with great difficulty to the work world and fared poorly in their careers.

HOME VALUES ASSESSMENT

1. In your household, do your children have regular chores for which they are responsible?

2. Do you as parents encourage your children to earn extra money through odd jobs and entreprenurial activities?

3. Do your children know the direct relationship between personal effort and reward because you don't provide free cash for the asking?

4. At home, do you engage in cooperative work projects with the kids as a way to make the experience more pleasurable and to model positive work habits?

5. As parents, do you hold the line and not pay in advance for work unfinished or for projects poorly done?

THE FIFTH HIDDEN KEY: TEACHING YOUR CHILDREN GOOD MANNERS AND SOCIAL SENSITIVITY IS A MUST.

Rationale: A sound understanding of people and related social skills is a basic requirement for success at work and for fulfilling relationships with loved ones.

Dick and Jane's parents knew what good manners were, but they were also very protective. Whenever there was a problem, they automatically took their child's side. At home, they didn't insist on good manners at all times. It just didn't seem that important. And, because parents were so busy and under pressure so much of the time, they weren't always paragons of politeness themselves! The kids learned through neglect and negative example that they didn't have to respect anyone's needs or rights except their own. As a result, they grew up with little empathic understanding of relationships or others' emotional needs.

These self-centered attitudes caused Dick and Jane many problems later in life. You already know that eventually most career paths require strong people-skills. In addition, solid relationship skills are needed in every facet of life beyond work: to create a mutually fulfilling relationship with a spouse, to be a positive parent, and to get along well with friends. Only naive parents neglect this vitally important part of their children's education. No matter how intellectually talented, men and women without interpersonal sensitivity, good manners, and well-developed relationship skills are at a disadvantage.

HOME VALUES ASSESSMENT

1. Do you insist that your children be polite and exercise basic good manners in public and at home?

2. As parents, do you practice good manners in your marital relationship so your children can learn directly from you?

3. When there is a problem, do you insist on getting all parties together to talk it out and find a reasonable solution?

4. If your child has been rude or insensitive, do you insist on a sincere apology personally delivered?

5. Do you as parents refuse to excuse children's rudeness or disrespect toward you just because they are angry or upset?

THE SIXTH HIDDEN KEY: YOUR CHILDREN ARE TAUGHT SOUND MONEY MANAGEMENT SKILLS BEGINNING EARLY IN LIFE.

Rationale: To effectively manage increasingly complex family finances and to prevent stress and conflict that stem from financial irresponsibility, well-developed money management skills are required.

Parents who fail these days to teach their children financial management skills limit their ability to live the good life later. Though making an adequate salary, many well-trained men and women live from one financial crisis to another because they lack these critical skills. And, research has shown that one of the major sources of stress for individuals and families is fiscal mismanagement. These days, maintaining a middle-class family's economic stability is quite comparable in complexity to running a small business. And, the family's finances must also be continually adapted to constant change and evolving needs.

Now let's look at Dick and Jane's experience. As they grew, they consistently received more than adequate spending money. And, spend they did—every bit of what they received and whatever else they could coax out of compliant parents who wanted their children to have all they themselves didn't have. With more allowance than needed, Dick and Jane had no need to budget or save for anything. Why should they? They got virtually everything they wanted just for the asking. Further, they developed a most cavalier attitude about possessions. When something was broken or lost, it was replaced almost immediately. Years later, when Dick and Jane entered the real world, they were traumatized by their lack of training in money management.

HOME VALUES ASSESSMENT

1. As a strong parenting value, do you mandate that your children save at least some of their money for future purposes?

2. Do you provide the kids with a set and limited weekly allowance which requires them to budget what they spend?

3. As parents, do you limit *your* use of credit and not permit your children to use your credit cards?

4. If one of your children breaks a toy in anger or maliciously damages property, do you insist on repayment?

5. As parents, do you reinforce care of possessions because the kids know they won't automatically be replaced if misused?

THE SEVENTH HIDDEN KEY: A WELL-DEVELOPED ABILITY TO RELAX AND PLAY IS TAUGHT BY PARENTS.

Rationale: Because of emotional fatigue resulting from constant mental work and from the intellectual demands of getting through each day, regular relaxation is necessary to promote health and enjoy life.

The effects of technological complexity on health and well-being are only now being understood. These days, work is rapidly evolving away from manual labor in the direction of constant mental work using high levels of intellectual skills. And, the complexity of living requires that individuals continue to think and learn at home: to operate a new microwave oven, to keep up with tax changes, to help a child put together a "simple" toy. Such mental work requires tremendous energy and leads to emotional exhaustion if not followed by adequate relaxation time. Because of the nature of today's work, parents must teach their children how to relax, not as a bonus for hard work well done, but as a health mandate.

As with most of their childhood friends, the pressures on Dick and Jane to succeed were constant. However, as they grew older, having been consistently protected by parents from life's realities, they also became quite insecure. Not only did they not achieve much, but both children were chronic worriers because they had not learned the skills necessary to cope well with challenges, problems, and setbacks. Their anxieties and fears prevented them from enjoying life even when they had the time. And, because they couldn't relax, they didn't gain the emotional benefits of time away from work. Stress symptoms, chronic negativism, and personal discontent were the result.

HOME VALUES ASSESSMENT

1. As parents, do you regularly take time for yourselves and with the children to enjoy pleasant and relaxing experiences?

2. When relaxing, do you focus on enjoying the experience rather than meeting goals, having products to show for your time, or intensely competing against others?

3. With the kids, do you as parents encourage quality time spent in relaxation as essential for health and well-being?

4. In competitive games, do you encourage the kids to do their best, but still play for fun instead of always needing to win or to be the best?

5. Do you as parents help your children appreciate the beauty around them and enjoy life's simple (and inexpensive) pleasures?

Parenting for "Goodness of Fit"

The basic thesis of the Hidden Curriculum of Success is that while good grades and a solid formal education are certainly important, they are simply not enough these days. It's a naive, but easy trap to assess potential for success by narrowly focusing only on how a child is doing at school. This parental stance completely misses skills essential in the marketplace and in life itself that are not necessarily reflected in schoolwork at all!

As a way to keep your child's education at home *and* at school in clear perspective, keep in the forefront of your mind "goodness of fit." This requires that you use as a framework for assessing your child's educational progress the expectations of the marketplace and life in general. To illustrate this important point, consider yourself to be an employer for a moment. Then think of the qualifications you would seek in a candidate for a job. Beyond formal educational requirements and necessary credentials, here are the qualities most often sought: initiative, getting along well with people, a positive attitude, able to work independently, trustworthiness, perseverance, willingness to learn, punctuality, ability to handle responsibility, honesty.

What is interesting, however, is what you probably didn't mention: The individual's IQ. The prestige of the school attended. Perhaps not even grades. Now take another look at the above qualities. You will notice that virtually all of them reflect life values that are part of the Hidden Curriculum of Success that is either taught or neglected at home. *The question that parents must continually assess is whether the values and skills taught at home are congruent with the values and skills expected at work and in life itself.* When they match, that's "goodness of fit!"

With the increasing complexity of contemporary lifestyles, you must now realize that the Second Curriculum is steadily becoming more important for parents to recognize and teach. The rationale is simple. The skills and values that together define this critical learning are most easily learned gradually and with parental guidance all through the developmental years. Conversely, these skills are most difficult and often traumatic to learn after a young adult has left the family. And, regardless of economic status, those children whose parents actively teach the Hidden Curriculum of Success gain a tremendous advantage over those who must "catch up" by learning it later in life.

To their credit, some savvy parents have been teaching this home-based curriculum all along. And, more parents are actively beginning to do so. However, even under the best of circumstances it's not an easy task. To do it well, there are several commitments that you must make as a parent.

PARENTAL COMMITMENT #1: TO *CLARITY* OF FORESIGHT. Teaching the Hidden Curriculum necessitates that you clearly understand the issues and accept the importance of your role as a parent in determining your child's ultimate success. Remember that your children will get no grades for learning this home-based curriculum. You will have to rely on common sense, your awareness of deeper values, and your observational skills to assess progress and to ultimately prevail in your teaching.

PARENTAL COMMITMENT #2: TO *CONTAINMENT* OF MATE-RIAL GIVING. You may not be rich, but you probably have more to give to your children materially than your parents had to give to you. Therein lies the problem. To learn the same basic values that you did to succeed in life requires direct teaching on your part and some degree of struggle by the kids. When everything is given to them, children don't develop character. As a parent, the question for you these days is more difficult than in the past: "If you have it, are you strong enough *not* to give it so that your children will grow up to be healthy achievers?"

PARENTAL COMMITMENT #3: TO *CHARACTER* IN YOUR PAR-ENTING. Make no mistake about it, the kids will take all they can get from you. That's immaturity speaking. And, these days children are able to place tremendous psychological pressure on parents to get what they want. Vulnerable parents often easily give in to the "every-one's doing it so it must be right" attitude toward parenting. You must have strength of character to resist these powerful influences. And, you must have enough self-trust and personal resolve to be a bit different than everyone else.

A final point. The values reflected in the Hidden Curriculum of Success are actually quite traditional. But with more complex con-temporary lifestyles, these basic values are more difficult to see and to teach effectively. If you do, the rewards for you and for your children will be great. Because you provided "goodness of fit" for your family, your children will "fit in" as well-rounded, competent adults. If you don't, after two hundred years a bit of wisdom inscribed on a Revolu-tionary War rum horn may yet apply to you as a parent: "Ye prudent forseeth the evil; ye simple pass on and are punished." So be it.

Chapter 3

Creating Essence of Family: Building Your Child's Security System from Within

You've seen the enlistment posters for the Armed Forces. They promise all kinds of new experiences. Travel! Learning opportunities! Excitement! What most couples don't realize is that similar opportunities are also available through parenting. Just take a look. Parenting provides it all.

TRAVEL:

—taking the kids back and forth to activities every day.

—moving constantly from room to room picking up clothes, toys, and other possessions.

—exploring local fields and woods in all seasons to find your kids.

EDUCATIONAL OPPORTUNITIES:

—to learn about the latest fad items (and how much they're going to cost you).

—to hear exotic languages as you seek to interpret the meaning of "nerd," "awesome," and "bad" which means good.

—to realize how far "out of it" you are these days in contrast to your kids who are "with it."

DAILY EXCITEMENT:

—as you break up territorial skirmishes between two kids who "didn't do anything!"

—as you calm your spouse who has totally "lost it" and who wants a ride to the nearest psychiatric facility for a long rest.

—of the hunt as you seek clever ways to be alone with your partner with your children systematically stalking you.

Ah, yes. That's the good life as every parent knows. There are plenty of such activities in every household. However, paired with these realities is another one: effective parenting, that is, raising healthy achieving children, is steadily becoming more difficult. And, part of what is producing this complexity is massive changes in the fabric of the family and in society as a whole. Unfortunately, many of these changes are destructive to what is known about positive parenting and raising healthy achieving children. And, the effects of these changes on families, both adults and children, are unfortunately becoming more serious.

The bottom line is that parents must be aware of these factors and how they psychologically affect children over the long term. Then, aware parents must be able and willing to take the appropriate steps to counter these negative trends as much as possible. As a starting point, here are the three major contemporary erosion factors that have deleterious effects on raising healthy achieving children.

EROSION FACTOR #1: RAPIDLY ACCELERATING SOCIAL CHANGES. The typical family environment these days is much different than it was even ten years ago, much less when parents were growing up. The advent of complex technology, more restrictive laws, crowding, and rapidly evolving social values have radically changed the way children grow up and what they experience while doing so. These changes over which parents do not have complete control significantly impact on the development of positive self-esteem and the personal security of children.

EROSION FACTOR #2: INCREASING EXTERNALIZATION OF SELF-ESTEEM. There are many influences these days that seek to link a sense of personal adequacy to external factors. Neither children nor adults are immune to development of these destructive linkages. The emotional reality is that healthy children and adults must have within themselves a positive feeling of adequacy that is relatively independent of externals. Creating internal self-esteem in children these days is immensely more difficult because of the many powerful influences both in the kids' social environment and at home.

EROSION FACTOR #3: THE PROGRESSIVE NEGLECT OF FAMILY LIFE. There can be little doubt that life within the family has changed radically in recent years. "Home" easily becomes a place to eat and sleep for children and their parents. However, personal security and positive self-esteem develop primarily from a close and supportive family environment during the critical developmental years. The problem is that shared family experiences are easily neglected. As parents begin to feel overwhelmed with responsibilities, the priority placed on establishing an emotionally healthy family life sinks.

Busy parents must keep one distinction in mind: *standard of living and quality of life are not the same thing for you or for the kids.* All too often, achieving parents have succeeded in considerably raising their standard of living. At the same time, quality of life in terms of personal fulfillment and family togetherness may have diminished to the point of nonexistence. It is critical that parents accept the importance of a strong family life to effectively counter the destructive trends that have become part of life as we live it these days. In this chapter, factors that erode self-confidence and personal security in children are considered in some detail in order to expand parental understanding. Then, tips on creating a healthy family life in spite of these influences are provided.

Negative Social Changes

Years ago, families lived in small and usually close-knit communities that changed only very slowly. As a result, it was quite easy for men and women to draw a sense of security from the relatively unchanging environment around them. However, in recent years, coping with constant change has become a way of life. Nothing stays the same for long anymore. And, unfortunately, these rapid changes extend from the largest cities to the smallest towns and hamlets. Further, the pace of change seems to be accelerating.

The net result is that without the benefit of a stable and relatively unchanging external environment, children must develop a base of personal security that is carried within. This kind of security must be built slowly through the developmental years from positive experiences in a loving home environment. To underscore the importance of stable family experiences these days, take a look at the massive social changes that parents must cope with and that children now face at ever younger ages.

CONTEMPORARY CHANGE #1: THE BREAKDOWN OF EXTENDED FAMILIES. Geographic areas where families, including cousins, aunts, uncles, and grandparents all live within five miles of one another and get together regularly have almost disappeared. Increased mobility results in only sporadic contact with an extended family, thereby increasing isolation of family members. These same trends are also steadily eroding the cohesive ethnic communities that once existed in many cities as the young leave to seek their fortunes elsewhere.

CONTEMPORARY CHANGE #2: THE "GHETTOIZATION" OF TOWNS AND CITIES. Related to the above is the diminished intergenerational contact seen these days. Years ago, men and women of all ages lived in healthy mix on every street. Now towns are increasingly divided into ghettoes defined by age. There are areas where the young and unattached (or college students) live. Other sections are dominated by young marrieds. The same is true for established and maturing families. Then there are special areas for retirees and still others for the aged. The result is that children are not regularly exposed to other age groups and the wisdom they offer.

CONTEMPORARY CHANGE #3: STEADILY INCREASING CAREER MOBILITY. Now and in the foreseeable future, men and women will find their careers taking them on a lifelong odyssey from community to community. The days when a man or woman will live and work in a single community for a lifetime are rapidly coming to an end. Some individuals are transferred by their companies. Others find career opportunities in new locales and move there. And, evidence suggests that in the future, individuals will have multiple careers instead of the traditional single one.

CONTEMPORARY CHANGE #4: NEIGHBORHOODS ARE CHANGING TO SUBDIVISIONS. A true neighborhood is a street or mini-community where everyone knows one another. Parents socialize over the back fence, drop in on one another, and otherwise keep in touch. Now, in many subdivisions the corner of one home is less than one hundred feet from the corner of the next. But, the adults who live in these homes typically do not know their neighbors except to wave "hi" as they drive in and out of the driveway. Note: In subdivisions, parents keep in touch only indirectly. Your kids play with other kids on the street. The kids talk among themselves about what their parents are doing. Then they go home and inform their parents about what's happening in the "neighborhood."

CONTEMPORARY CHANGE #5: THE RISE OF GENERAL IMPERSONALITY. With ever larger numbers of people inhabiting a given amount of space, logic would dictate that more sensitivity to others would develop. Yet, the opposite is occurring. With more people and large bureaucracies, impersonality is growing in every part of life. The desire to keep other people at a psychological distance becomes a strong need most apparent in larger cities. However, this same impersonal attitude now pervades even small towns. The problem is exacerbated by a decline in common courtesy toward others.

CONTEMPORARY CHANGE #6: CONSTANTLY CHANGING TECHNOLOGY. There is little question that use of sophisticated technology has become part of daily life. However, with each advance comes change and increased complexity. Nothing is simple anymore. A microwave oven comes with an eighty-five page procedure manual. New radios have only buttons, not knobs. Simple toys require the skills of an engineer to assemble. Rapid technological change erodes stability. It also necessitates mental work and constant learning just to keep up.

CONTEMPORARY CHANGE #7: LIFELONG FRIENDS ARE A SCARCE COMMODITY. With increased geographic mobility, deep and longstanding friendships have suffered. With frequent moves, friendships are increasingly transitory—viable only until the next move. The resultant impersonality is making it ever more difficult to meet people, to maintain a social support system, and to develop solid friendships when a move to a new locale is made. Loneliness in the midst of crowds is becoming endemic as every mental health professional knows.

CONTEMPORARY CHANGE #8: CHILDREN ARE MUCH MORE MOBILE. In days gone by, most of the time the kids could be found within the range of a shout from the back door. Now, with so many extracurricular involvements, even small children regularly travel long distances from home. Conversely, the kids spend little time in their own "neighborhood" (such as it is) and even less time at home. With this kind of childhood mobility, home is often a coordination center where parents and children say "hi" and work out scheduling problems as they pass on the way to their respective destinations.

CONTEMPORARY CHANGE #9: INCREASING DEPENDENCY IN AN ERA OF SPECIALIZATION. Fixing a TV used to be as simple as replacing a vacuum tube. Now you need a specialist who is knowledgeable about circuit boards. Simple maladies that used to be treated by parents now require medical specialists. With increasing dependence on specialists to get anything done or fixed, individuals no longer feel as much in control. Their sense of self-sufficiency wanes and a sense of helplessness becomes stronger. As a result, more personal insecurity is generated.

CONTEMPORARY CHANGE #10: NECESSITY FOR HIGHLY COMPLEX INFORMATION PROCESSING. Sociologists say, with truth, that this is the information age. Specialized information is expanding so rapidly that it is difficult to keep up. And, new and more detailed information is provided to the individual daily. New tax laws. New findings on health and nutrition. New information necessary to your profession. Constantly barraged with new and relevant information that must be learned, men and women find it nearly impossible to relax and feel comfortable with what they already know.

How Externalized Adequacy Is Created

It is most disturbing these days to assess the number of subtle and not-so-subtle influences that tend to externalize self-esteem in virtually all youngsters. An externally-based sense of personal adequacy is one that depends on factors outside oneself to feel personally acceptable. Along with social influences that promote the development of externalized self-esteem, there are also equally powerful family influences that do the same. Compounding the problem are parents who have externalized self-esteem themselves and easily pass this shallow orientation to personal adequacy on to their children.

The parent who suspects an externally-based definition of personal adequacy would do well to assess this question: "If I am what I do/wear/have in the bank, then what am I if I don't?" If you "aren't" when you "don't," then you are vulnerable. There are five major problem linkages that promote attachment of self-esteem to externals. Savvy parents must be aware of all of them and counter their effects as much as possible by providing a strong family environment with healthy values for the kids.

PROBLEM LINKAGE #1: SELF-ESTEEM IS ATTACHED TO SUCCESSFUL ACHIEVEMENT. This most common problem develops when parents begin to selectively respond with approval to their children. Positive responses occur only when a child performs well or successfully meets a goal. Otherwise, parents fail to respond positively or, worse yet, don't respond at all! As the result of this selective parental reinforcement, a child easily develops an emotional linkage such that feeling personally adequate occurs only when the child has been successful. Conversely, when there is substandard achievement or little success, a child with this linkage has no emotional basis for positive self-esteem.

Adequacy Drive: "I am acceptable and can be loved only when I am successfully achieving and meeting goals, so I can't ever stop."

PROBLEM LINKAGE #2: SELF-ESTEEM IS ATTACHED TO WINNING COMPETITION. Parents who encourage unchecked competition with others and the need to win ("Winning isn't everything, it's the only thing!") often inadvertently communicate to their children that unless they are "top dog" in everything, they are utter failures. This effect is exacerbated by parents and other influential adults who are extremely competitive themselves. These are the kinds of adults who unmercifully berate the kids at ball games and in every similar endeavor. Every performance problem or mistake, however minor, brings a personal putdown.

Adequacy Drive: "If I'm not Number One, I'm a personal failure so I've got to win at all costs."

PROBLEM LINKAGE #3: SELF-ESTEEM IS ATTACHED TO USE OF CERTAIN PRODUCTS. The advertising industry in this country is quite psychologically sophisticated. And, the average person is exposed to a multitude of advertising messages each day. A major advertising strategy is to link an individual's personal adequacy to use of a particular product which, of course, is for sale: "Use our cologne and your sex life will change within minutes." "If you don't have the proper logo on your clothes, you aren't with the 'in' group and everyone will know it." This problem linkage, incessantly reinforced, works so well that it is worth billions of dollars in retail sales each year.

Adequacy Drive: "I am acceptable and can feel good about myself only as long as I am using the right products and have all the proper possessions."

PROBLEM LINKAGE #4: SELF-ESTEEM IS ATTACHED TO PEER GROUP BEHAVIORAL NORMS. The influence of a child's peer group steadily increases with progress through school. By early adolescence (ages 11-17), peer group influence is in full and powerful bloom. To be "acceptable" means abiding by peer group values and behavioral standards. And, the standards set by children are emotionally shallow and highly external in nature: Who your friends are. Wearing the right clothes. The social status of your girlfriend/ boyfriend. Being invited to the right parties. Cliques form, excluding those who do not or cannot conform. Those who are accepted must rigidly maintain peer group standards to remain in the clique.

Adequacy Drive: "I am acceptable only as long as I am accepted by my peer group and strictly adhere to *its* values right or wrong."

In a variation of this theme, parents who perceive a child to have a peer acceptance problem (real or perceived) rush in to help out. The perceived deficit may be a physical disability, shyness, emotional immaturity, or lack of social skills. Parental response is to insure (*i.e.*, buy) acceptance by providing a child with more and better possessions than all peers. At a superficial level, this ploy sometimes works, with others developing at least tolerance of the child with everything. However, deep down, that same child is usually aware of the contingency: "I am acceptable only as long as I have more and better possessions than anyone else." Wise parents promote lasting self-esteem by helping a child address and resolve relationship issues. "Possession impression" just doesn't work in the long run.

PROBLEM LINKAGE #5: SELF-ESTEEM IS ATTACHED TO PARENTAL STATUS NEEDS. Successful and achieving parents are sometimes insecure themselves. Often they are driven to reassure themselves of their adequacy in material ways. One major avenue to do just that is to impress others with what they can provide for their children. Expensive clothes, electronic equipment, expensive fad items or toys, and cars are all used to create a "successful" image and to "one-up" others. This vicarious competition with other parents often seriously undermines the self-concepts of children. It is also detrimental to healthy achievement motivation because so much is given to the kids instead of letting them earn it.

Adequacy Drive: "What is important is not who I really am but the image that I can create in others' eyes."

Security Measures for Parents

Accelerating social changes and the influences that link personal adequacy to externals make it crucial for parents to provide a stable family environment for their children. Internally-based self-esteem founded on unconditional love by parents and a healthy base of experience in a close-knit family are the only workable countermeasures to these unfortunate social trends. With a positive sense of self based within, a child grows to adulthood able to cope with rapid change. That same child is also able to keep priorities deep and healthy because self-esteem is not contingent on external factors.

Despite these pervasive social problems over which parents have only limited control, it is still entirely possible to raise healthy achieving children. To help these parents do just that, here are a dozen security measures that can be implemented at home to promote the development of positive self-esteem and personal security in your children. While most are based on common sense, it is surprising how easily they are missed by well-intentioned but busy parents during their children's important developmental years.

SECURITY MEASURE #1: TALK CASUALLY AND CONSISTENTLY WITH YOUR CHILDREN. Parents who are experiencing too much stress or who are burned out often withdraw from one another and from the kids. Communication deteriorates to exchanges based on bickering and irritability. To insure that the kids develop positive feelings and experience healthy acceptance, you must regularly take time to chat casually with your children about anything and everything. It's a powerful message: "I'm interested in you."

SECURITY MEASURE #2: BECOME ENTHUSIASTIC ABOUT A CHILD'S INTERESTS. Early in life, a child is highly motivated to obtain parents' positive involvement and approval. A child is also a natural and creative "doer." Parents getting excited and enthusiastic about what a child does (even if it's messy and far from perfect) promotes development of a positive sense of self as well as achievement motivation. However, parents must be sensitive to giving encouragement and support without taking over.

SECURITY BUILDER #3: MANDATE FAMILY TIME TOGETHER AT ALL AGES. Children have many more outside activities these days than at any time in the past. And, parents are busier keeping up with their responsibilities. This combination often results in a nonexistent family life. To counter this trend, parents must mandate regular family time together, even at the expense of some extracurricular activities. One meal a day eaten together as a family is the rock-bottom minimum.

SECURITY BUILDER #4: COMMUNICATE UNCONDITIONAL ACCEPTANCE TO YOUR CHILDREN. One of the most effective counters to developing externalized self-esteem is unconditional love. That is, caring and acceptance expressed to a child just for being: "I love you just because you're you." "You're growing up to be a delightful young man/woman." "We're so glad you're our child." These kinds of messages regularly heard develop a core of self-acceptance in a child that is a powerful defense against needing externals to define personal acceptability.

SECURITY BUILDER #5: AFFECTIONATELY TOUCH YOUR CHILDREN OFTEN. Far too many children these days grow up without ability to establish emotionally intimate relationships. A major reason is that busy parents often don't affectionately touch one another and just as frequently don't affectionately touch their children either. There is no more emotionally important way to communicate personal acceptance and love than a spontaneous hug, an arm around a shoulder, a gentle pat on the back, or a peck on the cheek.

Note: The absence of physically expressed affection by parents often creates in children a deep need for touching and being held. Meeting this important emotional need often leads to premature sexual involvement by young adults of both sexes at adolescence. Sex is traded for the experience of physical closeness which is absent at home.

SECURITY BUILDER #6: DEVELOP FAMILY TRADITIONS FOR YOUR CHILDREN AND YOURSELVES. Traditions in families create a sense of continuity with the past. These are annual rituals that take place during holidays, vacations, birthdays, or anniversaries. Active participation by the whole family in such traditions helps build a positive family history composed of fond memories. These memories are a stabilizing factor later in life for the kids who must cope with the uncertain and everchanging world around them.

SECURITY BUILDER #7: CREATE "REMEMBRANCES" FOR DEVELOPMENTAL EXPERIENCES. The strong "throwaway" orientation of contemporary culture heavily contributes to a feeling that everything, even relationships, is transitory and superficial. A sense of the enduring is important for children. Arrange school pictures in a personal album, give special (but not necessarily expensive) gifts on significant occasions, save selected drawings or school papers. These memorabilia help create a sense of personal history and continuity for the kids. A treasure chest or hope chest to keep these remembrances in is an added bonus.

SECURITY BUILDER #8: HELP YOUR CHILDREN APPRECIATE LIFE'S SIMPLE PLEASURES. It is easy for a child these days to live in a "high tech" world packed with glitzy electronics, loud noise, video arcades, and fast cars. Adults and children living in this kind of abstract world easily lose touch with deeper feelings and appreciation of the beauty that surrounds them. Walking on the beach at dawn, enjoying a picnic in the woods, or lying on your back watching the clouds go by are important experiences for children to share with parents. These experiences promote personal depth and inner peace in parents, too.

SECURITY BUILDER #9: CAREFULLY CONTROL THE TELEVISION SET. One of the most powerful factors that undermines a quality family life these days is overinvolvement in television. Not only does too much television stifle natural creativity and the curiosity of children, but it also fragments entire families when television watching becomes a higher priority than quality family time. For parents and for the kids, too much television is tremendously isolating and compromises the kinds of experiences on which personal security is built.

SECURITY BUILDER #10: HELP CHILDREN BUILD A SPIRITUAL DIMENSION TO THEIR LIVES. An appreciation of the order in the universe and belief in a Higher Being bring with them a sense of stability. And, a spiritual dimension to one's life helps immensely during the bad times which almost inevitably come. A well-developed personal faith also keeps personal values deeper and stronger. For parents, involvement in a church helps create a needed sense of community with others. For the kids, an added bonus for church membership is a peer group with healthy values during highly vulnerable periods of development.

SECURITY BUILDER #11: HELP DEFINE AND CELEBRATE DEVELOPMENTAL MARKERS WITH YOUR KIDS. In other words, be a bit sentimental with your children. At birthdays. Graduations. A child's first part in a school play. When your child receives an honor or an especially good report card. These are times to be there to share the experience and celebrate. Celebrations need not be expensive. All they require are the good will and the positive feelings that make these times memorable for children. The emotional scars left in children by parents who consistently "weren't there" for these important events may last a lifetime.

SECURITY MEASURE #12: HELP YOUR CHILDREN DEVELOP A HEALTHY SENSE OF HUMOR. It is well-known that the ability to step back from personal problems and see the funny side of life is a most valuable attribute. It's also a solid sign of mental health. A well-developed sense of humor not only helps keep life in perspective, but it also serves to release tension. Conversely, the natural optimism of children can easily be squelched by pessimistic and cynical parental attitudes that can easily pervade every aspect of life at home.

Building Internal Strength

As the saying goes, "The future just ain't what it used to be!" And, neither is the present. These days, parents often become as vulnerable as their children to the negative effects of rapid change and the externalization of self-esteem. Staying emotionally healthy is a whole new ball game now when compared to just a few years ago. And, a decade from now, the process will surely be more complex than today.

Ironically, while negative social and family changes continue unabated, the basic emotional requirements for dealing well with life's problems remain virtually identical to any other time in history. However, the task of building internal strength within children has become steadily more difficult. In the past there weren't as many options available. The values encountered in the community at large were virtually the same as in the home. Now, parents must instill those same values in their children at the same time that the family lives within a diffuse, often impersonal, everchanging, socially superficial environment. That's not easy, but it can be done.

At this point, you know now that there are good reasons to make the changes needed to create and maintain essence of family in your home. As a way to summarize many of the points already made and to reinforce your commitment to a healthy family life, here are the four major justifications for making these important lifestyle changes.

JUSTIFICATION #1: SUCH CHANGES ARE MENTALLY HEALTHY. Psychologically, positive self-esteem and a sense of inner control are highly related. And, by extension, inner control is highly related to career success and getting along well in life. An individual whose personal adequacy is based within copes better because such a person has more capacity for self-direction despite negative external influences.

JUSTIFICATION #2: BUILDING INTERNAL SECURITY IS PROTECTIVE. The person who cannot cope with change and who has externalized self-esteem is highly vulnerable. Often change becomes threatening, something to be resisted. Along with discomfort with change comes inability to deal well with failure when those external things needed for self-esteem are lost or unavailable.

JUSTIFICATION #3: PERSONAL CHARACTER DEVELOPS STRENGTH. Character can be defined as being able to do what is right, not what is easy. It is an inner strength that a person with positive self-esteem and internal security carries within. This kind of personal strength cannot be compromised as easily as in an individual with external criteria for defining personal adequacy.

JUSTIFICATION #4: DEEPER LIFE VALUES ARE KEPT IN HEALTHY PERSPECTIVE. It is very easy for an individual without an internal base of security to spend years focusing only on those things needed to support a fragile, externally-dependent sense of self. A secure person with positive self-esteem is able to keep important values in healthier perspective and is not as influenced by social superficialities.

It is ironic how frequently couples who began their lives together with healthy priorities somehow lose them over the years. Is it possible to recover what has been lost as lives became busier and more complicated? Of course . . . but it takes effort, some psychological savvy, and lots of perseverance. When you put your knowledge and commitment to work, everyone benefits from the results. But it doesn't have to happen. Keep in mind that a house is not a home . . . unless you make it so.

The legitimate question is whether a real family lives at your address. As a successful achiever, providing the house may be easy. On the other hand, "home" is a warm place in the heart that endures for a lifetime. That's the hard part. It's the legacy of positive parenting and the essence of family. Your family. Unfortunately, these days there are lots of houses that aren't really homes although parents and their children live there.

Chapter 4

From B. C. (Before Children) to A. D. (After Departure): Survival Tips for Parents

There is no doubt about it. Your decision to begin a family was a big one. Virtually overnight, your status changed from easygoing couple to responsible parents. You accepted society's mandate to raise your children to be competent in the marketplace, upstanding as citizens, and successful in relationships. You began a new phase of your life together, and you took it very seriously. While your life had been steadily becoming more complicated for years, with the children it has become incredibly demanding. Recently, in the back of your mind, there has been a nagging awareness that your marital relationship has substantially changed and that it is now vulnerable. Your perception may very well be correct.

As time has passed, you may have both become concerned because you know now that being a close couple and being parents at the same time is much more difficult than you had anticipated. Your time and energy are spread so thin that you don't seem to have time for one another anymore. Everything else seems to take priority. Contrary to your early fantasies about how it would be, you have found that living day-to-day as a successful family in mainstream America is mighty hard work. For illustration, let's look at some before and after pictures of Vince and Virginia.

They were both in their midtwenties when they met and fell in love. Just out of college and novices in their respective disciplines, Vince and Virginia worked hard, but they also had time for the fun things in life. As young marrieds, they spent most of their free time together talking, laughing, playing, and creating new adventures to experience. Together they had a good income; their lives were simple and emotionally fulfilling. Vince and Virginia were best friends and lovers.

They were happy and carefree. Life was good.

A dozen years later, the picture has changed radically. Now Vince and Virginia have become established. At work, both have been promoted into positions of responsibility. They have purchased a nice home in a good neighborhood and have two cars. To their delight, Vince, Jr., and Andrea, their children, have come along. As solid citizens, both Vince and Virginia have become involved in community affairs and their church. To a casual observer, these dedicated young parents are upstanding citizens and responsible adults who are doing all the right things. They are making it in America . . . or are they?

The reality is that Vince and Virginia live in a daily pressure cooker. Their careers take more time than ever. They have a commitment to doing the best they possibly can for their children. But the lawn needs to be mowed and the house requires constant upkeep. They have been having trouble with one of the cars lately, and it is hard to find the time for their church and community responsibilities. Vince and Virginia are in constant motion from morning to night, all day every day. They are both tired and unhappy. They know something is wrong. Before they became so successful, they could pack up and go to the beach for a weekend on an hour's notice. Now it would take a month of very careful planning to do the same if they could do it at all!

Early on, when life was simple, Vince and Virginia were at the very top of the priority list for one another. Over the years, they have slowly slipped to the absolute bottom. For this very typical couple and for the untold numbers of their contemporaries, the changes that have come with success and with parenthood are nothing short of dramatic. And, they're certainly not all positive. From being friends and lovers, a couple's relationship inexorably evolves into a lifestyle devoted exclusively to managing and parenting.

In a nutshell, over the years, parenthood has replaced Pollyanna. And, as responsibilities increase, it is quite easy for couples to begin to take their marital relationship entirely for granted as they continue to live together but grow apart. Accompanying these insidious changes is a constellation of negative feelings that steadily grow within a now burdened and embattled couple. Here's the sequence of what happens as emotional barriers to intimacy in a marital relationship grow.

INTIMACY BARRIER #1: HOME LIFE BECOMES PRESSURED.
Early in a couple's life together, home is a refuge from the stresses of

work. Later, many more responsibilities loom at home. Fix-it jobs, routine housework, and maintenance of cars and other property all require more time and energy, to say nothing of the needs of a spouse and children. The result is that life after work becomes as pressured as the workplace. Home was once a sanctuary. Now coming home provides no relief.

INTIMACY BARRIER #2: THE NEED TO GIVE TO OTHERS CONSTANTLY. As responsibilities grow, you feel a consequent necessity to respond to them. In other words, to give of yourself to others in every area of life. Giving constantly to others without giving to yourself or receiving in return brings with it resentment and anger. As these feelings grow, others, even loved ones, are perceived as interested only in selfish taking, completely insensitive to the needs of the giver.

INTIMACY BARRIER #3: DEFENSIVE ISOLATION EMERGES. For self-protection, a spouse and children are consistently and irritably pushed away. "Leave me alone!" is the dominant theme of parental communication. However, as others learn to keep their distance, this defensive ploy backfires. A sense of personal isolation and loneliness grows in the place of neglected relationships. These feelings are typically accompanied by a perception that no one really cares.

INTIMACY BARRIER #4: A SENSE OF DISILLUSIONMENT GROWS. Accompanying all of the above feelings come several nagging doubts: "Is this what success and parenthood are all about? Have all the sacrifices been worth it? Is this what I've worked all these years to attain?" All the good things in life and in a once close relationship have somehow disappeared. Because of the growing distance between parents, these feelings often can't be talked out. Over time, disappointment grows more intense.

As did Vince and Virginia, most likely you enjoyed life B.C. (Before Children). Way back then, life was simple and you probably didn't even realize it at the time. At that point, you probably weren't as successful in an economic sense, but you sure had a good time. Now you are in the middle of the difficult years, but you also realize that there is life A.D. (After Departure) of the kids. Perhaps the major task that you as parents face is to preserve your relationship as a couple by keeping it healthy and strong in the meantime.

It's all too easy to live together but grow apart. However, the rationale for placing a high priority on your relationship together is easily missed. If you fail to stay together emotionally as a couple during these critical years, you *and* the children lose. As partners in marriage, you will not be as fulfilled or as happy as you could be. And, if you do not have a healthy marital relationship, you cannot be as effective in your parenting. And, in the end, after the kids are gone, what will you have left of your relationship? To prevent these problems, here are some ideas about how to renew your relationship as a couple right now and put the parents back in parenthood.

The Parents' Cohesiveness Checklist

Sometimes the distance that slowly grows between two parents is felt acutely, but the reasons have not been clearly articulated. The following statements make up the Parents' Cohesiveness Checklist. It pinpoints specific negative changes that lead to a persistent sense of estrangement that weakens a marital bond. Read down this checklist. The more statements you check as true, the more likely it is that you are not really emotionally together as a couple anymore. As a way to rebuild that wonderful closeness you once had, both you and your spouse should review these fifteen items carefully. Then talk about the results and decide to make needed changes together.

_____   1. When family members want to talk, you put them off with an indefinite "later" and then never get around to it.

_____   2. These days, much of your spouse-to-spouse communication is often fragmented and tinged with impatient irritation.

_____   3. When you and your spouse are around the house, both of you are constantly working or watching TV without spending quality time together.

_____   4. Most of the content of your "discussions" with your spouse involve the misbehavior of the kids, how much money is being spent and where, and how overburdened you feel.

_____   5. You tend to use very direct questions when you "talk" to family members these days.

_____   6. Because there are so many demands on you, you irritably push your spouse and the kids away because you basically want to be left alone.

_____   7. In contrast to years ago, you and your spouse rarely go out to enjoy yourselves without the kids anymore.

_____ 8. You have little or no time these days to see friends or to pursue the leisure interests or hobbies you used to enjoy.

_____ 9. Your physical relationship has been steadily going downhill because you are so tired all the time.

_____ 10. You find yourself complaining incessantly, and what you say to others is often critical and negative.

_____ 11. You are not as courteous and polite to one another as in the past.

_____ 12. There is not much left of the playful banter or horsing around you once used to enjoy together.

_____ 13. Because you're so touchy, you easily say nasty things or put one another down for no real reason at all.

_____ 14. Affectionate touching of your partner has virtually disappeared beyond the perfunctory peck on a cheek now and then.

_____ 15. These days, there is very little in the way of spontaneous compliments or encouraging one another.

Corrosive Pressures

As a responsible parent interested in doing your best, you live each day in a social milieu of powerful influences that can have a decidedly destructive effect on your couple's relationship. As these corrosive pressures take their toll, you begin to respond more and more to external demands and expectations. Within, by minute increments over the years, you lose sight of your sense of self and your life together as a loving couple. What you have really lost is not only the ability to take care of yourself physically and emotionally, but also the deeper value system that you need to maintain that important sense of inner control, perspective, and direction.

Here are the seven major corrosive pressures that, without your vigilance, will constantly eat away at your ability to feel good about yourself and grow together as a couple. A decision statement is attached as a remedy to each one.

CORROSIVE PRESSURE #1: YOUR SELF/SELFISHNESS LINE IS BLURRED. A major reason you do not feel good these days is that you have lost the ability to give to yourself. Behind this neglect is a fear that if you give to yourself when there is lots to be done or someone else wants something, you are being selfish or somehow bad. Then you begin to feel guilty. The result is that you opt to give to others to a fault, especially to the kids with their insatiable demands, to avoid the guilt that quickly builds if you don't. You get nothing because it has become so emotionally difficult to justify giving to yourself.

Your Decision: You must begin to treat yourself as important. Start giving to yourself and facing that irrational guilt instead of running away from it. Realize that giving at least a little bit to yourself is absolutely essential to make everything else seem worthwhile. Further, the only way to keep giving to others in positive ways is to give at least a little bit to yourself along the way.

CORROSIVE PRESSURE #2: YOU HAVE NO RESPECT FOR YOUR PHYSICAL AND EMOTIONAL LIMITS. Long ago, you worked hard, but you also found plenty of time to "get away from it all." These days, you are acting like Superman and Superwoman. Because so many responsibilities, expectations, and obligations are assaulting you from every part of your life, you are now burning the candle at both ends. Because of your "limitless" efforts, you have become highly self-abusive. And, you rationalize your self-destructive behavior nicely. But, the fact is that you just don't feel good too much of the time these days.

Your Decision: Make a clear commitment to your health by improving your eating, sleeping, and exercising habits at all costs. Build in some time to be together and relax. And, do it by saying "no" or cutting out some of the extraneous demands on yourself. Keep in mind that with age, you become more vulnerable to physical problems that stem from the pressured lifestyle you live each day.

CORROSIVE PRESSURE #3: YOUR LIFE HAS BECOME CONTROLLED BY THE PERSISTENT DEMANDS OF CHILDREN. With the passing of years, your priorities have subtly, but powerfully changed. Now you give to the kids, not to yourself or to your marriage. Any responsible parent knows from experience that children require time and energy and commitment. On the other hand, there is a vast difference between healthy caretaking and giving in to the insatiable demands of children. Once you begin to overgive of your time and attention, it becomes a trap. The children want more and more as you continue to give and give.

Your Decision: Back up and get control of yourself. You must set reasonable limits and abide by them. Only you can decide when enough is enough. Give your children what they need rather than what they want. Define this line clearly to yourself and to the kids.

Then hold that line! You and the kids will all be healthier in the long run. And, your children will learn to occupy themselves without relying on you for entertainment.

CORROSIVE PRESSURE #4: YOU ARE DRIVEN BY THE FEAR THAT YOUR CHILDREN WILL BE FAILURES. Today, "making it" economically is a longer, much more sophisticated process than it was even a single generation ago. Your awareness of the demands of the marketplace creates a fear that drives you. That fear and your sense of responsibility to your children motivates you to provide them with a fantastic array of sometimes expensive "enrichment" experiences. While your efforts are laudable within limits, your fears have caused you to carry the extracurricular education of your children to the point of eroding the stable family life that children need to emotionally thrive. And, constantly carrying the kids from place to place also interferes with time you need to keep your couple's relationship strong.

Your Decision: Start right away to make *family* enrichment a very high priority. A healthy family life is extremely important to the later success of your children. It provides a sense of security and a base of positive experiences that help cope with uncertainty for a lifetime. Beyond that, creating a family environment in which you as parents are also emotionally nourished is necessary to attain that same goal.

CORROSIVE PRESSURE #5: YOU HAVE BEEN SEDUCED BY MATERIALISTIC VALUES. Achievement-oriented parents interested in becoming successful find it very easy to begin defining their self-worth through external criteria. Your salary level, your address, your social status, even your children's achievements become the major foundations of your self-esteem. As you become progressively externally-focused in a very materialistic society, you more easily lose deeper values. As this happens, you begin to live superficially with much more personal vulnerability.

Your Decision: Begin right away to rediscover the basics together. Strong and loving relationships, personal fulfillment, and enjoying some of life's simple pleasures are more enduring than any "things." As you begin to redefine yourself internally, you will regain the ability to relax and be yourself in a delightful new way. Positive experiences together and a good relationship are definitely "keepers" that help maintain deep and healthy priorities.

CORROSIVE PRESSURE #6: YOU HAVE FALLEN FOR THE "NEIGHBORHOOD NORMS" TRAP. It is a paradox that parents who live in close proximity to one another in the suburbs are often psychologically isolated these days. Impersonal subdivisions have replaced true neighborhoods. Intermittent, casual contacts with neighbors are the norm. The result is that you have slipped into taking many of your cues about parenting from what you observe others doing up and down the street. You are reluctant to be different so you go along with the crowd. You tend to do what your kids tell you other parents are doing.

Your Decision: At all costs, make the time to think out the issues rather than slipping into highly questionable neighborhood norms. Make it a point to talk over basic parenting issues and decisions with your spouse. Decide together that maintaining solid life values is worth the feeling of being different than everyone else. Then coordinate your efforts and do what makes sense even if it is not what everyone else is doing.

CORROSIVE PRESSURE #7: YOU HAVE BECOME CONDITIONED TO RAPID CHANGE. Everything changes so quickly these days that practically nothing seems stable and enduring. You have become so used to rapid change that when anything gives you a problem, you easily shift into a "throwaway" ethic and get rid of it. TV channels, relationships, communities, and possessions have all become too replaceable. With this type of destructive social ethic, it is easy to seek something new instead of searching for what is deeper and ultimately more fulfilling.

Your Decision: Realize that what it takes to make a relationship healthy and strong will never change. A good relationship always requires time and energy and commitment. However, the results will be worth it to you both. Your first step must be to stop taking your couple's relationship for granted. Then commit yourself to "hanging in" and making your relationship all that it can be for you both.

Survival Mandates for Parents

At this point, you understand some of the pychological pressures that result from an interaction of unhealthy environmental influences and unresolved issues within yourself as a parent. It is likely that these same pressures will remain very powerful and even become more intense in the future. That places the burden on you as a couple to look within for what you need to survive parenthood in style. It would be an excellent idea to begin your search for a deeper and more enduring relationship right now. Make it an ongoing project, one that will ultimately draw you as close together as you used to be. After all, if you do not deserve a bit more out of life than you are giving yourselves these days, who does?

Here are listed a dozen specific survival mandates that perhaps have been weakened or lost over the years. By readopting these basic values that you once shared and using them as the basis for making decisions as parents, you are creating an emotionally healthier environment in which you and your children can thrive.

SURVIVAL MANDATE #1: KEEP THE PARENTAL RELATIONSHIP PRIMARY IN THE FAMILY. Far too frequently children drag parents through life according to the *children's* immature whims. It is not a healthy situation for you or for the kids. The children must come *with you* until they become self-supporting adults. When you re-establish this fundamental priority within the family, you will be more able to give to yourselves as parents and to guide your children with more perspective.

SURVIVAL MANDATE #2: STRIVE TO REACH AGREEMENT ON WHAT YOU WANT OUT OF LIFE. Agreement on the basics of what you want together as a couple, on the fundamentals of parenting, and on what is right and good is most helpful to keep you both going in the same direction. Do not neglect talking about these issues frequently. A wise saying states: "If you don't stand for something, you can fall for anything." It is best if you stand together as a couple.

SURVIVAL MANDATE #3: DEEPEN YOUR COMMITMENT TO "MAKING IT TOGETHER." Over the past two decades, far too casual attitudes toward relationships, including marriage, have been the norm. However, this situation is now changing. Basing your relationship on a deep commitment to working out differences or problems is far healthier than the "if it doesn't work out, we'll split" orientation. Nurture this value in your relationship because couples who have it not only stay together, but find that life is easier and more deeply fulfilling when it is shared.

SURVIVAL MANDATE #4: SHOW AFFECTION TO ONE ANOTHER DAILY. One of the greatest liabilities that come with children and a busy lifestyle is neglect of the "affection connection." Lots of nonsexual physical touching, along with expressions of caring and love, are important to both of you to feel good every day. It is an easy, but terrible mistake to assume your partner knows how you feel. If you really mean it, make it known through your words, gentle touches, and caring responses.

SURVIVAL MANDATE #5: NURTURE A SPIRITUAL DIMEN-SION TO YOUR COUPLE'S RELATIONSHIP. Virtually every survey of the best marriage relationships that last mentions this value. It centers on belief in a Supreme Being who transcends mere mortals. This kind of personal faith, whether nurtured through a formal religious affiliation or in other ways, produces a healthy inner strength that is a buffer against the vicissitudes of life. It also keeps your values centered in deeper meanings rather than on seductive superficialities.

SURVIVAL MANDATE #6: LEARN TO RESOLVE CONFLICTS IN HEALTHY WAYS. Conflicts are inevitable in even the best of relationships. A major difference between a marriage that works and one that does not lies in whether the couple involved can resolve differences in ways satisfactory to both. Strive for open discussion, healthy give-and-take, and flexible compromise instead of hitting below the belt, or worse yet, denying the problem and refusing to deal with it.

SURVIVAL MANDATE #7: SPEND QUALITY TIME ALONE REGULARLY. As a busy parent, it is very easy to forget that you had a relationship as a couple before the children came along and that you will have one after they are gone. Keep firmly in mind that relationships require that you spend time together enjoying one another. It's deceptively easy to avoid one another while spending a lot of time together under the same roof. No doubt about it, couples who play together stay together.

SURVIVAL MANDATE #8: MAKE SURE THAT YOU REMAIN EMOTIONALLY SELF-SUFFICIENT. A strong marriage requires two capable adults who relate to one another as such. In many marriages, however, one spouse may lament: "I have three children— Johnny, Janie, and my husband/wife." In such relationships, one spouse has slipped into the role of dependent or irresponsible child. It is only when *both* partners remain competent adults that they can not only do what needs to be done, but also lean on one another in healthy ways when necessary.

SURVIVAL MANDATE #9: PRESERVE MUTUAL EMPATHIC SENSITIVITY AND RESPECT IN YOUR RELATIONSHIP. In short, do you support your partner with consistent words of encouragement? Is there willingness to help one another? Do you call home to inform your partner if plans change or you will be late? These kinds of responses are only characteristic of individuals who have emotionally accepted marriage as a true partnership. In those many marriages without it, a vital aspect of being together is missing.

SURVIVAL MANDATE #10: PERSONAL GROWTH AND CHANGE ARE AN ACCEPTED PART OF YOUR MARRIAGE. Personal development, essential to positive self-esteem, requires change that almost certainly will affect the marital relationship. Healthy relationships allow mutually supportive change. However, acceptance of change and accommodation of the necessary adjustments in your primary relationship require mutual trust that must be carefully built and never violated.

SURVIVAL MANDATE #11: MAKE THE TIME TO CHAT WITH YOUR PARTNER EVERY DAY. One of the surest indicators of growing distance between spouses lies in not taking the time to touch base every single day. This time to coordinate schedules, to inquire about how each partner's day went, and to relate interesting happenings is vital time that must become an important part of your daily routines. When you are comfortable with one another in this way, then you can talk more comfortably about the deeper and more emotionally-loaded issues that will inevitably confront you both.

SURVIVAL MANDATE #12: EACH SPOUSE HAS A PLEASANT PERSONAL INTEREST THAT IS BEING PURSUED. To make all your efforts and sacrifices seem worthwhile, you must have something that is just for you. It is a personal involvement that you pursue, just for you, just for the fun of it. This kind of activity is usually separate from your partner and should be relaxing and fun. It is the one area of your life where you give just to you and because you do, it makes being together as a loving couple and as responsible parents much easier.

Managing to Be a Couple

Few parents would argue with the fact that parenting is tough, and, in a very complex and everchanging world, it is getting tougher. The skills needed for success are more subtle. The training required to "make it" financially takes longer. Parenting your children well through the difficult developmental years is much more complex. As parents striving to do the very best you can for your children, you are vulnerable to inadvertantly losing yourselves as a couple. Although surrounded by neighbors, you are psychologically isolated. Although economically successful, you may not be really happy. With so much to give within you, you are resentful because you seem to be getting so little back these days. It is far past time to reverse these trends.

The bottom line is that you must begin to treat your marital relationship as one of primary importance if you are going to thrive as a couple and be the best parents possible. What you have lost are your hopes and your dreams and the part of life that is fun loving and effervescent. That part of both of you has been buried beneath your many responsibilities and obligations for too long. For you and for your children, it really is time to back up, define a bit more clearly how you want to live, and then adopt the survival values that are the building blocks of a new life together.

It takes time, but when you rebuild the closeness you once had, you will both begin to feel better inside. You will become a delightful couple again who also happen to be good parents in lieu of a worn-out twosome just managing to survive day to day. Along with these positive changes come some healthy side effects.

SIDE EFFECT #1: YOU WILL MODEL A HEALTHY RELATION-SHIP FOR YOUR CHILDREN. How sadly common it is for children to grow to adulthood with no idea about what a healthy adult relationship is like because they have never seen one. As you renew your relationship with your partner now, you will be creating a solid foundation for your children to do the same later. It's a subtle, but powerful asset in the later fulfillment of your children.

SIDE EFFECT #2: YOU WILL BE ABLE TO DRAW STRENGTH FROM ONE ANOTHER NOW. From "Leave me alone, I've got enough problems" evolves a new spirit as you draw together again. "We're a real team and we can handle anything together" becomes your couple's byline. It is a good feeling to know that you are not alone when times get tough. With this same unity, the good times are even more fulfilling.

SIDE EFFECT #3: YOU WILL BE PREPARING FOR LIFE AFTER THE CHILDREN LEAVE. Busy and responsible parents who cease to be a couple wind up strangers at the breakfast table after the last child leaves. By rebuilding your couple's relationship now and sharing with one another every day, you will really be together, finding life even richer and more exciting than you thought.

Yes, Vince and Virginia, there is life after parenthood right now, but only if you make it so. Best friends and lovers. That is how you started your life together. With success you became managers and parents with practically nothing at all left over for yourself. Now you are going to do something about that sad state of affairs. Love that lasts is one in which you both grow together every single day. And, good parenting these days certainly requires a "together" couple. It's a mistake to put it off until later. Later may be too late . . . for you and for the kids.

Any time is a good time to get your priorities in order. And, it's easier to prevent the problems that come from skewed priorities than it is to correct them once destructive marital patterns have become deeply ingrained. A very wise individual once defined mature love not as two individuals gazing into one another's eyes, but rather as a couple walking hand in hand in the same direction. The simile is perceptive and one that today's parents with their hectic schedules must carefully consider. In the end, all you really have is each other. "Hey, stranger, let me take your hand. Let's talk about *us* while we walk."

Chapter 5

Going Down the Tube: Television Can Weaken or Enhance the Family

It has been more than four decades since television has come into the home. Immensely more sophisticated now, it has evolved to become *the* most popular form of entertainment in America. Television is cheap. Television is easily available. It is interesting, exciting, and educational. With its current global scope, there can be little doubt that television has done more to expand the awareness of those who watch it than any other form of media. Adults and children sit for hours on end before the set. Many are obviously gaining from its ability to stimulate. Too many others, however, are using these same hours to avoid facing issues that relate to healthy family life, success, and personal well-being. Aided and abetted by their television habit, they are going down the tube while sitting in front of it!

The point is that television, with its tremendous potential, can enhance the family if properly used. Conversely, an overdeveloped television habit can also fragment the family and interfere with learning essential life skills. As a prime example of the latter, let's peek through the window at the Mellow family. Living in the suburbs and reasonably successful, the Mellows are typical in many ways. However, changes have occurred over the years, especially since the children have come along. Some of the closeness has disappeared. They don't talk as much, and they hardly ever go on family outings as they did in the past. And, by slow increments over several years, television has come to dominate the life of each family member.

MICHAEL MELLOW: Dead tired after a hard day's work, Mike does not feel much like talking when he comes in. Instead, he flips on the evening news during dinner. Shortly thereafter, he retires to his favorite chair to indiscriminately watch television until it is time to go to bed. This habit goes on day after day, weeks on end. He does not like family members interrupting while he is watching and responds with irritation when they do. Throughout the evening he periodically snacks. The pattern is much the same on weekends. Mike also dozes constantly while watching.

MARY MELLOW: After working in the mornings, Mary returns home and turns on the TV immediately after unlocking the front door. She is very involved in afternoon serials and becomes extremely upset when she misses a day for any reason. However, even when her shows are not on, the TV is on because she finds it uncomfortable without the background noise even though she is in another room. When friends drop by (they don't come much anymore), they must either watch her serials or talk only during the commercials.

MARSHA MELLOW: A bright eleven-year-old, Marsha will watch anything, anytime. She enjoys children's shows, but recently she has also become absorbed with her mother in afternoon soaps. She hurries home from school each and every day to watch them. In addition, she habitually does homework in front of the television set. Her grades have suffered as a result. In the evenings and on weekends when there is a conflict about what to watch, she goes to her room where she has her own television set to watch "her" shows.

"LITTLE MAC" MELLOW: Almost five, Little Mac has grown up on television. He loves cartoons, and it is hard to get him involved in anything else. He turns on the television set whenever he feels like it. While he is watching, family members know that he is quieter and does not need as much attention. Whenever he becomes bothersome, he is gently ushered to the nearest TV to distract him. On the flip side, he habitually ignores parental instructions. He isn't very interested in playing with neighborhood children anymore because there is TV to watch at home.

Take a moment to count the number of highly questionable television habits that have developed over the years in the Mellow family. In the good old days, Mike and Mary rarely watched television because they had so many other interesting things to do: talk with one another, see friends, take walks, play tennis, or just goof around. As the family became more established and successful, two dramatic changes have occurred that can be seen clearly only if viewed over a span of years. First, quality leisure activities were given up because there was so much to do. Second, Mike, Mary, Marsha, and Little Mac have developed abusive television viewing habits that have further eroded the quality of life within the family.

It would be patently ridiculous to blame all of these changes on television. In fact, there is little question that television is *fantastic!* At no other time in history has there been such a blend of quality entertainment, educational shows, and news programs so easily available so constantly to so many. The real problem is that television becomes a too-passive alternative when other pressures on various family members become intense. Gradually, television comes to dominate the family, fragmenting it internally. As a responsible parent, now would be a good time to take stock of your current lifestyle and to examine closely how much TV your family is watching and for what reasons. To help clarify your thoughts on the subject, here is an overview of some of the healthy uses and chronic abuses of television.

Television Can Isolate Parents

Certainly children are attracted to television. It is only natural, with the very high levels of stimulation it provides. However, far too frequently, unhealthy use of television by the children begins with parental modeling. In a nutshell, as parents' lives become more complicated with more to do each day, Mom and Dad become increasingly fatigued because they are spending so many hours working. In other words, busy parents burn out trying to keep up with their myriad responsibilities.

Most of the time, along with the low-level depressive state that characterizes burnout comes a dramatic increase in television viewing time. Clinical experience reveals that this is especially true of men. On the other hand, the quality of that viewing time clearly deteriorates. In front of the set, the individual is not laughing, excited, or involved in the shows being watched. Rather, that person is found sitting, stonefaced, worrying and mulling over problems during extended hours of viewing time.

Under these conditions, personal burnout deepens with its negative impact on the emotional health of the individual. Beyond these effects, however, the quality of life after work in general and the marital relationship in particular begin to slide. Two people, once close, begin to grow apart. To be more specific, here are seven characteristic family-life changes that occur as television becomes the dominant focus of family members.

FAMILY-LIFE CHANGE #1: OUTSIDE INTERESTS BEGIN TO FADE. As low-quality television viewing time goes up, time spent seeing friends and pursuing leisure interests or hobbies correspondingly declines. Parents spend much more time at home, but become increasingly isolated from one another and the family as time passes. As this emotional withdrawal occurs, they find it increasingly difficult to get excited about much of anything.

FAMILY-LIFE CHANGE #2: FAMILY COMMUNICATION SHUTS DOWN. To put it bluntly, television-dominated families don't generate much quality communication. Communication problems affect critical parent-to-parent dialogue as well as parent-to-child interactions. The person you want to talk to is perennially watching television and does not want to be distracted by having to respond. Individual isolation worsens with time.

FAMILY-LIFE CHANGE #3: UNHEALTHY HABITS ARE EXACERBATED. Individuals who overeat, drink, or smoke are likely to do so more when they are spending long, low-quality hours in front of the TV set. Children also quickly pick up the habit of snacking while watching TV. These unhealthy habits heavily contribute to a lack of physical fitness, and also exacerbate parents' awareness that they are not feeling good emotionally or physically these days.

FAMILY-LIFE CHANGE #4: A DEEP LETHARGY SETS IN. In other words, an inertia problem develops. As a very passive lifestyle dominated by excessive television viewing time evolves, a deep lethargy slowly but surely sets in. It is a fact that lethargy breeds lethargy. The more you sit around, the more you feel like sitting around; that is exactly what happens in front of the television set.

FAMILY-LIFE CHANGE #5: INTERPERSONAL INTIMACY DECLINES. With more television time, once close marital partners spend less time enjoying one another and participating together in quality leisure activities. The quality of their communication also diminishes. They become irritable and bicker more, which drives them farther apart. Necessary communication increasingly focuses on problems. Affectionate touching disappears as do words of encouragement and support. The gulf widens.

FAMILY-LIFE CHANGE #6: LIBIDINAL ENERGY DIMINISHES. Along with other changes already occurring, sexual energy is concurrently decreasing. The quality of a couple's physical relationship goes downhill as lethargy sets in because of what is happening in front of the TV in the living room. Not infrequently, television is used actively to avoid a partner. It is well-known that libido often dramatically weakens when there are other negative emotions—fatigue, anger, stress, or worry—are present.

FAMILY-LIFE CHANGE #7: A VICIOUS CIRCLE BEGINS. As the emotional needs of the family members are not met, they have a tendency to retreat to even more television time. An already-negative family situation begins to spiral downward and feed on itself. Sometimes one family member sees what is happening and pushes for change, but pleas fall on deaf ears. Eventually, everyone unhappily gives up as the family settles into a low quality, television-dominated, monotonous lifestyle.

Television, Children, and Success

Much of the current controversy about the impact of television on a child's development centers on program content. However, a more subtle level of influence must be of equal if not greater cause for concern to responsible parents. Such parents must carefully consider the psychological *structure* of television as it impacts on learning the skills necessary for success later in life. Those parents who conscientiously monitor the content of shows watched by children, but who fail to limit sheer time spent in front of the set, may win a battle but lose the war.

Here are listed the seven major structural impact problems of television that can impede or distort a child's ability to learn critical life skills. A counterpoint as it relates to success is provided for each.

STRUCTURAL IMPACT #1: CREATIVITY AND IMAGINATION ARE DULLED. A child's natural creativity may have little or no outlet when virtually all free time is spent watching television. Similarly, imagination, the rich internal world that is the font of creativity, may be dulled by constant stimulation from external sources via television. The TV child just doesn't get as much practice using natural creativity.

Counterpoint: The capacity for innovation and for solving problems creatively is a critical ingredient in career success. Creative outlets also keep life interesting and become an important form of emotional expression for many adults and children.

STRUCTURAL IMPACT #2: AN ASOCIAL LIFESTYLE IS PRONE TO DEVELOP. With a child constantly glued to the television set, interest in seeing friends may wane and sometimes disappear. Little ones watching TV together have little opportunity for cooperative play or meaningful interaction. As a result, a child may remain excessively isolated from peers at a critical time in development when key social skills are typically learned.

Counterpoint: Strong "people skills" are needed to "make it" in virtually every career or profession. These same skills are needed for healthy relationships and a strong family life later.

STRUCTURAL IMPACT #3: TASK PERSISTENCE MAY DE-CREASE. Television attracts children because of its constant high levels of visual and auditory stimulation. Scenes change every few seconds. However, in reality, completion of meaningful tasks may require persistent efforts without much external stimulation at all. A child who becomes addicted to the constant stimulation and change characteristic of TV may lose the capacity to stick with important projects that become dull or routine (as most do).

Counterpoint: Hard work and persistence despite frustration and monotony are almost always required to reach meaningful personal and professional goals.

STRUCTURAL IMPACT #4: PERSONAL INITIATIVE MAY WEAKEN. In sad partnership with burned-out adults, children who watch too much television do not want to do much except watch more television. Unless parents dictate otherwise, as long as television is available, that is what children will choose. With time, many children lose the capacity to occupy themselves without external stimulation. When the TV is off, their constant lament is "I'm bored."

Counterpoint: Success in almost any endeavor requires initiative and the ability to create personal challenges and stimulating activities without having them provided by others.

STRUCTURAL IMPACT #5: ATTENTION SPAN MAY BE SHORTENED. Another problem with the constant barrage of stimulation and scene changes on television is that a child's ability to focus mentally may be compromised. As children become used to constantly changing external stimuli, internal thought processes may become increasingly fragmented. This is often accompanied by high levels of distractibility in tasks requiring steady concentration.

Counterpoint: Solid problem solving skills and many other essential life tasks require a well-developed ability to concentrate and focus attention for reasonably long periods of time.

STRUCTURAL IMPACT #6: EASY SOLUTIONS TO PROBLEMS ARE EXPECTED. Television characters or cartoon figures solve the most difficult life problems with the greatest of ease. Uncomfortable emotions, the various steps involved, and the time framework necessary to deal with real problems are presented on TV in a highly compressed fashion, often with critical parts completely absent. The child comes to expect the same in real life.

Counterpoint: To cope well with anxiety and frustration while struggling with very complex problem situations is absolutely necessary for success at work and for healthy relationships that last.

STRUCTURAL IMPACT #7: THE MATURATION PROCESS IS INHIBITED. Children who are allowed to spend too much time watching television often remain emotionally immature. The process of "growing up" requires give-and-take, trial-and-error interaction with the real world. It also necessitates testing and refining work skills, not to mention learning to deal well with people. The TV child misses much of this critical practice, along with the ongoing parental guidance that facilitates emotional and cognitive maturation.

Counterpoint: To get along well in the world requires judgement and skills that come only from a broad base of personal experience with "what works" and what doesn't in particular kinds of situations.

Healthy Television Habits

Although overuse of television can have an extremely detrimental impact on individuals within the family and on family functioning as a whole, it can also have an enriching impact if its use is controlled and if viewing time is selective. By making deliberate efforts to modify use of television in the home, you as parents will begin to move the entire family in the direction of cohesiveness, better communication, a healthier lifestyle, and more fulfilling relationships.

As a way to get started, here are a number of television guidelines for you to seriously consider adopting within your home. Keep in mind that *you* may be abusing television just as much or more than the children. To gain the benefits from more controlled use of TV, *both* of you as responsible parents must agree on and cooperate in making these needed changes.

TELEVISION GUIDELINE #1: TURN OFF THE TELEVISION SET DURING MEALTIMES. At breakfast and lunch, but especially at dinner, the TV should be off. Meals may be the only time the entire family is together during any given day. Eating together should be made into quality time to chat comfortably about stimulating topics of interest, the day's activities, or family concerns. This just cannot be done with the distraction of television.

TELEVISION GUIDELINE #2: CREATE AN EDUCATIONAL BALANCE IN VIEWING TIME. In short, make it a point to mandate that documentaries, educational programs, and daily news get relatively high priority during viewing time. It is the only way to utilize fully the tremendous potential of television to expand knowledge, awareness, and understanding. Watch such shows *with* the children whenever possible.

TELEVISION GUIDELINE #3: INSIST THAT CHILDREN ASK TO WATCH TELEVISION. In homes where television viewing is uncontrolled and indiscriminate, children perceive TV as a right, not a privilege. It is probably well past time to break that unhealthy habit by insisting that children ask permission to watch television. In this way, parents regain control of program content and also television viewing time.

TELEVISION GUIDELINE #4: ELIMINATE TELEVISION AS AN ELECTRONIC BABYSITTER. Television does keep children quiet and occupied, but it backfires over the long run. When children do not have the opportunity to learn to entertain themselves, their dependency on television consequently grows. Then when parents do try to limit viewing time, the kids don't know what to do with themselves and nag parents to death.

TELEVISION GUIDELINE #5: PARENTS MUST BREAK THE "FLIP ON" HABIT. Think for a moment. When you return to the house, what do you do right after you unlock the door? If you habitually go immediately to the TV and flip it on, you have developed a very bad habit. You probably find the background noise of television comforting even though you are two rooms away. Start getting used to having the TV off by not turning it on until there is a particular program you want to see.

TELEVISION GUIDELINE #6: DO NOT DO HIGHLY COGNITIVE WORK IN FRONT OF THE TV SET. It is a fact that you cannot concentrate fully on two intellectual tasks at the same time. You may have slipped into trying to do office work while watching television. In addition, children will do homework in front of the tube if parents permit it. In either case, concentration is limited and quality of work typically suffers as a result. Make it a point to carry out intellectual work in a quiet place without the distraction of TV and insist that the children do the same.

TELEVISION GUIDELINE #7: USE TELEVISION FOR "FAMILY SHOWTIMES." Some television programming is excellent in content and quality of entertainment. Make watching high-quality shows a family affair. Gather the family together to watch, and make some popcorn while you are at it. Then, when the program ends, turn the TV off. This kind of television viewing pattern contributes to a quality family life instead of eroding it through indiscriminate overuse.

TELEVISION GUIDELINE #8: WHEN FRIENDS DROP OVER, TURN THE TV OFF. Time and again, adults cordially invite friends over to visit. Then when the friends arrive, those same adults sit watching television and do not want to interact! Children often do the same. Have the courtesy to turn off the TV when friends stop by if you want them to keep coming. The only legitimate exception is when you invite friends over specifically to view a special program together.

TELEVISION GUIDELINE #9: DO NOT PERMIT CHILDREN TO HAVE TELEVISION SETS IN BEDROOMS. A television set in the parents' bedroom is questionable, but permitting children of any age to have sets in their bedrooms is clearly out of line. The bedroom is a prime study area that is compromised when there is a personal TV in it. In addition, children tend to isolate themselves even more from the family by habitually retreating to their rooms to watch "their" shows.

TELEVISION GUIDELINE #10: COLD TURKEY ON THE "CHANNEL CHANGING" HABIT. One of the most irritating habits that a family member can fall into is trying to watch two or three programs simultaneously. This is done by changing channels back and forth every few minutes. This is highly distracting to others and represents an inability of the individual doing it to focus on and enjoy just one show. By breaking this pattern, you secondarily improve your ability to relax by learning to become more deeply and pleasantly involved in just one activity.

TELEVISION GUIDELINE #11: WORK TOWARD FAMILY AGREEMENT ON TELEVISION VIEWING SCHEDULES. How much, what, and who watches should all be subjects for serious family discussion. Clear guidelines understood by all, especially the children, help bring indiscriminate viewing under solid parental control. Open discussion also helps parents make healthy decisions about family-life priorities and their own television viewing habits.

TELEVISION GUIDELINE #12: DO NOT SLEEP OR DOZE WHILE WATCHING TELEVISION. If you are tired, take a nap or go to bed. Dozing for hours in front of the television set often interferes with quality sleep when you do turn it off. On the other hand, a conditioned response is likely to develop in which you quickly "nod off" when the TV is on even though there is something interesting you want to watch. Also, keep in mind that some of your "fatigue" may be nothing more than lethargy generated by too much television!

The Breaking Away Process

By regaining perspective on healthy television viewing habits, perhaps you have also regained perspective on vital aspects of the good life that you have given up as you have become more established at work and in your community. You realize only in retrospect just how many once-fulfilling and deeper life values you have slowly lost. And, because of your loss, the kids are not learning healthy values, either. Perhaps only now are you becoming acutely aware of how much television has become a too-passive alternative to living well and really enjoying life these days. With the help of a television habit, you and your family may have been living together, but growing apart for years.

To further your awareness of the insidious role too much television has on family life, here's a diagnostic point to consider. True or false. *On a reasonably regular basis, your entire family spends an evening at home pleasantly occupied in activities of personal interest. You and your children do not necessarily have to be doing anything together during these times. However, during these evenings at home, the television set does not go on for one minute!* If your answer is TRUE, you are promoting healthy lifestyle values within the family. Unfortunately, a True answer is a rarity these days. It underscores the dependency of family members on TV and the family life lost as a consequence.

While television is certainly not the only cause of family problems and distance between family members these days, its easy availability does exacerbate them once internal fragmentation of the family begins. It's best to consider overuse of television as both a symptom and a cause of family problems. Daily, you experience the negative effects of a life after work dominated by television. It doesn't feel good. You see the changes in your children as they model you. You lament the passing of the closeness and the fun times you once shared. A good sign is that your concern about you and the kids and too much television is growing.

Deep in your heart, you know it is time to get back to some basics because the alternative is to let the family continue to go down the tube. As you and your partner make the commitment to change your television viewing habits as a way to recover control and create a healthier family environment, you know it is not going to be easy. It will take time and it will be frustrating at first. As you begin the process, it is helpful to understand the three basic phases of breaking away from your family's chronic and indiscriminate television viewing habits.

BREAKAWAY PHASE #1: SHOCK/DISEQUILIBRIUM. When the television set is off, what do you do with the massive amounts of time you used to spend sitting in front of it? Every family member begins to feel the resulting personally uncomfortable void. Parents and children are together more, but without the psychologically comfortable distraction of television. All family members may be irritable and at loose ends during this time. Consequently, parents must guard against returning to old habits just to relieve the tension.

BREAKAWAY PHASE #2: TESTING/ADJUSTING. Once initial shock has passed and with continuing parental commitment to change, individual family members (including the children) begin to actively experiment with new activities to fill the time void. Family members begin to regain the closeness they once had because they are spending increased time together and interacting more. However, frustrations and tensions do continue as old habits are broken down and a new family lifestyle evolves through trial-and-error by all family members.

BREAKAWAY PHASE #3: ACTIVE STABILITY. Gradually, from initial disequilibrium, a new family stability emerges. It is characterized by healthier values and by a higher quality family life. There is more communication within the family, individual members are more active, and a sense of togetherness grows. As time passes, parents must continue to be vigilant to ensure that new values remain. However, with their new perspective, parents quickly make any needed corrections. These parents, through personal experience, remain acutely aware of the negative effects of the passive alternative waiting in the living room.

One last point about the effects of television on children: in practically every international study done on the physical fitness of children, American youngsters rank virtually at the bottom. Too much passive time spent watching television does much to produce these sad results. The evidence is clear that physical fitness is highly related to maintaining positive health throughout life. And, regular activity helps keep energy levels high. Help your children develop more active lifestyles with benefits that will last a lifetime. Then, consider doing the same yourself! You'll feel better.

When you became a parent, you made a commitment to do the very best you could for your children. But you also made a commitment to yourself as parents to enjoy life and one another every day. Somehow, too easily, both commitments silently slip away as life becomes complicated. With more than a little bit of truth, someone once remarked: "Nostalgia is like a grammar lesson. The past is perfect. The present is tense." How true for too many who long for the good old days when life was easy and simple. You were more active then, too. Perhaps it can never be exactly that way again, but it surely can be better than the way you've been living recently. To make that happen for you and for the kids, bring back some control and start actively living life again instead of passively watching it pass by on a screen.

Chapter 6

Commanding Respect at Home: Effective Parents Define Themselves Clearly

In the best of all possible worlds, genuine respect would be granted automatically. Relationships would be characterized by caring communication, much more tact, and deep sensitivity to others' needs. Everyone would feel good because each would experience consistent kindness and emotional support. Alas, such is not the case. Such wishful thinking flies in the face of human nature. The fact is that relationships between people, no matter what their ages, require setting boundaries for interaction. These behavioral boundaries are tested and defined during the development of relationships. Employees test their supervisors. Students test their teachers. Adults test one another and children test their parents.

These testing responses are actually behavioral probes. Individuals push at one another until they meet resistance. The point of resistance then becomes a behavioral boundary that then helps define how to relate to that particular person. Unfortunately, some individuals grow to maturity without ever learning to create these kinds of essential boundaries for their relationships. These mild-mannered men and women don't manage well in their relationships at home or at work. They don't set and enforce limits. When they're abused, they make excuses that rationalize being victimized by others, even children. Examine for a moment these very common relationship problems.

Bob's parents constantly take advantage of his good nature. Whenever they need something, it's Bob they call rather than his brother who lives much closer to them. His brother simply says no when a request is excessive or frivolous. Bob doesn't. He does what his parents want and then secretly resents them.

Bob's Excuse: "It's okay, I guess. That's just the way they are and they'll never change."

Amy, a young parent, has a close "friend" who continually borrows from her. The problem is that nothing gets returned. Needed clothes, sports equipment, and garden tools now reside somewhere in her friend's home. Amy can't bring herself to ask for them back. On the other hand, Amy's occasional requests to borrow from her friend are usually politely declined.

Amy's Excuse: "If I confront her, it will hurt her feelings and she's my friend."

At the office, John has a silver-tongued colleague who time and again manages to talk John into taking over some of his work, claiming that a critical problem necessitates this. John acquiesces because he fancies himself a good person always willing to do a good turn. In point of fact, John's kindness allows his colleague more time to socialize.

John's Excuse: Repeat over and over: "It just wasn't the right time or place to bring up the subject."

Andrea's two children pretty much get what they want from her, whether it is new toys, staying up late, or pressuring her to relax the rules about doing their homework. They've learned that when they accuse her of being a "bad Mommy," Andrea quickly gives in to their requests. The kids have her right where they want her.

Andrea's Excuse: "They don't mean to take advantage. They're just being kids. They'll learn as they grow."

The obvious theme that runs through all of these scenarios is that one individual, covered by a legitimate-sounding excuse, is being constantly taken advantage of by another. A more subtle commonality is that though all these individuals are resentful, they have varying levels of awareness of their anger. Bob, Amy, John, and Andrea are all psychological victims. Because they have not been even minimally assertive in their relationships, they suffer as a result.

As a critical relationship skill, assertiveness can be defined as "the ability to openly but tactfully communicate feelings, positions, or expectations to others and follow through with them in ways that protect personal integrity and engender respect by others." Needless to say, healthy assertiveness is a crucial parenting skill. The bottom line is that the ability to make assertive responses is part of any good relationship. Assertive responses define who you are and the values you live by. However, don't neglect to note that the definition of assertiveness involves responses that generate *respect* by others, but not necessarily their *approval*.

Basically, the healthy assertive individual is able to tactfully maintain self-respect even though others, including children, don't get their way. For the nonassertive parent, this is a difficult choice to make. Furthermore, for the parent who is just learning these skills, some common confusions about assertiveness must be clarified.

CONFUSION #1: ASSERTIVENESS AND VERBIAGE. Assertive responses simply don't require being highly verbal. The fact is that many reserved individuals are quite assertive. They are quiet and say little, but they do mean what they say. When such individuals do speak, others listen.

CONFUSION #2: ASSERTIVENESS AND AGGRESSION. This distinction is crucial. Aggression is characterized by an attack on someone else. Often, the intent is to punish or to overpower another person. The assertive person, however, strives to keep communication open, solve problems, and protect personal rights.

CONFUSION #3: ASSERTIVENESS AND CONTROL. Attempting to control other people or situations totally misses the point of assertiveness. Healthy assertive responses are based on self-control. Inner control is used to actively choose responses that protect personal integrity and get things done.

Let's face it. It's not always fun to be assertive. And, others won't always like your assertive responses. However, in the long run, tactfully assertive individuals develop fulfilling and reciprocal relationships along with positive self-esteem. Nowhere is this more true than in your relationships with your children. On the other hand, while assertiveness superficially sounds quite simple, it is actually a quite sophisticated interpersonal skill. Here's a primer to help parents learn to command respect in relationships with children and others as well.

The Origins of Passivity

While there seems to be a genetic predisposition toward interpersonal reserve, it is abundantly clear that pathological passivity is learned. With few exceptions, the emotional origins of nonassertive behavior lie in family interactions during the early developmental years. In other words, most passive individuals were directly trained to be so through consistent reinforcement of these behaviors by parents who directly linked assertive responses with negative consequences. As a result, specific fears became emotionally linked to assertive responses, and these fears were carried into adulthood.

Understanding these interaction fears is the first step in confronting and resolving them. Conversely, unless these problems are overcome, parents are not free to develop into fully functioning adults, and their relationships with their children will be seriously compromised.

INTERACTION FEAR #1: IF YOU ARE NOT ASSERTIVE, YOU WILL BE REJECTED. Quite frequently, adults who are unduly passive had parents who emotionally withdrew from them when they were assertive. Given the "cold shoulder" and rejected by important adults, a child learns to associate assertive responses with being alone and abandoned; this results in the belief that only very passive and compliant behaviors in relationships will keep others emotionally close. An irrational but understandable emotional link is created.

INTERACTION FEAR #2: FOR BEING ASSERTIVE, YOU WILL BE SEVERELY PUNISHED. It is unfortunate that many insecure parents associate virtually any assertive responses in their children with outright defiance of their authority. As a result of such "misbehavior," the children are punished, sometimes severely. Thus a child learns that assertive responses are very bad, and in order to avoid punishment, the child becomes passive. An all-too-common variation occurs when an alcoholic parent consistently beats children for even the most minor infractions.

INTERACTION FEAR #3: WHEN YOU ARE ASSERTIVE, YOU ARE BEING SELFISH. It is not uncommon to find nonassertive adults who have learned to be excessively compliant through constant accusations of selfishness by parents. For meeting legitimate personal needs, the child is accused of denying others (usually a martyristic and manipulative parent). The message sticks because being labeled selfish is so emotionally painful. The result is a guilt-ridden adult who has become irrationally responsive to others' needs.

INTERACTION FEAR #4: ASSERTIVE RESPONSES ALWAYS LEAD TO BEING PROVEN WRONG. To some parents, an assertive response by a child, or any other kind of independent action, becomes another opportunity to prove once again that parents know best. "You should have listened to us!" is the message by these parents who seem to want to keep their children dependent. To avoid being wrong or failing and never being allowed to forget it, the child learns to rely exclusively on others' judgement to guide personal behavior. **INTERACTION FEAR #5: BEING ASSERTIVE IS COMMITTING A MORTAL SIN.** In some families, openly stating opinions or values that even mildly differ from those of the parents is equated with sin. "Honor thy father and thy mother" is distorted into, "You must completely agree with us in all ways or you are sinful and bad." This relationship dynamic often has its origins in parents who are so dogmatic and emotionally rigid that *any* questioning of their value system by anyone is highly threatening to them. **INTERACTION FEAR #6: WHEN YOU ASSERTIVELY TAKE A STAND, YOU WILL BE HELD RESPONSIBLE.** "It's never safe to take a risk" is the message of very conservative parents to their children. Ingrained in children is the value that security needs are absolutely paramount in a dangerous world. By not rocking the boat or in any way risking what you have, you will always be safe. The problem is that with this very passive stance, you will never grow either.

Note: It is entirely possible for children to develop any of these Interaction Fears from years of observing the negative consequences of assertive responses being meted out to siblings without necessarily experiencing such consequences directly. The long-term emotional effects are the same.

Diffusing Your Messages

As a way to get started on building new relationships with your children, it is wise to look for and completely eliminate some common communication errors that are characteristic of passive individuals. After all, the major determinant of effective assertive responses lies in how well you communicate your needs, values, and expectations. Unfortunately, one of the worst habits of the too-passive individual is to diffuse and blur communication at critical times. The net result is that: 1) the message intended is never received by a child, 2) what is said is not taken seriously, or 3) a child is relieved of responsibility for personal actions.

Clear, direct responses are the essence of assertive communication. As a way to "clean up" what you say, make it a point to eliminate completely each one of these five diffusion habits. When you have accomplished this alone, you will have made a giant step in the right direction.

DIFFUSION HABIT #1: YOU TEND TO BE TOO "TACTFULLY" INDIRECT. *Example:* "The reactions of your new friends are, well, interesting." (Translation: "I don't approve of your friends' lack of manners, and I dislike your hanging around with them so much.") In a nutshell, the nonassertive parent is often so "tactful" in order to avoid hurting others' feelings that what is said is excessively obtuse or dishonest or both. It is entirely possible to be more direct and tactful at the same time. When you do so, you reveal your values, thereby setting the stage for more trust in you as an honest and forthright person.

DIFFUSION HABIT #2: YOU SUPPLY YOUR CHILDREN WITH AN EXCUSE. *Example:* "You've been getting up late every morning for school, but I know you're not a morning person and it's so hard to get moving so early." When your responses provide a ready-made excuse, a child gets the message that what has been done is okay when it is definitely not all right. It sets the stage for continued abuse of you as a parent or of the rules that must be respected. Further, you are perceived as wishy-washy, passive, and not willing to follow through to make sure you and the rules are given due accord.

DIFFUSION HABIT #3: YOU APOLOGIZE TO THE KIDS FOR MAKING ASSERTIVE RESPONSES. *Example:* Three hours after assertively telling his son to pick up his room: "I'm sorry I talked to you that way, son. I know you would have cleaned up your room on your own." Baloney! Neither this father nor any other individual has to apologize for an appropriately assertive response to someone else. When an apology is made after the fact, it is usually the result of guilt or fear that has built up in the "assertive" individual. To relieve these uncomfortable emotions, the apology is made. The problem is that those parents who always "undo" assertive responses toward children aren't respected.

DIFFUSION HABIT #4: YOU CONSISTENTLY OVERQUALIFY YOUR DIRECTIONS. *Example:* "I need the garage cleaned up by Friday because I'm going to paint. But, it could wait until next week. I might not even need it done at all if I can get to the walls." This message is unclear and confusing because it is qualified so much. A flat statement with a clear expectation (the first sentence above) would prevent miscommunication and stand a better chance of getting the appropriate response from children. For more assertive parental communication, take out the and's, if's, and but's and insert clear, concise statements in their place.

DIFFUSION HABIT #5: YOU SHIFT RESPONSIBILITY FOR YOUR ACTIONS TO OTHERS. *Examples:* "Everyone thinks that . . . ." "Your father/mother says that you should . . . ." "Your teacher wants . . . ." Here, the authority of a parent is diminished by shifting responsibility for assertive statements to others. This ploy lets the nonassertive parent off the hook, but also places that father or mother in the role of messenger without any real authority. If responsibility for getting something done is yours, then assume that responsibility by making assertive statements beginning with: "I want you to . . . ." You will be perceived as a much stronger and more together parent when you do.

Controlling Your Anger

No discussion of assertiveness can be complete without addressing the problem of anger. The facts are that parents who feel overwhelmed with responsibility, frustrated by the emotional trials of parenting, and neglecting their own emotional needs at the same time, often begin to feel angry. Under these conditions, a number of destructive uses of anger can develop. While anger is certainly not an inappropriate emotion, it can destroy relationships if it is not expressed in healthy ways. Here are some of the more common emotional misuses of anger, along with suggestions for resolving them.

EMOTIONAL MISUSE #1: ANGER AS PART OF ACQUIRED IMPATIENCE. As life becomes busier and more complicated, there is a tendency to speed up to get everything done. The result is hurry sickness. You work faster, talk faster, drive faster. And, you become more impatient with anyone or anything that gets in your way. Accompanying your impatience is anger generated by the multitude of frustrations you experience each day. It gets worse with time.

Resolution: An important first step is to stop fighting the natural flow of life around you. Plan what needs to get done with plenty of time built in for inevitable glitches. Keep reminding yourself to remain calm and save your energy because much of what is frustrating you simply can't control.

EMOTIONAL MISUSE #2: PSYCHOLOGICAL DISPLACEMENT OF ANGER. This bad habit is also known as the "kick the cat" problem. You become angry in one situation where it would be difficult or impossible to express anger directly (*i.e.*, to a boss at work). The anger is then held in or suppressed until a safe target becomes available. Then it comes out unabated. Easy targets? The kids or a spouse at home.

Resolution: First, calm down and try to deal tactfully with the real source of your anger. Or, find a compassionate listener to talk out the situation, thereby diffusing angry feelings. As a bonus, an objective listener can also help you see your own blind spots and alternative ways of responding.

EMOTIONAL MISUSE #3: ANGER AS A MOTIVATIONAL TECHNIQUE. Sometimes called KITSE (Kick in the South End) motivation, this use of anger is favored by those who believe that the only real motive for doing anything is intimidation. Typically, fear is produced through outbursts of intense anger accompanied by dire threats. Along with resentment, an adversarial relationship develops with those on the receiving end of this kind of motivation.

Resolution: Learning to positively reward others, children in particular, for work well done, is at the core of overcoming this problem. First, though, you must train yourself to see what has been done right or well. Then build on it through encouragement, support, and positive strokes to encourage cooperation.

EMOTIONAL MISUSE #4: ANGER TO REDUCE INTERNAL TENSION. Here, tension and frustration arising from the pressures of a hectic day are suppressed, especially while in the workplace. However, once you have left, internal tension is easily transformed into anger and directed toward any opportune target. After an angry outburst, you become calm again because your tension has been reduced. In the process though, you may have damaged a relationship.

Resolution: The best way to overcome this problem is to create a transition routine to follow the day's work. The best transition techniques involve some physical activity to work off built-up tension—a short workout, a walk, a bicycle ride. These same activities allow you to "downshift" before you must deal with the kids.

EMOTIONAL MISUSE #5: ANGER RESULTING FROM GIVING TOO MUCH TO OTHERS. Frequently, busy parents find themselves responding to the needs of others in every part of their lives. But, a problem occurs when those same parents lose the ability to give to themselves. Resentment grows with resulting outbursts of anger. The emotional message is simple: "I'm giving so much to everyone else. Why isn't anyone giving anything back to me?"

Resolution: As a first step, recognize that you have created this problem for yourself. Then begin to give some time for pleasant and fulfilling diversions to yourself. Make sure you pursue these activities regularly. To do so, you will have to break some bad giving precedents, but it's worth it to all involved.

EMOTIONAL MISUSE #6: ASSERTIVENESS JUSTIFIED BY RIGHTEOUS ANGER. Many basically passive people can be assertive only when they are very angry. First, they allow others, including children, to push them to the brink. Then self-righteous anger is called up as the impetus required to take a stand and push back. Because this anger has been building up over time, its intensity is sometimes frightening when it emerges.

Resolution: Two fundamental changes are called for here. First, make a commitment to confront even small problems when they occur instead of letting them pass and becoming resentful. Then learn to respond to such problem situations in direct and firm, yet tactful ways. Because your anger does not then build up internally, it is easier to control.

Making Assertiveness Work for You

Now that you're more direct in your communication and you have brought angry outbursts under some modicum of control, you are ready to continue your progress by learning some additional assertiveness techniques. However, you must understand that as you bring your new parental responses into play, you are in effect changing the rules of the relationships you have already established with your children. You will "come across" in a new way, and it will take time and consistency for new ways of relating to become comfortable for both of you. Persistence does count here, so don't permit your discomfort or the reactions of the kids to stop you.

Here are a number of assertive suggestions to try. Read them through carefully so you understand each one. Then consciously begin integrating one or two at a time into how you communicate with your children. When these become comfortable, then move on to others. As you strive for consistency, though, give yourself some room to goof up now and then.

ASSERTIVE SUGGESTION #1: STATE YOUR EXPECTATIONS EARLY. Passive parents often assume that others, even children, somehow know what is wanted or will do what is expected without being clearly told. This easy but erroneous assumption leads to needless problems simply because others, especially children, aren't mind readers. Things will go more smoothly when you make it a point to always communicate what is wanted or needed ahead of time.

ASSERTIVE SUGGESTION #2: CLEARLY CONCEPTUALIZE IS-SUES BEFORE STATING THEM. When faced with a problem, many parents have an immediate impulse to respond strongly and emotionally. It's much better to take a little time to think through the issues and then state your case in a direct, reasonable, and rational way. It will more likely be really heard and accepted when you do. Even children respond positively to calm clarity.

ASSERTIVE SUGGESTION #3: STRIVE FOR CONSISTENCY OF RESPONSE. A bad parental habit is to let a mood determine discipline or enforcement of limits. If you're feeling good, you let things go. If you're tense or frustrated, you strictly enforce every rule you ever made! This is very confusing to others, especially children. It is wise to set reasonable limits and then consistently encourage children to abide by them.

ASSERTIVE SUGGESTION #4: STATE YOUR VALUES AND EX-PECTATIONS WHEN THERE IS NOT A PROBLEM. It's a mistake to state your values as a parent only after a problem has erupted. Rather, make it a point to talk frequently about right and wrong, values for living, and how to get along through casual discussions and informal conversations. Comment on and reinforce these kinds of behaviors in the kids when you observe them. And, talk about them when there is no problem.

ASSERTIVE SUGGESTION #5: CHOOSE YOUR ISSUES CARE-FULLY. Often, newly assertive men and women confront others, even their children, too often. As a result, the kids may turn off because all they hear is a barrage of criticism. Sometimes it is better to remain silent. Healthy assertiveness requires that you consciously choose the issues you want to deal with. Through your selectivity, you gain more control, thus maximizing the possibility of a positive outcome.

ASSERTIVE SUGGESTION #6: DESCRIBE YOUR ANGER OR HURT. It's certainly all right to be angry or upset or hurt. These are not inappropriate emotions. However, there is a tremendous difference between describing your feelings to someone else and acting them out. The fact is that the motivation for acting out negative emotions is usually punitive. For a better response, describe your feelings and attack only problems, not people.

ASSERTIVE SUGGESTION #7: REMAIN MATURE EVEN IF OTHERS DON'T. It's a mistake to initially approach a problem calmly and then let the immature responses of children provoke you into similar immature responses! Under these conditions, you can't be a healthy model for the kids and they learn little about how to deal effectively with relationship problems. Further, your calmness and tact will have a quieting effect on the kids as well as keeping the interaction more positive.

ASSERTIVE SUGGESTION #8: USE ASSERTIVE NONVERBAL CUES. If you're going to be taken seriously, your nonverbal responses must be consistent with what you are saying at the time. Give full attention to the child you are speaking to while maintaining good eye contact. Emphasize key words. Use your silence for reinforcement. Make appropriate (but not aggressive) gestures to underscore what you say. Then, the kids will know you mean it.

ASSERTIVE SUGGESTION #9: FOLLOW THROUGH FOR CREDIBILITY. In other words, avoid giving ultimatums. Even small children know from experience when empty threats are being made. To establish your credibility, state reasonable expectations and the consequences that will result if they are not met. Then follow through consistently. Respect by others is gained only from their sure knowledge that you mean what you say.

ASSERTIVE SUGGESTION #10: PRACTICE WHAT YOU PREACH. Small children are perfectly capable of spotting a hypocrite. "Do what I say, not as I do" is not a way to enhance your credibility when being assertive. It's a good idea for all parents to listen to what they are telling their children and then examine their own responses for consistency. Then you avoid the "Why should I do it if you don't?" responses from the kids.

Communicating Your Self

The journey from fearful passivity to full adult maturity and effective parenting is sometimes a long one. It is definitely not accomplished overnight, and in many ways it's emotionally difficult. In fact, it's risky business. The bottom line, however, is that the self-defeating equilibrium that has been established in your present relationships with the kids must be changed. As you change your patterns and back up what you say, your children will react. They liked the old you who they could manipulate, who had little credibility, and who could be ignored most of the time.

As you learn to communicate in firm, definitive, and tactful ways, you will feel more in control from within. You will finally be free of old fears and able to fulfill all your potential as a person and parent. And, as you come into your own with new ways of relating, you are actually changing some longstanding, but questionable values from within. These values from your past were based more on negative early experiences and fear than on knowledge of healthy functioning and positive relationships.

These value changes are most clearly represented by shifts in some basic priorities within you. There are three that will make you a really together and much more effective parent.

PRIORITY SHIFT #1: YOUR SELF-RESPECT TAKES PRECE-DENCE OVER APPROVAL. You now realize that being liked when the price tag is your self-respect just isn't worth it. With this shift, you are able to stand on principle when the situation calls for it whether you get approval in return or not. This is an inner strength that has become part of your character, and you're an emotionally stronger parent as a result.

PRIORITY SHIFT #2: INTERNAL CHOICE TAKES PRECE-DENCE OVER EXTERNAL EXPEDIENCY. In the past, your parental responses have been excessively determined by fears or by your need to be liked. Now, you have developed the ability to determine what you do and how you do it on the basis of a wider range of internal choices. As a result, these days you are capable of doing what is right as a parent, rather than what is easy.

PRIORITY SHIFT #3: REALITY TAKES PRECEDENCE OVER FANTASY. Only after you have become more assertive can you fully appreciate how unrealistic and fantasy-like your expectations of relationships have been. Now that you have accepted some basic parenting realities, you're not as disappointed in your relationships with the kids as you have been in the past. And, you know how to create emotionally fulfilling relationships that last.

By way of summary, it should be pointed out that a sound principle of communication states that *you* teach others how to respond to you through your reactions to them. In other words, you and only you are responsible for the quality of your relationships with your children. The fact is that if you're a mild-mannered parent, you can only move forward by teaching your children to respond in better ways. The teaching process will be ongoing, but the earlier you start, the easier it will be.

Your core parental curriculum must be consistently communicated through assertive responses that are more than hollow words. Clear and consistent communication must be backed by character and commitment. Yours. Without these changes, the price tag for your passive parenting can be high indeed for the entire family. Probably commenting about nonassertive parents, a very savvy individual once derisively remarked: "Blessed are the meek. They always get out of your way before you have to push them!" And so it is with the ways of the world . . . and with kids . . . unless you're willing to assertively teach otherwise.

Chapter 7

Getting Kids to REALLY Talk Back: Parental Communication Promotes Expression or Suppression

In virtually all areas of your life, the ability to communicate is extremely important. How and what you say and under what conditions determines the quality of your relationships, your success at work, and the effectiveness of your parenting. Early in life, young men and women often communicate openly and quite expressively to one another; however, with the complexity of an established mainstream middle-class lifestyle full of obligations and responsibilities, communication patterns change. And, for the most part the changes are not particularly positive. Nowhere do these changes have a greater impact than on parents' relationships with their children.

How you verbally relate to your children during some of the most hectic and busy years of your life greatly influences their health, happiness, and ultimately, success later in life. Let's take a look at a very common phenomenon. It's one that frequently puzzles and distresses concerned parents.

At the elementary school where she is a student, nine-year-old Kimberly frequently seeks out a teacher's aide to talk over things important to her. Quite a few of her friends have also found this same aide very easy to talk to because she takes the time to really understand.

Don, now twelve and on the verge of puberty, needs to talk about some of the confusing changes going on within him. When he needs to talk, he knows the perfect person. He finds his friend Jim's mother. She always makes him feel better about himself.

At home, with both of her successful parents usually available, Ann almost always finds a few moments to be alone with her father when she has a problem to solve. She finds that he is compassionate, yet quite direct when he needs to be.

In the boarding school that he attends, Kevin has found that the maintenance man in charge of his dormitory is the best sounding board for his concerns. He has formed a close bond with this man, and their conversations are very important to Kevin.

Several commonalities run through each of these situations. First, it is safe to assume that all children have a need to talk to adults about what is going on in their world. And, it is extremely important to the maturational process to have caring adults to relate to openly and without fear. Second, all of these young people have found someone in their particular environments to talk to about problems and personal concerns. Third, these relationships are important and deeply valued by the children who establish them. The adults involved are often remembered for a lifetime.

Now take a closer look at these relationships. With the exception of Ann, not one of them involves the parents! Even Ann seeks out her father, but not her mother when she needs to talk. It is this selectivity that concerns, hurts, and distresses parents. "Why not me? I care and I'm the parent" is their lament. The central issue lies in understanding that children will "open up" only to adults they trust and who respond in ways that make them feel good. *Your status as a parent isn't much of a determining factor in whether your child will really talk to you.* The way you communicate, though, makes all the difference in the world.

Parents are too often shut out of the private inner world of their children because of problem patterns of communication. As a sad result, parent-child relationships cannot be as deep or as emotionally fulfilling as might be possible. And, the level of trust (or distrust) established with a parent because of that parent's communication style may easily affect for a lifetime the quality of a relationship with a particular child. To learn how to talk to your children in healthier ways, you must first understand three common distortions that insidiously creep into the speech patterns of busy adults and that serve to undermine open communication.

SHUTDOWN #1: YOU ATTEMPT TO CONTROL ALL CONVERSA-TIONS. Parents, in their role as caretakers, often try to excessively control the behavior of children via a dominating style of communication. "I'm in charge, here" is the unmistakable tone of their parental responses. As a result, a child often withdraws because free and open dialogue is not possible under such conditions.

SHUTDOWN #2: YOUR FOCUS IS ON GETTING INFORMATION QUICKLY. Basically, children need time to express themselves as do many adults. When a chronically impatient parent comes on like an interrogator every time a child wants to talk, the "conversations" usually go nowhere. Savvy parents are patient and help their children express feelings and thoughts instead of exclusively seeking only raw information as quickly as possible.

SHUTDOWN #3: YOU QUICKLY IMPOSE YOUR VALUES OR JUDGE PREMATURELY. It is not uncommon to find parents becoming very evaluative when "talking" with their children. "I know best" is their theme and "Do what I tell you" is their mandate. As a result, a child may never learn to explore situations and make sound personal decisions because adults are constantly being so "helpful."

The bottom line is that open and expressive communication is healthy—for your relationships and for your health. The same goes for your children. Intimacy also depends on how you communicate. It's such a good feeling, especially for a child, to talk things out with someone who cares. There are definitely ways to relate that will set the stage for your children to trust you enough to let you into their inner world. If you teach them not to trust you, you will never really know them. Then everyone loses. Here are some of the do's and don'ts of opening up your communication with the kids. By using some of these same techniques, your relationships with other adults may just improve as well!

Styles of Emotional Suppression

Parents frequently give tremendous lip service to wanting open communication with their children. Yet, when their communication styles are examined closely, a direct contradiction is found. Parents respond in ways that suppress a child's desire to communicate, particularly when the issues are emotionally-loaded or controversial. Some parents simply don't take the time to listen to a child's thoughts and feelings. Others are threatened by any conversation that is emotional in tone. Still others have a high need to impose rationality and logic on everything in their world, including the kids.

If you truly want to become a deep and meaningful part of your child's life, a good idea is to first assess how you are communicating these days. You may be inadvertently using suppression techniques. Regardless of your rationalizations, each carries a message: "What you have on your mind isn't important to me" or "I don't respect what you're saying." If you care enough, you will eliminate each and every one of them from your repertoire of responses to children and to other adults as well.

SUPPRESSION TECHNIQUE #1: YOU EMOTIONALLY BETRAY YOUR CHILDREN. *Examples:* Telling friends or family members something your child has said in confidence. Constantly reminding (or kidding) a child about something sensitive that was said to you.

There is no question that betrayal will cost you dearly in terms of the depth of your relationships with your children. Each time you betray a child, you are sending a clear message to that child not to trust you. Such betrayal blatantly communicates your disrespect for a child's thoughts or feelings. That message isn't lost on the child; he quickly learns not to open up to you. Keep in mind that what is important to a child may not seem significant to you, but at all costs you must respect it anyway.

SUPPRESSION TECHNIQUE #2: YOU TELL A CHILD WHAT IS BEING FELT. *Examples:* "You're angry, but you just won't admit it." "I know you're feeling bad about what happened. Why don't you just say so?"

This easy mistake is in some ways understandable. Children often have a difficult time articulating feelings, and sorting out emotions is an important emotional skill; however, adults who are always quick to label a child's feelings from *their* perspective inhibit their child in learning to express what is being felt. The poor kid doesn't have a chance because adults are always jumping in and imposing what they think is going on. Often they're wrong! Eventually a child gives up and shuts down.

SUPPRESSION TECHNIQUE #3: YOU DENY A CHILD'S FEEL-INGS. *Examples:* "You really don't feel that way deep down." "There's nothing to cry about, so you can't feel sad."

In this common type of parental response, an important adult simply negates a child's statement of feelings. In effect, the child is told: "You don't know what you are feeling." Hogwash. Most of the time, a child does know what is being felt and those feelings are quite real. A child may need help to define particular feelings, but denying them altogether is in fact denying the reality of the child's emotional self. This in turn leads a child to question the validity of personal feelings, resulting in emotional confusion later in life.

SUPPRESSION TECHNIQUE #4: PARENTS REFUSE TO RESPOND TO QUESTIONS. *Examples:* To a child's question about sex: "You'll learn more about that later." To a child's question about drugs: "That's awful. Only bad people do it. Let's talk about something more pleasant."

These responses represent some of the more blatant avoidance techniques used by adults. And, they are not lost on the kids. This kind of parent is not comfortable enough to respond to sensitive issues or questions so they don't. When children notice such avoidance and conclude that there is something mighty interesting about the subject, they go to other sources (or personal experience) to find out more. A better way is to respond honestly and openly to all inquiries at the child's level of understanding. The kids will continue to ask because you try to help them find answers.

SUPPRESSION TECHNIQUE #5: YOU EMOTIONALLY MANIPULATE A CHILD. *Examples:* "You be good or I'll tell your father/ mother what you said." "I know you don't care what I feel so you just go on and do what *you* want to do."

In a nutshell, these kinds of responses by parents come under the general heading of emotional blackmail. A child's statements or emotional vulnerabilities are used to control the child's behavior in unfair ways. This is heartily resented by any child. When parents do this consistently, the child on the receiving end learns not to trust others, and this distrust often carries over to interfere with close relationships as an adult. Only parents who are emotionally immature themselves betray children in this way.

SUPPRESSION TECHNIQUE #6: PARENTS OVERREACT TO A CHILD'S STATEMENTS OR BEHAVIOR. *Examples:* A parent becomes hysterical when a child makes an off-the-cuff statement about not going to college. Parents "freak out" when a son or daughter dates someone they don't like.

When a child brings into the open an emotionally-loaded issue, what is often being sought is a reasonable sounding board. Parents who overreact shut off needed communication with that child at a very critical time. Ironically, parents who make strong attempts to dissuade or control a child's behavior under these circumstances only reinforce the child's resolve to do it anyway! In any kind of touchy circumstance, a much better outcome usually results when you stay neutral at first and keep communication wide open.

SUPPRESSION TECHNIQUE #7: PARENTS MAKE LIGHT OF A CHILD'S FEELINGS. *Examples:* Constantly taking conversations to a humorous level when a child is expressing feelings. Repeatedly kidding a child about a sensitive emotional issue.

By and large, these ploys communicate the adult's unwillingness to take the child's feelings seriously and to respond in caring ways. Sometimes adults do this in a naive attempt to make a child feel better. The net effect of this communication pattern, however, is to teach the child that it's not worth it to open up because no one will really listen and respond. Interestingly, adults who do this to a child usually do it to other adults as well. Most often the cause is a parent who is uncomfortable with emotional intimacy and has a corresponding need to keep all interactions superficial.

SUPPRESSION TECHNIQUE #8: THERE IS CONSISTENT COMMUNICATION OF DISTRUST. *Examples:* To a child who visited a friend's house when parents weren't home: "You didn't break anything, did you? Did you make a mess?" To a child who returns from a stay with cousins: "Were you polite? Did you thank everyone? You didn't leave your clothes lying around, I hope!"

These queries communicate an implicit assumption that a child will surely misbehave if not under direct parental control at all times. However, a barrage of these kinds of suspicious and distrustful questions may trigger withdrawal, refusal to communicate, or expressions of anger. Parents would do better to respond in ways that reflect the positive aspects of a child's experiences: "I'll bet that Jimmy's house is really neat!" "It must have been lots of fun for you to see your cousins again." When a parent responds to a child's excitement, communication stays open. Problems encountered will usually emerge for discussion because the interaction is nonthreatening.

Softening Exercises

For parents whose communication has inadvertently become suppressive, excessively information-oriented, or highly controlling, there are certainly strategies to "relax" the way you respond to others. While these softening techniques are particularly important when talking to the kids, they are also very helpful in modifying the way you respond to friends, a spouse, or colleagues at work. When you're able to switch gears to a more easygoing way of responding when the situation calls for it, you will find that relationships become more open and easygoing as well.

Here are outlined several softening exercises for you to practice. While not easy to master, each one reflects a negative communication habit you have drifted into as your life has become busier and more complicated. Make it a point to practice each one of these. You may be pleasantly surprised at how much difference they make.

SOFTENING EXERCISE #1: REDUCE USE OF THE PRONOUN "YOU." As a first step, make attempts to carry on conversations without this excessively overused pronoun. Be especially aware of using "you" to begin sentences when you're discussing problems. When this happens, what you say quickly develops an accusative tone. With a barrage of "you's," the other person is usually put on the defensive. Or, what is said is experienced with a strong demand quality and accompanying psychological pressure that is often resisted. In a nutshell, using "you" now and then isn't bad, but overusing it can certainly create communication problems. For better results, substitute statements beginning with "I," or, in a neutral way simply describe the situation or what happened.

SOFTENING EXERCISE #2: AVOID USING ANY "W" QUESTIONS. The "W" questions are those that begin with Who, What, Where, When, and Why. For good measure, throw in questions that begin with "How," too. Overuse of such questions comes across as interrogation, not conversation. This resultant blunt and intrusive tone reflects a need for lots of information quickly. Most of the time, the person on the receiving end of such questioning defensively withdraws. Even children become suspicious and react this way to "hard" questioning. If you want the kids to really talk to you, drastically reduce your use of "W" questions.

SOFTENING EXERCISE #3: ELIMINATE ALL QUESTIONS FROM CONVERSATION. This is the ultimate test of communication skill. Believe it or not, it is entirely possible to talk with a child (or another adult) for long periods of time without using a single question. Good conversationalists do it all the time. As practice, make a game of it. As you and a partner talk, monitor one another for use of questions. The first person to use three questions loses! It's difficult in the beginning, but keep in mind that your frustration is also an index of your reliance on questions when conversing with others.

Now let's stop for just a moment to address a common question as these "relaxing" communication techniques are attempted, particularly the last one. If questions aren't to be used, then what can be substituted in their place? Here are four of the most common ways to respond in lieu of questions. Integrating all of them into your response style will soften it even further.

QUESTION ALTERNATIVE #1: MAKE QUESTIONS INTO STATEMENTS. It is relatively easy to turn an intrusive question into a softer statement. It also helps to get rid of the "you's" and "W" questions that are so overused. *Examples:* Change "What did you do?" to "Something happened here." Change "Why didn't you call like you promised?" to "I didn't receive the call I expected."

QUESTION ALTERNATIVE #2: MAKE USE OF EMPATHIC COMMENTS. In short, empathic comments are brief statements that communicate your sensitivity to another person's feelings or current situation. When used, they encourage that other person to continue talking because you emotionally understand. *Examples:* "That's awful." "I do know how you feel." "That's a hard situation to be in."

QUESTION ALTERNATIVE #3: SELECTIVELY USE SELF-DISCLOSURE STATEMENTS. These responses communicate your willingness to open your inner world of feelings and experiences to another person. Personal self-disclosure invites the other person to continue to respond in kind. *Examples:* "When I was young, I was shy, too." "Sometimes my feelings are just overwhelming." "I feel the same way when that happens." **Note:** Do recognize that self-disclosure can easily be overdone with the result that you take over the conversation!

QUESTION ALTERNATIVE #4: SIMPLE LEADS. Leads communicate your attentiveness with subtle encouragement for the other person to continue talking. As with self-disclosure statements, they can easily be overused. However, used with discrimination, simple leads convey your concern and interest in what is being said. Back them up with nonverbal reinforcers such as good eye contact and nodding. *Examples:* "Uh-huh." "Go on." "Please tell me more." "Hmmmmm." "Very interesting."

Other Communication Techniques

As you become more aware of your personal communication style, sit back from time to time and listen very objectively to what you are saying and how you are saying it. Be particularly sensitive to how you respond to your children. It is entirely possible that you may be shocked at the rather low quality of your communication these days. Despite your desire to have close and open relationships, the way you are responding may communicate demands, your need for control, and a lack of sensitivity to the kids' feelings.

Let's face it. Good relationships are built on open and trusting communication. To the extent that the way you relate doesn't reflect true caring, then once close relationships may grow distant and new ones may never blossom. To remedy this problem, your communication must become less emotionally threatening. Here are a number of opening techniques to help you accomplish just that.

OPENING TECHNIQUE #1: BEGIN TO LISTEN A LOT MORE. In other words, let the other person talk. Refrain from quickly jumping in with your thoughts and feelings. With constant interruptions on your part, the other person will often shut down in frustration. A wise maxim states that you have two eyes and two ears, but only one mouth. The interpretation is easy. Look and listen twice as much as you speak.

OPENING TECHNIQUE #2: REFRAIN FROM USING "TRIGGER" WORDS OR PHRASES. These are emotionally-loaded comments, provocative statements, or put-down labels that are sure to cause the other person to react emotionally and negatively. These trigger words or phrases develop in every close relationship, even with kids. Because the only possible response to trigger words and phrases is hurt, mature individuals respect others enough not to use them, and consequently communication stays more open.

OPENING TECHNIQUE #3: WHEN YOUR CHILD INITIATES DISCUSSION, TAKE TIME IMMEDIATELY. The time when a child is really concerned enough to talk openly about an issue or problem may be very brief. If, during those critical times, you habitually communicate that you will be available only "later," your child will quickly give up on you. To keep communication channels open, take the time to hear out your child's concerns even if it's not totally convenient.

OPENING TECHNIQUE #4: REWARD YOUR CHILD FOR TALKING ABOUT FEELINGS. Parents often neglect this easy and very important part of communicating with a child. Approval statements can be very simple: "I'm so glad you told me. Now, I understand."

These kind of comments powerfully communicate how much you value your child's openness. Combined with a hug or a kiss (or both!), there is no better way to communicate your interest and sensitivity.

OPENING TECHNIQUE #5: WHEN DISCUSSING PROBLEMS, STAY NEUTRAL IN THE BEGINNING. When you jump the gun and immediately become highly judgmental when a son or daughter is trying to explain a problem, open communication is inhibited. It is far better to stay quite neutral in the beginning until all the facts emerge. Once all the details are out on the table, then the situation can be more easily discussed in an open way that will help discover the solution that is most satisfactory to all involved.

OPENING TECHNIQUE #6: HELP YOUR CHILD MAKE PER-SONAL DECISIONS. It is extremely beneficial later in life for a child to have learned and practiced sound decision-making skills all through the developmental years. One way parents can facilitate this process is to help a child sort out all the relevant factors in problem situations, define possible courses of action, and examine the consequences of each one. As the result of open dialogue with an understanding parent, a child learns how to evaluate situations from various perspectives and then decides on the best way to respond.

OPENING TECHNIQUE #7: TALK TO YOUR CHILD ALL THE TIME. Parents who communicate consistently with their children frequently have more open relationships with them. Talking about everything, during good times and bad, from emotionally deep issues to light banter, and doing it in a way that signals your sensitivity and respect of a child's inner world is a tremendous plus. It's a lesson that backfires when a child learns that parents only pay attention when there's something wrong!

Knowing a Child's World Within

Of three things parents can be sure. First, all children experience many emotions, some of which are very strong. Second, no matter what they are, these feelings are valid. They are an important part of a child's inner reality. And, adults must accept these feelings as such. Finally, the child's way of coping with feelings may be inappropriate or emotionally immature. The fact is that feelings reflect a tender and vulnerable part of a child's growing sense of self. Parents are allowed entry to their child's inner world only if they are deserving. To be deserving, you must be trusted by that child.

A deep relationship is simply not possible without being permitted to share in a child's emotional world. Children, as well as adults, are under no *ipso facto* obligation to share their inner world with others, even parents. It is a shame that so many parents, through the way they communicate, teach their children to hide important parts of themselves and their experiences. Only a superficial shell is revealed. With the richness within defensively hidden, parent-child relationships are kept quite shallow. Parents and their children who become emotionally isolated from one another suffer needlessly.

Beyond the day-to-day satisfactions of an open and expressive parent-child relationship, improved communication provides benefits that will help your child live well emotionally for a lifetime. To be specific, there are four of them.

EMOTIONAL BENEFIT #1: FEELINGS ARE ACCEPTED. Parents who suppress feelings within the family teach children that particular feelings, or emotions in general, should be hidden and never expressed. A healthy child not only learns that all feelings are valid, but also learns to express each of them in mature and sensitive ways.

EMOTIONAL BENEFIT #2: TRUST IN OTHERS INCREASES. In families where emotions are denied or made light of or where the child is controlled using feelings, deep distrust often develops on the part of the child. For personal protection, a child thus learns not to reveal the inner self because the only consequences of doing so are negative.

EMOTIONAL BENEFIT #3: THE DEVELOPMENT OF INTI-MACY. Intimacy depends on enough trust in someone else to share the inner world of hopes and dreams and feelings and fears. Self-revelation is also necessary for self-acceptance. This process is the only way to know someone else deeply and grow together in emotionally fulfilling ways.

EMOTIONAL BENEFIT #4: PERSONAL HEALTH IS MAIN-TAINED. The relationship between appropriate emotional expression and emotional and physical health is being clearly established through ongoing research. Significant internal pressure and negative health consequences result from consistently denying feelings or suppressing strong emotions.

In a world that demands high levels of achievement to succeed, the importance of a rich emotional life can easily be neglected in parents and children. With constant emphasis on rationality, the inner illogical world of feelings is frequently negated. In an information age, relating focuses too often on the exchange of data in lieu of deep, emotionally-based communication. Someone has said that a mind without a heart is nothing, and it's up to parents to make caring expressions of the heart as important as statements of fact. For their children. For themselves.

Although there are no short cuts, a good way to begin is to watch what you say and how you say it, to the kids in particular. While your children may not be able to pinpoint exactly what the communication problem might be, they do know with certainty whether they are comfortable with you or not. It's up to you to spot communication problems that have developed. Then you must do something about them. It's amazing how much difference eliminating a few negative communication habits will make with children and with other adults.

An old adage that is unfortunately too true for too many parents is worth repeating: "While your eyes are the windows to your soul, your mouth may not be the doorway to your brain!" Perhaps it's time to think about what you say to the kids *before* you say it. And, the best rule of thumb is simple. If in doubt, don't open your mouth. Zip your lip, as the saying goes. You'll usually come out better. With your spouse. With friends. Certainly with your children who need to talk with you, but often can't.

Chapter 8

Growing Up Responsible (Part 1): Parental Discipline and Success Are Related

Take a moment to remember your childhood: surely there were many carefree days filled with adventure. Just as surely there were times when you felt that being a child was the worst thing in the whole world. You felt powerless, harassed, and overwhelmed by parents who just didn't understand. You may have even thought that they didn't care at all about you or your feelings. During these interminable periods of misery, you wondered whether you would ever grow up. But, of course, you did.

Looking back with more objectivity, you are easily able to see the positive part your parents played in your present success. In the best of all possible worlds, your parents were singularly important in preparing you for competent adulthood although you probably didn't understand, much less appreciate, their efforts at the time. Or, sadly, you may be part of another sizeable minority who became successful without much helpful parental involvement at all. You may have made it in spite of your upbringing!

However, the probability is that those individuals who become successful later in life likely had parents who were both caring and effective in their discipline. Yet, social values toward discipline are not static. They wax and wane over the years in rough synchrony with the times. A decade or so ago, "permissive parenting" was much in vogue. Recently, and inevitably, the pendulum began to swing in the opposite direction toward stronger parental control and more active guidance for children. This trend reflects the "back to basics" movement that is currently exerting a significant influence on parenting in this country.

Despite its obvious social value and psychological necessity, the process of implementing parental discipline is still widely misunderstood and mired in controversy. As a way to begin examining the developmental underpinnings of discipline and its effects, consider these individuals.

—At age four, Anna eats her lollipop now instead of waiting until after dinner as she was told.

—Nine-year-old Tommy gets mad and hits his best friend who has just teased him about his new braces.

—A college sophomore at nineteen, Jackie can't resist a late night party even though she has an important test in the morning.

—Brett, in his late twenties and a talented stonemason, can't find work because he usually finds other interesting and distracting things to do instead of getting to work on time.

—Now forty-two, Betty is a reasonably successful interior designer; she has to be because she's an incurable impulse buyer who is constantly in debt.

—Jim at fifty-five has never let his work interfere with his social life, and as a result his career has never blossomed as he once hoped it would.

Now comes the key question. What do all of these individuals have in common? The answer is that the kinds of choices such individuals make share one basic characteristic. In key situations, such men and women consistently gravitate toward what's easy and what's fun rather than what's right and what's responsible. And, they persist in doing so despite the sometimes serious consequences of their choices. As a result, their ability to respond in mature ways that reflect personal competency has been seriously compromised.

In a child like four-year-old Anna, this kind of immature choice can be excused because the ability to choose self-denial over pleasure is not yet developmentally possible. With age, however, the lack of ability to make choices reflecting a commitment to higher-order goals becomes a progressively more serious liability when it comes to success. At this point, some definitions will help bring the relationship between this critical skill and parental discipline into focus.

DEFINITION #1: SOCIALIZATION. Socialization is the process of teaching a child the values and behaviors that are necessary for adaptive social living. These values and behaviors reflect generally accepted criteria of adult maturity and are also related to fulfilling relationships and to achieving economic success.

DEFINITION #2: PARENTAL DISCIPLINE. Parents are given primary responsibility for socialization of their children. Parental discipline is the process of creating external boundaries for the child's behavior and positively and negatively reinforcing conformity with them to create the capacity for that child to make similar choices as an adult.

DEFINITION #3: SELF-DISCIPLINE. The most desired product of socialization and parental discipline, self-discipline is the ability of the child to make responsible choices based on internalized values and personal commitments despite easier or more pleasant alternatives. In short, self-discipline is the ability to choose what is right instead of the path of least resistance.

As you can see, the concept of parental discipline as "making a child behave" is both narrow and naive. With its tremendous implications for the future of the child, *parental discipline reduced to its fundamentals is really Consistent Caring Communication about Choices and Consequences (the 5 C's of discipline).* As a parent, the positive impact you can have on your child's future depends on: 1) how well you understand the behaviors necessary for responsible and successful adulthood, and 2) how effectively you can help each of your children learn these behaviors during the approximately eighteen years the child is in your primary custody.

The Pleasure-Prone Child

Consider for a moment the sheer magnitude of the task that parents face during the socialization process. Every child comes into the world completely unsocialized and totally incapable of functioning in a socially acceptable and responsible manner. Compared to a mature and competent adult, the child's way of relating is very primitive. While acceptable early in life, with age this immature way of responding becomes socially inappropriate and increasingly dysfunctional.

There are three major characteristics that together define the primary response pattern of young children. Each of them must be overcome during the process of socialization for personal responsibility and competency to develop.

PRIMITIVE MOTIVATION #1: THE CHILD'S RESPONSES RE-

FLECT TOTAL IMPULSE EXPRESSION. In other words, the child responds to stimulation of various kinds in a completely uninhibited way. There is little or no control nor is there a sense of propriety. Impulse expression is total, spontaneous, and without regard for consequences.

PRIMITIVE MOTIVATION #2: THE CHILD'S BEHAVIOR IS GUIDED BY THE PLEASURE PRINCIPLE. Freud believed, correctly, that a child's basic motivation is simple to define and that it has dual thrusts: to maximize pleasure and to minimize pain. This primitive motivational system, called the Pleasure Principle, determines virtually all of a young child's choices.

PRIMITIVE MOTIVATION #3: THE CHILD'S ORIENTATION IS NARCISSISTIC IN NATURE. Put simply, young children are highly "me" oriented and inherently selfish. "What I want is most important" is the basic theme of their responses. A child's view of the world is one in which everything revolves around self as the center without regard to others' needs or feelings.

The Self-Disciplined Adult

During long years of training in the home, the impulse-ridden, pleasure-seeking, self-centered child must be radically transformed if a mature and competent adult is to emerge to take his or her place in society. Of all the skills necessary for responsible adulthood and career success, not one is more important than self-discipline. The primary bridge between the psychologically autonomous adult who does not need external limits to function and the immature child is the parent. And, the primary instrument for creating the capacity for self-denial is effective parental discipline.

Basically, what must occur during the parenting years is that the very primitive motivational system of a child must be broken down. In its place must be built a more sophisticated capability that is both socially adaptive and that reflects personal accountability. However, the motivational system mandated by society for success and personal responsibility is, psychologically, a monumental task requiring many years to learn. Clearly, it is best taught through years of effective parenting at home.

The capability for emotionally mature choices and personal responsibility can best be explained this way. The individual, virtually from childhood on, will be confronted again and again with choices of a particular type. There are always at least two options.

OPTION #1: TO CHOOSE THE IMMEDIATE AND PLEASURABLE. On one hand, there is usually an option to do something fun that you would love to be involved in right now. This choice is typically the easiest although it may be wrong, short-sighted, or immoral. However, the payoff is virtually instantaneous. At a superficial level, or to an immature individual, it is usually the more attractive choice.

OPTION #2: TO CHOOSE SELF-DENIAL AND A HIGHER ORDER PAYOFF. On the other hand, in any situation involving this kind of choice, there is usually another option that is not much fun either because it entails work and energy output or because it may be unpleasant. However, if this choice is made, the payoff will be more significant in the long run than the immediate, pleasure-oriented alternative.

Now the question. Confronted with this kind of choice over and over again throughout life, what option does the responsible individual exercise? Look at these examples. After insulting a friend in a fight, does a teen apologize or walk away and ignore the affront? With chores to do, does a child do them or go out to play when a friend knocks? There's a backlog of homework to get done, but a terrific party is going on just down the hall in the dormitory. What does a college student do? Several kids decide to try some drugs. What choice does each one make? A young couple is saving for the down payment on a new home, but there's a terrific buy on a new sports car that one of them has always wanted. What do they do?

The bottom line is simple. *If an individual cannot voluntarily choose self-denial over immediate pleasure, that person cannot be personally responsible, build mature relationships, or succeed in the work world!* It's the task of parents to help a child learn this capability through effective disciplinary procedures which increase the probability that self-discipline will develop. At its psychological root, self-discipline is no more than the ability to do what's right rather than what's easy or wrong. It is choosing long-term payoffs instead of immediate pleasure. It is standing by personal values instead of going with the crowd. Without this crucial ability, emotional maturity is simply not possible. Nor is personal responsibility.

Now consider presenting a three- or four-year-old this choice: "If you want this lollipop, I'll give it to you right now. On the other hand, if you will wait until tomorrow morning and ask me again, I will give you five lollipops just like this!" Virtually all children this age will immediately grab the lollipop offered right now. But look objectively at the choice offered. By waiting less than twenty-four hours, the payoff increases by five hundred percent! That's not a bad deal in anyone's book, but a small child's choice is wholly determined by impulsivity, pleasure-seeking, and narcissism.

The fact is that no child of three or four years has the capacity to make the kind of choice that involves self-denial. At this age, children have no future perspective nor are they developmentally ready to make choices based on long-term goal attainment. However, by age seven or eight this capacity should be developing. One signal is a child who begins saving dimes and quarters for a larger toy instead of spending every cent in a video arcade or on candy bars. That's voluntary self-denial in the service of a higher-order goal. It's also the beginning of being responsible and personally accountable.

While this kind of choice is emotionally difficult to make, it is absolutely necessary for success later in life. It is well-developed in the healthy achiever, but the fact is that it is usually not learned without effective parental discipline all through the developmental years. In point of fact, it does not have to be learned at all! It's very easy to overlook just how many adults in this world have never learned this crucial skill. These emotionally immature and psychologically impaired adults pay a very heavy price for this deficit. Relationships suffer. Personal fulfillment becomes elusive. Career aspirations disappear.

The Products of Self-Discipline

At this point, it will be illustrative to examine the important implications of the capacity for self-discipline. Parents often miss just how broad the social consequences can be for not helping their children learn self-denial. Self-discipline can be broken down into nine interrelated responses, all of which are the products of effective parental discipline, and all of which are widely recognized as socially valuable.

DISCIPLINE PRODUCT #1: THE BASIS FOR INTERPERSONAL TRUST IS CREATED. Trust can be defined as knowledge, based on experience, that another person will follow through on a commitment or responsibilities. The follow-through frequently necessitates resisting temptations and pleasurable alternatives in order to do what needs to be done. Viewed in this way, self-discipline is one of the bedrocks of trust between individuals. There is no sound basis to trust the undisciplined.

DISCIPLINE PRODUCT #2: THE CAPACITY TO WORK TOWARD LONG-TERM GOALS BECOMES POSSIBLE. Reaching long-term goals with payoffs sometimes far in the future requires self-denial in the present. In additon, the ability to work toward distant goals with no immediate payoff is closely related to going places in the work world. This skill necessitates not only faith in personal capabilities, but also the capacity to resist the many seductive diversions along the way that would thwart ultimate success.

DISCIPLINE PRODUCT #3: AN ADAPTIVE PERSONAL VALUE SYSTEM IS CREATED. A child who cannot say no or deny personal pleasure has no consistent value system. Choices will be determined by what is immediate and what is pleasurable regardless of what is intellectually dictated by deeper values. In other words, the situation defines the choice, not the person. And, an individual who does not control personal choices is not only immature, but also a hypocrite who is usually able to cleverly rationalize irresponsible behavior.

DISCIPLINE PRODUCT #4: THE BASIS FOR INTERNAL CONTROL DEVELOPS. Maturity can be defined as the ability of an individual to make reasonable and responsible choices about how to respond to various life situations. It means that the individual must have enough internal control to make choices that are not based solely on impulses, emotions, or self-gratification. Inner direction requires that an individual step back to assess a situation objectively and then to consciously decide how to respond maturely even if it's not fun!

DISCIPLINE PRODUCT #5: ANTICIPATORY AWARENESS IS LEARNED. A child learns judgement in two important ways: 1) from directly experiencing the consequences of actions and 2) from parents' explanations of the consequences of actions. However, to consider the future implications of an act, the individual must have the capacity to stop and think it out before going ahead. Those individuals who have not learned to check their impulses usually experience many more problem consequences of their behavior than those who have the capacity for self-denial.

DISCIPLINE PRODUCT #6: INTERPERSONAL SENSITIVITY AND RESPECT ARE INTERNALIZED. It is well-known that ultimate career success depends at least as much on people skills as on technical expertise. Teaching children appropriate social behaviors through the disciplinary process is important to developing healthy relationships both at work and at home. The fact is that good manners and social sensitivity—both highly desirable social skills—require that personal needs be put aside to meet the needs of others instead.

DISCIPLINE PRODUCT #7: THE FOUNDATION FOR FISCAL RESPONSIBILITY IS ESTABLISHED. In no other area is the lack of responsibility found in adults as frequently as in money management. This skill involves the ability to save for large purchases or to prepare for the future. It is the capacity to pay off loans or obligations despite other more pleasurable ways to spend money. Effective money management absolutely requires self-denial. The fact is that lack of fiscal self-discipline is one of the most commonly reported causes of stress and conflict in families.

DISCIPLINE PRODUCT #8: THERE IS LESS VULNERABILITY TO DELINQUENCY AND DANGER. Let's face it. Drugs, fast cars, deadly sexually transmitted diseases, and increased mobility present more danger these days for children. For this reason alone, it is imperative that a child be disciplined at home as a way to learn self-discipline and the ability to say "no." While it is always hard for a child to say "no" in the face of peer pressure, the ability to do so is much more likely to occur when there has been effective discipline implemented at home by knowledgeable parents.

DISCIPLINE PRODUCT #9: THE FOUNDATION FOR POSITIVE SELF-ESTEEM IS BUILT. The capacity for self-control and the ability to direct efforts toward personal goals is highly related to self-esteem. Conversely, individuals with little self-discipline usually have sagging self-esteem because capacity for meaningful choices and the ability to reach long-term goals becomes extremely difficult, if not impossible. In such men and women, self-esteem is further eroded because the "good life" and its rewards are so elusive.

Principles of Discipline

When emotionally healthy discipline is an ongoing part of family life, children grow toward adulthood with a substantial edge that makes success easier and life more fulfilling. Conversely, it is not difficult to find biologically mature adults who are essentially impulsive, who orient their lives excessively toward seeking pleasure, and who are selfish in their relationships. In most instances, these grown men and women were raised in families where discipline was weak in its implementation, distorted in its orientation, or emotionally destructive (or all of the above).

To help children internalize key values and learn the skills necessary for success, parents can use a number of discipline principles as guidelines. However, it is a fact that very few, if any, parents are highly skilled in every one of them. As you peruse these principles, assess your strengths and weaknesses in implementing parental discipline. Then maximize the positive and direct your energies toward strengthening your weak areas. Both you and your children will benefit.

DISCIPLINE PRINCIPLE #1: DEVELOP SHARED PARENTAL VALUES ABOUT DISCIPLINE. For effective parenting, it is imperative that both parents, even if separated or divorced, agree on values about what is right and what is wrong. It is just as critical that both parents agree on the nature of discipline and how it should be carried out within the family unit. Accomplishing these objectives requires ongoing dialogue between parents about the children and their activities. If parents disagree, they should back one another up publicly and work out differences privately for best results. This way, it is difficult for children to play one parent against the other.

DISCIPLINE PRINCIPLE #2: PARENTS MUST TAKE EQUAL RESPONSIBILITY FOR DISCIPLINARY ACTION. "Just wait until your father/mother gets home!" is clearly a cop out on discipline. A good rule of thumb is that the younger the child, the more immediate the disciplinary action must be in order to be effective. With both parents sharing responsibility for discipline comes the perception that they are acting together as one. Further, it prevents the destructive perception by children that one parent is the "heavy," while the other is passive and weak.

DISCIPLINE PRINCIPLE #3: DISCIPLINE MUST ALWAYS FOCUS ON THE CHOICE AND ITS CONSEQUENCES. A child who is disciplined for somehow being "bad" is probably not going to gain much from the experience. Discipline, after all, is really education about life, living, and getting along well. Along with disciplinary action, the child must be helped to conceptualize the choice made, other ways of responding, and the consequences of each alternative. In this way, parents through their discipline become actively involved in helping a child refine judgement and thus to make better choices in the future.

DISCIPLINE PRINCIPLE #4: TAKE CARE TO DISCIPLINE WITHOUT DAMAGING YOUR CHILD'S SELF-ESTEEM. One of the most self-defeating habits a parent can fall into is to associate discipline with humiliation or shame, name-calling, or ridicule. These practices directly attack a child's sense of self at an age when it is undeveloped and vulnerable. It is entirely possible to disapprove of a child's behavior without rejecting the child. When this is done, the child's self-esteem is left intact to grow in positive ways. Then, later in life, mistakes and failures can be accepted more gracefully because they do not represent personal negation.

DISCIPLINE PRINCIPLE #5: DO NOT NEGLECT TO GIVE ON-GOING POSITIVE REINFORCEMENT. When a parent consistently responds only to the negative in a child without acknowledging the positive, several problems are created. First, the child learns that, "I can never do anything right." This perception of self is most damaging to the growth of confidence. Second, sooner or later the child learns to turn off the constant barrage of criticism. When a parent takes the time to consistently acknowledge and reinforce the positive with praise, then that child is more likely to listen to and respond well to criticism.

DISCIPLINE PRINCIPLE #6: START TO DISCIPLINE YOUR CHILDREN WHEN THEY ARE YOUNG AND NEVER STOP. Reasonable discipline, started early, is much more easily accepted by a child all through the course of development. Because growing up is never easy, consistency helps immensely. Unaware or naive parents often excuse inappropriate behavior in young children, sometimes even seeing it as "cute." However, the story is different when an undisciplined teenager begins to raise the roof. The point is simple. It is most difficult to begin to discipline late and have it accepted. It's better to start early and never stop.

DISCIPLINE PRINCIPLE #7: CREATE A BASELINE OF UNCONDITIONAL ACCEPTANCE OF THE CHILD. One of the keys to effective discipline is to communicate, on a regular basis, your unconditional love and caring for each child: "I love you just because you're you." "I'll always love you, no matter what happens." "I'm so glad that you're my son/daughter." Such statements communicate a deep acceptance by parents that is independent of personal actions. However, such parental caring does not mean that all behavior will be accepted or tolerated. But, children who are sure of parental love can more easily accept discipline because they know it is an expression of caring.

DISCIPLINE PRINCIPLE #8: AFTER DISCIPLINARY ACTION, FORGIVE AND FORGET. In simple terms, once disciplinary action has been taken for an infraction, then get back to your normal way of relating to that child. Parents often make mistakes on two extremes. Some are extra nice after punishing a child to alleviate their own guilt for the punishment. Others continue to punish the child after the fact through constant reminders of what was done and how bad it was. In poor marital relationships, parents do the same to one another. In either situation, it is not a way to build a healthy relationship.

DISCIPLINE PRINCIPLE #9: MAKE DISCIPLINE A PRIVATE AFFAIR. Business management practices emphasize giving positive feedback publicly, but relating criticism privately. The same is true for parents. The reason for this guideline is that public humiliation, whether in front of friends, siblings, or in the grocery store, is extremely damaging to self-esteem. In fact, little else is more emotionally damaging to a child than repeated humiliation at the hands of parents. Make it a point to always discipline in private. You will protect the child's self-esteem, and your concerns will more likely be heard.

DISCIPLINE PRINCIPLE #10: LET THE CHILD EXPERIENCE "NATURAL CONSEQUENCES" OF ACTIONS WHEN FEASIBLE. When a child loses or breaks a toy through negligence, it should *not* be immediately replaced by parents to placate the child. The loss of the toy is the direct consequence of the child's action and must be experienced as such. In this way, the direct relationship between personal actions and consequences is created. In a broader sense, the child develops a sense of personal accountability and responsibility. No parental "punishment" is needed; the natural consequences of behavior are enough to facilitate learning.

DISCIPLINE ACTION #11: DO NOT ALLOW YOUR CHILD TO MANIPULATE YOU. Children are intuitive. By trial and error, they will soon zero in on your weaknesses and use them to get their way. Remember that a child's basic motivation focuses on self-gratification, not on doing what's right. If your vulnerabilities can be used to escape discipline, the child not only has control, but also is avoiding personal responsibility. Further, manipulative relationships usually deteriorate with time. It's up to you to learn your vulnerabilities and deal with them. Otherwise, they will be used against you to the detriment of your child's maturation.

DISCIPLINE PRINCIPLE #12: MAKE SURE DISCIPLINE FOCUSES ON YOUR CHILD'S NEEDS, NOT YOURS. A parent frustrated at work lashes out and unfairly disciplines a child at home. A small child playing has made a mess and is punished for not meeting parents' unreasonably high standards for order. In both instances, discipline has slipped from teaching a child adaptive values for living to meeting parents' questionable emotional needs. With such slippage, the child may be inadvertently taught maladaptive values or behaviors (to be passive and withdrawn, that neatness is more important than enjoying one's self). Check frequently on whose needs are being met by disciplinary action and what your child is *really* learning from you.

Parents and Preparation

There is no question about it. Growing up responsible is difficult these days. The world is more complex. Change is rapid. Children are barraged with stimulation from every part of their lives. In the midst of this sometimes confusing social milieu, you as a parent must still prepare your child to get along, to live well, and to "make it" in a world of future unknowns. Some of the best possible advice on discipline for parents and educators lies in the profound words of Dr. Maria Montessori, the founder of the Montessori schools: "The first idea that the child must acquire, in order to be actively disciplined, is that of the difference between good and evil; and the task of the educator lies in seeing that the child does not confound good with immobility, and evil with activity . . . . Our aim is to discipline for activity, for work, for good; not for immobility, not for passivity, not for obedience."

Further, to prepare your children effectively for responsible adulthood and success in life, you must have a solid and positive sense of who you are as a parent and what the parenting process is all about. Your time, your energy, and your commitment will be required. Your children *will* be children. Your resolve will be tested continually. To help keep your parenting in healthy perspective, keep these three fundamentals of discipline firmly in mind.

FUNDAMENTAL #1: CHILDREN NEED DISCIPLINE. Only the most unaware parents assume that children can grow up responsible without healthy discipline. As a parent, like it or not, you provide your child's primary frame of reference for living and relating. If you cop out on discipline, or if it is unhealthy, it may take years for your child to undo the damage and to forgive you for what you didn't do.

FUNDAMENTAL #2: CHILDREN RESIST DISCIPLINE. Just as consistently as you set limits, your children will just as consistently test them. Expect it. This produces the continuing dynamic tension that exists between the parental mandate to guide development and a child's needs to experience the new and the unknown. In healthy families, this dynamic tension is always present, although not always comfortable.

FUNDAMENTAL #3: CHILDREN RESPECT DISCIPLINE. Children respond with deeper and more loving relationships to adults who are able to discipline in firm but caring ways. Relationships almost always deteriorate with adults when children know they can abuse, control, or manipulate the adults. For your own good and that of your child, it is best to be a loving parent *and* a good disciplinarian.

From your own experiences, you have probably already learned that parenting in general and disciplining in particular will put you to the test. You already know there are no perfect children. In all probability, it has also come home to you that there are no perfect parents, either. As your children grow, so will you. They will see to it. You will learn about your vulnerabilities. Be confronted with your weaknesses. See the inconsistencies in your behavior. Be aware of the distortions in your perceptions.

You and your children will grow together—literally and figuratively —if you parent well. A perceptive parent who surely had been through it all once underscored this simple truth: "Who among us is mature enough for offspring before the offspring arrive? The value of marriage is not that adults produce children, but that children produce adults." As the song says, growing up is hard to do . . . for parents *and* for children. But, not growing up emotionally is worse . . . for parents *and* for children!

Chapter 9

Growing Up Responsible (Part 2): Parental Problems with Discipline Procedures

Ambivalence is simultaneous attraction and aversion. There is little question that most parents have at least some ambivalent feelings about discipline. Review for a moment the disciplinary "lessons" you received as a child from your parents. Undoubtedly, you didn't like most of them. Now, how do you feel when you discipline your children these days? More than likely, apprehension or even distaste wells up within you even though you know your children need discipline. It's emotionally difficult for parents and kids.

Now turn your thoughts to self-discipline. Negative feelings turn positive because you know how very important self-discipline is to success. You are also well aware that healthy parental discipline evolves into self-discipline and that you're responsible for producing that environment in your family. You like the product, but don't particularly care for the process necessary to build it. Your ambivalence about discipline is normal.

Like it or not, society gives to you—the parent—primary responsibility for preparing your children to function in mature and competent ways when they grow up. To fulfill this awesome responsibility requires commitment, awareness, and skill. Parents must constantly examine the "goodness of fit" between the values and behaviors they are reinforcing in the home and the skills society requires for success. Discipline as an active teaching process is the means through which a completely impulsive, pleasure-oriented, and self-centered child is transformed into a mature adult. Done well, the process works beautifully. On the other hand, a child can easily remain a child in an adult's body if parents have significant problems with disciplinary procedures.

A major personal issue with discipline is that positive parental involvement with children must be constant and consistent at a time in your life when you are busier and have more responsibilities than ever before. You may find yourself struggling for your own emotional survival every day. Under these conditions, it is difficult to give of yourself, but give you must. One result is that parents become easily frustrated with their children when their behavior is not responsible. In addition, the children are not particularly motivated to make the parental teaching process any easier. That goes with the territory. Furthermore, there are three other frustration factors that help turn parents' hair prematurely grey.

FRUSTRATION FACTOR #1: YOU MUST COUNTER "SIBLING DRIFT." Privileges that older children must earn or fight for are given to younger children earlier and easier. That process is "sibling drift." The net effect is less stringent parental discipline and consequently, diminished self-discipline in younger children. As a parent, you must exert constant energy to counter this trend so younger children grow up as responsible adults, too.

FRUSTRATION FACTOR #2: YOU MUST COMBAT SOPHISTI-CATED PSYCHOLOGICAL WARFARE. With age, children learn to read their parents like a book. Children pinpoint your weaknesses and vulnerabilities with deadly accuracy and then use them against you. Children want to have their way, and you want them to be competent and responsible. The pressure can be intense as children "hit your buttons" constantly.

FRUSTRATION FACTOR #3: YOU MUST ACCEPT THE "REPE-TITION REALITY." "Will they ever learn?" is the familiar lament of parents who become frustrated repeating the same instruction virtually daily. To this question, the answer is yes. Your values are being internalized, but very slowly. You may not see the results for years. In the meantime, repetition is reality and your frustration is real.

Despite the many frustrations, effective parental discipline is vital to each child's eventual emotional maturity, ultimate success in the work world, and capacity for healthy relationships. Discipline as consistent caring communication about choices and consequences is really education for life. From another perspective, discipline is a personal, perhaps even intimate, part of the relationship you have with your children. As such, however, it may arouse in you conflicts and uncomfortable feelings that compromise your ability to discipline well. A knowledge of some of the common problem areas with discipline procedures puts you as a parent in a prime position to grow beyond them. When you do, you will suffer less from the perils of parenthood, and your children will have a head start on growing up responsible.

Compensation and Compliance

Your early experiences serve as your primary frame of reference for parenting in general and discipline in particular. How your parents related to you as a child has a significant positive or negative influence on how you deal with your children now. As a general rule, the more deficient your parents were in disciplining you, the more likely you are to have unresolved conflicts that are interfering with healthy discipline in your family today.

Your parents may have been far too permissive with you or even ignored proper discipline. Conversely, your parents' style may have been too harsh and emotionally punitive. As a parent now, you may find that, in spite of yourself, you treat your children the same way your parents treated you (unhealthy compliance). Alternatively, you may find yourself going to an extreme in the opposite direction (unhealthy compensation).

Here is a way to pinpoint whether you exhibit this kind of parenting vulnerability. First, consider all parental discipline to fall on a scale from 1 to 10. Emotionally healthy discipline lies in the 4 to 7 range. Scores from 1 to 3 represent exceedingly lax and permissive parental responses to discipline. Excessively harsh and punitive discipline lies in the 8 to 10 range.

The next step is to rate your *dominant* parent on this scale from 1 to 10. Now comes the hard part; that is, rating yourself on how effectively you discipline your children. If you doubt your objectivity, it is often helpful to seek the opinions of others—a spouse, friends, even the kids. If the consensus is that you fall within the healthy range of discipline, there is usually little problem. However, when you *and* your dominant parent score outside the 4 to 7 range, there is typically a problem with either compensation or compliance. Using this scoring system as a framework for understanding disciplinary skews, examine these four major types of problems.

PROBLEM TYPE I: PERMISSIVE COMPLIANCE. *Parent score 1-3; your score 1-3.* Your parents copped out on discipline, and now you are doing the same with your children. You have many rationalizations for your actions, but none really holds water. One result is that because you are not in control of yourself most of the time, your children are out of control as well. Work on being more in control within, and then discipline consistently and effectively.

PROBLEM TYPE II: PERMISSIVE COMPENSATION. *Parent score 1-3; your score 8-10.* You realize the many detrimental effects that your parents' lenient or absent discipline had on you, and you have worked very hard to overcome them. You have committed yourself to making sure that the same problems are not passed on to your children. The point is that you have gone too far and have become too harsh and unduly restrictive. Loosen up just a bit and make it a point to become more positively involved with your children.

PROBLEM TYPE III: RESTRICTIVE COMPLIANCE. *Parent score 8-10; your score 8-10.* Though your parents were really tough on you growing up, you made it. You see your children growing up in an environment far too permissive for your taste. You want your children to learn the same hard lessons you did to build character. To an extent you are on the right track, but you are probably overdoing it. Restricting a bit less and personally teaching life skills a lot more would be a good idea.

PROBLEM TYPE IV: RESTRICTIVE COMPENSATION. *Parent score 8-10; your score 1-3.* Because of harsh treatment by your dominant parent, growing up was a painful process. Because it created problems for you, now you are going too far in the opposite direction with your children. In fact, you are creating a new set of problems for them by becoming too permissive. Tighten up your discipline to bring it into the healthy middle range to ensure that you do not suffer along with your children from the "spoiled child" syndrome.

Note: When each partner in a couple comes from significantly different parenting backgrounds, the marital dimension of compensation and compliance problems emerges. The result may be severe and continuing conflict about discipline in the home. In such instances, it is helpful for each spouse to rate both self and partner on the discipline scale. Then take the time to discuss the results to bring more consistency and cooperation to disciplinary procedures as a couple.

Disciplinary Soft Spots

Beyond correcting misbehavior and teaching life skills as the emphasis for disciplinary procedures, several specific behavioral areas need parental attention if children are to grow up well-rounded and responsible. It is naive to assume that parents are equally aware of and responsive to children's needs in each of these areas. In fact, it is frequently found that discipline may be quite "uneven" when all areas are considered. Some parents may even have a total blind spot in one area or another.

Here are the four major focal areas for discipline. Examine each one and then rank them from 1 (your weakest area) to 4 (the area where you are most responsive). Then begin to make the necessary changes to strengthen your disciplinary soft spots.

DISCIPLINE AREA #1: RESPECTING OTHERS' FEELINGS AND RIGHTS. *Examples:* Saying "please" and "thank you." Apologizing for a wrong. Getting along with friends.

No matter how technically competent the individual, real success in life is not possible without people skills. Surprisingly, this is the most common weakness in the parenting skills of successful adults. Such parents often emphasize academics while permitting their children to remain rude and insensitive. The solution is simple. Model interpersonal sensitivity and respect for your children, and systematically discipline them to do the same.

DISCIPLINE AREA #2: REINFORCING PERSONAL ACCOUNTABILITY. *Examples:* Bringing home and doing assigned homework. Doing chores at home. Following through on promises.

Accepting personal responsibility is a major key to success. Strangely enough, successful parents may not insist that their children be accountable. Meeting expectations and doing what needs to be done even if it is not particularly fun are the marks of maturity and competent adulthood. Begin to train your children early in life to accept responsibilities commensurate with their ages. Build on this base all through the developmental years.

DISCIPLINE AREA #3: ANTICIPATING CONSEQUENCES OF BEHAVIOR. *Examples:* Taking an umbrella if it looks like rain. Not hitting someone when you are mad because you will get in trouble. Getting to work on time to avoid penalties.

Anticipating the consequences of actions is perhaps a unique human capability; however, it is a habit that must be learned. If it is not, physical danger or punitive repercussions may result. Parents who permit their children to avoid the direct consequences of their actions do them a great disservice, one that is most difficult to correct later.

DISCIPLINE AREA #4: FUNCTIONING WITHIN DEFINED LIMITS. *Examples:* Coming home on time. Respecting school rules. Driving within the speed limits.

Learning to live by the rules is necessary not only to get along, but it is also critical for career success. Externally defined limits are a part of life that do not go away. On the other hand, the rules permit considerable freedom of action. However, if limits cannot be accepted, an "authority problem" surfaces. Without the ability to live within someone else's limits, an individual cannot be responsible. Teaching this to your children starts by disciplining them to abide by the most important limits of all: yours.

Destructive Emotional Control

As long as parental discipline remains Consistent Caring Communication about Choices and Consequences, it will probably be effective. However, it is easy for busy and frustrated parents with many responsibilities to focus on ways to merely control their children in lieu of effective disciplinary involvement. Unfortunately, parents learn many unhealthy and emotionally destructive ways as a means to exert control over their children. In the short term, these strategies may work. In the long term, parental control is purchased at the price of sometimes severe emotional damage to the children. The effects may not show up until adulthood.

Make no mistake about it. It is entirely possible to discipline effectively without placing your child's emotional health in jeopardy. Here are some of the more common ways that parents impose destructive or unfair emotional control on their children. Make it a point to eliminate each and every one from your repertoire of parental responses. When you do, you will feel better about yourself, and your children will grow toward maturity in an emotionally healthier environment.

DESTRUCTIVE RESPONSE STYLE #1: YOU PUBLICLY SHAME AND HUMILIATE YOUR CHILDREN. One of the favorite tactics of an immature parent is to publicly chastise and put down children. It is naively expected that the painful "public" nature of the response will ensure compliance with parental dictates. Too often, a spouse who "misbehaves" is held up for public ridicule in the same way. No response style is more emotionally damaging to self-esteem and breeds more resentment than public humiliation. The damage to children may last for years, if it can be completely overcome at all. Also, the parent who uses this highly dubious motivational technique loses, too. Others correctly perceive this individual to be tactless and blatantly insensitive.

DESTRUCTIVE RESPONSE STYLE #2: YOU CONSISTENTLY INDUCE GUILT IN YOUR CHILDREN. There is a wide gap between helping your child learn responsibility and making a child feel intensely guilty for every mistake. Parents who excessively indulge in this quasi-martyristic style ("You've let me down again") create guilt-prone children who may become emotionally paralyzed adults. The guilt-prone adult does not function well because of constant fear of being selfish, of alienating others, or of somehow disappointing someone else. As a result, individuality and autonomy cannot blossom. Keep in mind that if you seek to control your children through guilt, they may comply, but you will be heartily resented for it.

DESTRUCTIVE RESPONSE STYLE #3: DISCIPLINE IS BASED ON YOUR MOOD, NOT A CHILD'S ACTIONS. Children need consistently enforced behavioral boundaries in order to thrive emotionally. On the other side of the coin, there is no better prescription for inconsistency and unfairness than for discipline to be based on how you happen to feel at the moment a child violates a limit. One day, when you are feeling good, a serious problem may be overlooked. The next, a minor infraction may provoke a harsh punishment. When a child cannot predict how you will respond, then trust in you cannot develop. For self-protective reasons, a child may learn to maintain distance from you. Do yourself and your children a favor by finding healthier ways to relieve your frustrations so you can be fair and consistent.

DESTRUCTIVE RESPONSE STYLE #4: YOU INTIMIDATE YOUR CHILDREN IN ORDER TO MAINTAIN CONTROL. Making your children fear you is hardly the way to create a close and loving relationship with them. It also does not facilitate development of a sense of personal responsibility and willing cooperation. It is possible to control through intimidation, but the catch is that when you are not present, the "discipline" quickly breaks down. Administering abusive punishment and instilling fear in a child often breed rebelliousness and the probability of a counterattack later. Your use of this technique makes a very unflattering statement about you. It proclaims your naivete, your lack of sophistication, and your shallow perception of motivation.

DESTRUCTIVE RESPONSE STYLE #5: YOU PERSISTENTLY ATTACK YOUR CHILDREN'S SELF-ESTEEM. When you are upset and angry, you are likely to say anything and you do. When your children make mistakes or misbehave, you put them down with your name-calling and negative labels. In the process, you are rejecting your child as a person rather than disapproving of certain behaviors and directly teaching a better way. The fact is that healthy discipline does not involve an attack on a child's sense of self at a very vulnerable age. Too often, these favorite parental labels are internalized ("I'm stupid") to interfere later with adult functioning. For better results, correct without putdowns. Try this method with your spouse as well.

DESTRUCTIVE RESPONSE STYLE #6: YOUR DISCIPLINE IS BASED ON A MINDSET ABOUT A CHILD. Cross out the word that does not apply: "When there is a problem, my child is always/never at fault." When you respond in this way, you have developed a positive or negative mindset about your child. As a result, you cannot see your child clearly. On one hand, you may view your child as perfect and therefore never, ever at fault. Alternatively, your child may be seen as a perennial troublemaker who is always the instigator of any problem. In either case, you are blind and unfair. Your "perfect" child will never learn accountability. Your "troublemaker" will learn to lie and blame others to escape your inevitable wrath. Everyone loses.

DESTRUCTIVE RESPONSE STYLE #7: YOU COP OUT BY AT-TRIBUTING ALL MISBEHAVIOR TO "THE WAY CHILDREN ARE." Without doubt, this is the least acceptable parental excuse for not being actively and positively involved in disciplining children. This kind of aloof, "care less" attitude assumes that somehow, some way children will learn essential life skills and grow up to be competent adults without parental help. More likely, if you persist in responding this way, your children will remain emotionally immature and increasingly abusive of you as a parent, impulsive in their actions, and disrespectful of authority. Under these conditions, the magnitude of the problems children create grows steadily more serious with the years. Children and parents suffer intensely because parents were not responsible enough to teach their children to be responsible.

Regaining Your Credibility

Frustrated parents often complain that their children do not listen or that they totally ignore their parents when told to do something. Part of this perennial problem is very natural. Children are motivated to use avoidance behaviors when instructed to do something they do not want to do. Even under the best of circumstances, it is a rare child who immediately and without question responds to parental requests without the need to repeat them. On the other hand, parents often make this problem much worse by responding in ways that reduce the credibility of what they say to their children. Then, from low credibility grows even more frustration.

There is quite a variety of parental behaviors that diminish credibility. Use the following checklist to pinpoint yours. It goes without saying that you will find yourself somewhere on it because no parent is one hundred percent credible one hundred percent of the time. However, where your credibility is concerned, it is well worth it to make any needed improvements.

_____ **1. YOU AUTOMATICALLY SAY "NO" WHEN YOUR CHILD MAKES A REQUEST.** When you fall into this bad habit, your child quickly learns that "no" really does not mean no. Then, after some nagging and pestering, you stop to really listen to what your child wants and often the initial "no" becomes "yes." It is far better to listen carefully the first time a request is made. Then make a decision and stick with it to enhance credibility.

_____ **2. YOU RETRACT DISCIPLINARY MEASURES BECAUSE YOU FEEL GUILTY.** Sometimes this problem is caused by initially imposing punishment far too severe for the situation. Most of the time, however, it is your child's discomfort that creates your guilt. Not infrequently, a child learns how to exaggerate personal suffering to exacerbate your guilt and eventually get off the hook. When disciplining, be fair and then follow through all the way.

_____ **3. YOU LET YOUR CHILD FAST TALK YOU OUT OF DISCIPLINE.** Even young children become adept at finding "reasonable" excuses, rationalizations, others to blame, and clever deceits to avoid discipline. Gullible parents find themselves convinced that discipline is unfair and unwarranted under the circumstances described by a fast-talking kid. The more it works, the more you reinforce your child for learning all the glib skills of a con artist.

_____ **4. YOU AVOID CONFRONTING YOUR CHILD WITH WHAT YOU BELIEVE IS TRUE.** Far too many parents strongly suspect that their children are seriously misbehaving, particularly outside the home. Yet, they do not confront the situation early and directly. The reason? Then they would have to admit the problem exists and deal with it. While the situation gradually worsens, these blind parents continue to deny reality. Eventually, a very serious problem erupts that is even more painful for parents to admit and more difficult to correct.

_____ **5. YOU MAKE EMPTY THREATS AND GIVE ULTIMATUMS.** Your threats of dire consequences if your child does not behave is your emotional reaction to a problem situation. More often than not your threats are absurd and your child knows it. In the meantime, you steadily lose credibility. The best solution is to bite your tongue until you have calmed down. Then respond to the problem reasonably and follow through.

_____ **6. YOU UNDO OR SOFTEN YOUR PARTNER'S DISCIPLINARY ACTIONS.** You may conspire with your child to keep your partner from becoming aware of misbehavior, or you may covertly let a child escape consequences after discipline has been meted out by your partner. These kinds of responses strongly suggest a breakdown of communication between spouses. Moreover, your child easily learns how to use this breakdown to personal advantage.

_____ **7. YOU KEEP REPEATING INSTRUCTIONS.** Over time, children learn how many times a parent will repeat instructions before a limit is reached and disciplinary action is taken. Then, the children will simply ignore you until you are at your limit. Often, your breaking point is signaled by *tone of voice, not your words.* To correct this problem, take action immediately after your *first* request is ignored.

_____ **8. YOU LET YOUR CHILD CHARM YOU OUT OF DISCIPLINE.** This is manipulative affection or flattery at its worst. The problem is that it works so well with far too many parents. It is hard to discipline a child who is expressing undying love, incredibly deep affection, and unbelievable remorse for your benefit. If you cannot discipline fairly and consistently under these conditions, you may live to see your child become a "charming" adult manipulator.

_____ **9. YOU FEAR YOUR CHILD'S ABILITY TO PUNISH YOU.** Many children learn to punish their parents for taking disciplinary action. Ploys range from sullenness, lack of cooperation, and verbal cuts to passive-aggressive responses that may go on for weeks. Any parent who tolerates such behavior loses. This kind of child has learned how to avoid accountability through an indirect, but punitive counterattack on you. Then, you become apprehensive about discipline and your child grows up with no reason to respect authority. Do not let this pattern even start.

_____ **10. YOUR CHILDREN MOBILIZE PEER PRESSURE AGAINST YOU.** "Jane's parents let her do it." "Andy does it all the time." Despite misgivings and common sense, you give in. You are not strong enough or sure enough of yourself to be different. You go along with the crowd instead of carefully thinking out what is right and proper for your children. You will be a much better parent if you stick close to your values and not let your child's self-serving descriptions of peer behavior change your mind.

Doing What's Right, Not What's Easy

By way of summary, the intent of parental discipline is twofold. First, it is the major avenue through which children learn the direct relationship between behavior and consequences that results in personal accountability. Second, it is the process through which children learn the capacity for self-denial to obtain higher-order goals. The result is a self-disciplined, emotionally mature, and responsible adult. When this happens, skills necessary for healthy relationships and later career success are in place. The child with this training is most certainly advantaged in ways that far transcend material affluence.

To survive with flying colors the long and stressful process of helping your children to grow up responsible, parents need skills themselves. The patience of Job is definitely most helpful. The wisdom of Solomon is crucial. And, a goodly portion of plain old common sense is an absolute must. To this mixture must be added a parental commitment to do what is right, not what is easy. And, that commitment to doing what is right must be deep enough to risk being a bit different than neighbors up and down your street.

Beyond being an important part of your children's ultimate success, there are other important incentives for creating a consistent and healthy disciplinary environment in the home. Over the long run, three of these parental incentives stand out as critical to the emotional well-being of parents and their children.

PARENTAL INCENTIVE #1: YOUR CHILD'S PATH THROUGH ADOLESCENCE IS EASIER. At no other age are external boundaries for behavior needed more than during early adolescence (ages 12-17). By teaching your child to accept and abide by reasonable limits early in life, the chaos of the adolescent years is negotiated more easily by both parents and child. These years of turmoil are never easy, but they are far better than they might be if there has been consistent disciplinary involvement all along.

PARENTAL INCENTIVE #2: YOUR CHILDREN WILL PROUDLY MODEL YOU. As a caring and effective parent, you will create in your child not only a lasting closeness, but also a sincere desire to grow up to be just like you. In addition, your child will not have to "overcome you" on the path to responsible adulthood. Further, when your child becomes a parent, your values and skills will be proudly and consciously modeled. That is real success as a parent. Your valued place in an extended family that spans generations will be assured.

PARENTAL INCENTIVE #3: YOU WILL FEEL SO MUCH BETTER ABOUT YOU. The sure knowledge that you are in control from within is crucial to positive self-esteem. When you do not discipline effectively, you are likely to feel out of control and your children will likely be out of control too. Then, resulting negative feelings cause your self-esteem to plummet. With positive disciplinary involvement in your parenting, your self-esteem rises and your children grow up healthier.

Perhaps a final reminder about an aspect of discipline that is often forgotten is in order. For your disciplinary actions to be most effective, they must be balanced. It's all too easy to perceive discipline as punishment for an infraction. That's only half the story. Discipline, the teaching of personal responsibility, also must include consistent rewards for compliance with limits or for doing what is right, not what is easy. A child who hears only negatives and experiences only punishment turns off. Positive rewards—a statement of pride, a hug, a glowing report to a spouse or relatives—all create incentives to continue responding in mature and responsible ways.

In speaking about the positive side of discipline, one more point needs to be made. Studies of communication patterns reveal that positive feedback is not only less frequently given, but that *it is also more general than negative feedback.* It's illustrated by the difference between "Stop roughhousing on the furniture this instant!" and "You've been so good this afternoon." The child who is disciplined for inappropriate behavior usually knows exactly why. A child who receives positive feedback may not understand the specific responses that brought praise. The point is simple: not only give more positive feedback, but make it behaviorally specific for best effect.

For better or for worse, you are a parent. With no formal training, you have embarked on the decades-long task of helping your children grow to become competent and responsible adults. And, these days, that task is not only more sophisticated, but it is also more crucial because of the complicated and dangerous world within which your children must grow to adulthood. You have only your own experiences, the values you have developed, and a commitment to do what is best for your children to use as guides. However, your understanding of the issues and an ability to clearly conceptualize them are also crucial.

Perhaps speaking in reference to the children of effective parents, an individual in the know once commented: "Those who succeed usually don't have a big advantage, but they almost always have an edge." Your consistent, caring involvement blended with a healthy disciplinary environment throughout the developmental years is the biggest edge that you can possibly give to your children. The positive effects will last a lifetime. A final word. When it comes to discipline, paraphrasing the simple message of a familiar commercial is most apropos: "Don't let your children leave home without it!"

Chapter 10

Creating "Go for It" Confidence: Healthy Achievers Make Good Things Happen!

Tim is in the fifth grade. He's been a rather poor student all along. Testing revealed no learning disabilities, but Tim isn't achieving to potential. He just doesn't seem to care about homework. He'd rather spend his time making forts with his friends or just tinkering in the garage.

Annette lives just a few doors away. She's a very bright student and loves school. Always willing to tackle new projects, she's a rising star. When not at school, she reads and does extra projects. Her teachers are as proud of her accomplishments as her parents. Dedicated as she is, she is expected to go far by all who know her.

Now the question: "Which of these two students is motivated and which is not?" If you answered that Annette has lots of motivation and Tim has virtually none, you would be dead wrong! The fact is that both of these young people are highly motivated. The difference lies in where their energies are focused. Tim likes to tinker and work outdoors while Annette likes to study and learn within a classroom environment. The contrast between these two young people also debunks the myth of the "unmotivated" individual. As an adult or as a child, there is no such thing!

While everyone is motivated, the directions for personal motivation vary greatly from person to person. What parents are most concerned about in an "unmotivated" child is that that child is not achieving to potential in school. They realize how important learning is to success. They despair that their child whose energies are focused primarily on nonacademic endeavors will ever make it. Sometimes such parental fears are well-founded. Sometimes they are not. It requires close examination of the emotional reasons for achieving to tell the difference.

It may be that both Tim and Annette have healthy achievement motivation. On the other hand, for the sake of argument, let's look at some negative possibilities. Tim, for example, may not be academically-oriented because of past experiences that have been turned into emotionally painful failures because of parental attitudes. Thus, his nonacademic directions may be motivated by fear of more failures. On the other hand, Annette may be driven to high achievements because she has learned that that is the only way she can get any kind of positive responses from her parents. For her, successful achieving has become heavily linked to self-esteem. She can't ever stop.

In these typical situations, appearances are deceptive. Depending on prior experiences, the motivations of Tim and Annette could be healthy or unhealthy. These days, it is necessary for parents to understand the dynamics of healthy achievement motivation and how to nurture it within their children. As a starting point, let's look at the four components that make up a positive achievement cycle. Then let's add some parental attitudes and comments that may over time completely turn a child away from a desire to achieve in positive directions.

COMPONENT #1: THE RISE OF DESIRE. *Inner Experience:* "I really want that." Here a child becomes aware of an object of desire and a need to possess it. This awareness generates achievement motivation to obtain what is wanted.

Parental Negation: "You want it? Here, I'll buy it for you!"

COMPONENT #2: STRIVING AND REACHING. *Inner Experience:* "I'm trying! I'm trying!" Here basic motivation is channeled into creating and implementing strategies to attain the desired goal. Setbacks and barriers must be overcome and perseverance counts.

Parental Negation: "You'll never get there. Just look at all the mistakes you're making!"

COMPONENT #3: GOAL ATTAINMENT. *Inner Experience:* "I've done it! At last!" Here the goal is reached usually after hard work, problem solving, and personal sacrifice. With goal attainment comes learning about how to make things happen and a deeper sense of personal control.

Parental Negation: "So what's the big deal? Anyone can do that!"
COMPONENT #4: THE INTERNALIZATION OF REWARDS. *Inner Experience:* "It feels great! I want to do it again!" Reaching a goal may bring a sense of accomplishment, the goal itself may be rewarding, and others may provide positive recognition. Emotional rewards reinforce achievement motivation and generate a desire to repeat the experience.

Parental Negation: "You could have done much better if you had only tried harder!"

No doubt about it. Achieving for the right reasons is wonderful. It is not only deeply fulfilling, but also contributes heavily to personal growth, to an inner sense of control, and to the ability to live the good life. On the downside, parental attitudes can easily subvert achievement motivation into avoidance or foster high achievement for the wrong emotional reasons. It depends on your understanding of the basics of healthy achievement applied to the needs of a particular child. For parents who want to accentuate the positive and minimize the negative, here are some do's and don'ts to foster "go for it" confidence in your children.

The Qualities of Excellence

Any discussion of achievement motivation must focus on creating an environment where individuals feel good about being productive. It is interesting that in homes, in offices, and in classrooms, certain characteristics are almost always present when high morale and productivity are found together. This special environment is created by the attitudes and skills of those in charge. Whether that person is a parent, a teacher, or an office administrator, these qualities are exactly the same. So are the positive effects.

There are three qualities of excellence that together create this kind of positive growth environment with the family. Used in tandem, they promote healthy achievement motivation, personal growth, and positive self-esteem in children. Each one is outlined with a statement of the extremes that undermine healthy achieving.

QUALITY OF EXCELLENCE #1: YOU HAVE HIGH BUT REALISTIC STANDARDS FOR PRODUCTION. In other words, there is an expectation that everyone will work to potential. Parents don't tolerate goofing off or avoiding the tasks that need completion whether they are chores or homework. And, the expectations of parents tend to be reasonably attainable by children with hard work and dedication. When these goals are reached, the kids feel good and parents make it a point to provide positive feedback and approval. Although not everyone "makes it" all the time, most can and do *when they try*. On a continuum, the Parent of Excellence falls somewhat on the tough side of the median in terms of performance expectations.

The "Easy Does It" Contrast. At this extreme is the "slide" parent whose needs for approval from children interfere with promoting performance. Such parents are usually liked by children because their standards are so low. However, they are not respected because laziness and sloppy work, or avoidance of work altogether, are tolerated. As a result, children don't grow. No teacher who offers a "slide course" receives awards for excellence and neither do parents!

The "Purely Impossible" Contrast. These usually perfectionist parents set performance expectations so high that no one can meet them. No matter what has been done, it's not enough or it could have been done better. After a while, children become demoralized because of constant failure. Over time, achievement motivation diminishes because rewards in the form of parental approval are never there. The feeling is: "Why try? I can never do it right!"

QUALITY OF EXCELLENCE #2: YOU ARE FIRM BUT FAIR IN MAINTAINING CONTROL. The Parent of Excellence is clearly in charge and remains so with effective discipline. However, control is reasonable and implemented in healthy ways that children can accept. The kids are aware of parental guidelines and limits and know from experience that infractions will be confronted immediately. However, this kind of parent isn't rigid, either. Allowances are made on the basis of personal judgement or when special circumstances warrant. Children feel safe in bringing problems to you because you respond in helpful ways and are fair to all involved. On a continuum, your style lies somewhat on the tough side of the median on control and discipline.

The "Pushover" Contrast. "You can get away with anything" is the norm when this kind of parent is in charge. Simply ignoring the rules may work. If that isn't effective, manipulation surely is. This parent may shout a lot, but credibility is low because rules and limits aren't backed up. Any kind of flimsy excuse gets the child off the hook. The kids run wild and problems worsen because there is no real leadership or control. Chaos is king here.

The "Rigid Rulebook" Contrast. This parent is rigid and unyielding to absurdity. No excuses. No exceptions. This parent is incapable of bending even a little. This is the kind of parent who can't admit a mistake and when one has been made, hides behind false pride in not admitting it. This same kind of parent often creates power struggles with children that usually worsen with time. As the children get older, defiance deepens. Intimidation is habitually used as a motivational technique. This parent is perceived as impersonal and uncaring.

QUALITY OF EXCELLENCE #3: YOU DEVELOP HEALTHY INVOLVEMENT WITH YOUR CHILDREN. This kind of parent cares deeply and the kids know it. Although your standards for performance and discipline are tough, they are balanced by personal warmth, understanding, responsiveness, and sensitivity to the emotional needs and frustrations of the kids. You have a realistically upbeat style, and you regularly provide encouragement and positive feedback. You actively encourage personal development through your support, and you view making mistakes as part of the total growth process. Because of your healthy caring, the kids respect your leadership and like you as a person. As a result, they will work hard for you because you make them feel good about themselves. On a continuum, the Parent of Excellence falls somewhat on the "warm" side of the median.

The "Shielding" Contrast. This parent tends to be overprotective of the kids. With too much concern about personal feelings or pain, they often tend to subtly promote dependency rather than independence. To a fault, this parent may allow a child to avoid responsibilities or may even do the work for that child. The net result is that the child never learns to overcome problems with positive encouragement and support for independent action. "Here, poor baby, let me take care of you!" is the ethic. It keeps the kids immature.

The "Coldheart" Contrast. At this extreme, the parent exudes a rejecting "I don't care about you, just do it!" attitude. Often an individual with emotional problems related to intimacy, such a parent earns the disrespect and resentment of the kids over time. It is well-known that high performance and acceptance of discipline is the result when children perceive parents as caring and loving. Conversely, the kids can't be faulted for not giving that "something extra" to their work when parents are perceived not to really care.

Seven Achievement Killers

The vast majority of parents want the best for their children. And, they want to be proud of the kids as they grow toward emotional maturity, career competence, and personal responsibility. That's what a Healthy Achiever is all about. However, as parents strive to achieve these ends, they encounter many pitfalls along the way. Some lie outside of direct parental control; then parents must function on the sidelines as coaches and a support system. Other achievement problems, however, can be almost entirely prevented by parents who are aware of them.

Here are a number of achievement killers that parents must eliminate. Some are inadvertent. A few have their roots in parents' experiences growing up. One or two more result from distorted attempts to motivate. Sooner or later, all of them backfire to compromise the confidence of the kids, their good feelings about themselves, and the experience of success in an achieving world.

ACHIEVEMENT KILLER #1: SECURITY IS EVERYTHING. *Destructive Message:* "Never take a risk or you'll be sorry!"

Often these parents were small children during the Great Depression. Ingrained in them are extreme security needs: "Get a job and keep it." "Accumulate money in the bank, but don't ever spend it." "Always play it safe." These fears are then deeply ingrained in children in many subtle and not-so-subtle ways. The reality is that reasonable risks to meet challenges are part of healthy achieving. Parents who stifle this ability in the kids for whatever reason create an inadvertent, but destructive priority: "Security and stagnation are always preferable to reasonable risk and personal growth." Not so.

ACHIEVEMENT KILLER #2: COMPETITIVENESS WITH OTHER SIBLINGS. *Destructive Message:* "Achieve like your brother/sister or you're a failure."

Short-sighted parents frequently try to motivate one of their children by comparing the low achievements of that child to the high achievement of another, usually older, one. The message is powerful in its abilty to undercut the confidence of the child on the losing end of the comparison. At times, this message is so consistent that a child learns to not even try. Why? It's simple. To try and fail to live up to the standards of another sibling is emotionally more painful than not trying at all! Further, parents who constantly compare one child to another can create an enmity between those children that will impair their relationship for a lifetime.

ACHIEVEMENT KILLER #3: CONSTANTLY SOWING DOUBT. *Destructive Message:* "Most other people are smarter and more motivated than you are, so we don't think you can really make it."

These kinds of messages often are distorted attempts either to motivate a child or to prevent a child from experiencing failure by reaching too far. However, the plan usually backfires miserably. Instead of pushing harder, a child may become demoralized because parents are perceived to be doubtful about success. And, it is not uncommon for parents with this style to be negative about virtually everything a child does. Their nonsupportive and critical attitudes may permanently sabotage the development of "go for it confidence" in a vulnerable child.

ACHIEVEMENT KILLER #4: PROMOTING UNREASONABLE FEARS ABOUT EVERYTHING. *Destructive Message:* "The world is a fearful place so full of hidden dangers that you can't ever relax."

Most often, parents who promote the fears of children are excessively fearful themselves. They see potential danger everywhere. Typically, their lives are restricted because of the anxieties they live with. On the surface, they want to protect their children, but deep down they may want the kids to be exactly like they are. The messages are never ending: "The ferris wheel will fall." "You'll drown in that boat." "There are dangerous germs in that public bathroom." All fears are possibilities, but instead of teaching children to realistically assess danger and protect themselves, these parents instill fear and promote avoidance instead.

ACHIEVEMENT KILLER #5: TO GET WHAT YOU WANT, ANYTHING GOES. *Destructive Message:* "It's okay to be unethical or dishonest because the ends always justify the means."

These kinds of attitudes, now more frequently found in competitive parents than ever before, are a sad indictment of some of the superficial values endemic in society today. Parents encourage these kinds of attitudes by helping children to bypass rules. Or, they help the kids avoid the consequences of behavior by lying or otherwise covering for them. Teachers know just how common this practice is! Public figures who betray the trust of constituents and the rash of white-collar criminals who are caught these days are both a symptom and a cause of this growing problem. The bottom line is that parents must model and teach ethics. The consistent message must be: "You are accountable at all times. It is better to lose honorably than to win unethically."

ACHIEVEMENT KILLER #6: PLEASE US AT ALL COSTS. *Destructive Message:* "Your role in life is to fulfill us as parents by meeting our needs."

Here the emotional message becomes clear over time: the needs of parents are always more important than the needs of the child. And, if a child achieves at all, it is to meet the needs of parents rather than to develop personal skills and competencies. Too frequently, the needs of parents are questionable to begin with: to enhance a public image, to "one-up" other parents who have children the same age, to have *their* child in a prestigious career. Any or all of these needs may be promoted at the expense of a child's real talents and aptitudes. As time passes, most children become aware of parental needs and may either defy those needs and risk parental rejection or meet them at the expense of personal fulfillment.

ACHIEVEMENT KILLER #7: YOU CAN NEVER TRUST ANYONE. *Destructive Message:* "People will always take advantage of you, so keep your distance and never trust anyone else."

Unfortunately, when parents consistently reinforce this attitude, the emotional impact can be very powerful. What comes across is: "Don't ever get close to anyone. You'll always be let down or betrayed." This kind of defensive way of relating often compromises the development of emotional intimacy in relationships. At work, cooperation and teamwork may be impaired as well. These days, cooperative efforts are becoming even more important than unmitigated competitiveness. In the end, an overly suspicious person often winds up with poor relationships because of trust problems created by parents.

The Confidence Builder's Checklist

Volumes have been written on the specifics of creating healthy achievement motivation in children. However, in examining written materials, a solid core of suggestions occurs time and again. It is a mistake to think that it costs money to build achievement motivation in children. It doesn't. What it does cost, however, is some thinking through, some understanding, and some change in the way you communicate with the kids. When you come right down to it, it's the values communicated through parental responses to children that either encourage the development of achievement motivation or destroy it.

Let's face it, creating confidence is never easy. And, its basic source lies in positive experiences with achieving. While all children will not become high achievers as adults, with help all children *can* develop personal potential in this area. The "go for it" confidence that results will provide benefits for a lifetime whether focused on a career or turned to other personally fulfilling directions. Here is the Confidence Builder's Checklist to help you get started.

_____ **1. YOU UNDERSTAND THAT LEARNING TAKES PLACE IN MANY DIFFERENT CONTEXTS** besides schoolwork. It occurs in free and unstructured play, through trial and error in accomplishing personally meaningful tasks, by relating to peers, and in projects personally initiated and carried out. Although there are no grades for these activities, you realize their importance to the total development of children and mandate time for them.

_____ **2. YOU MAKE A CLEAR DISTINCTION BETWEEN "HELPING OUT" AND "TAKING OVER"** when the kids have a project. You make helpful suggestions and you get involved with what the kids are doing, but not too much. You are wary of getting conned into taking over and doing it for the kids. Instead, you let the kids set the tone and make their own mistakes without any "I told you so!" recriminations.

_____ **3. YOU TREAT FAILURE AS AN INEVITABLE AND NECESSARY PART OF SUCCESS,** and this positive value is always evident in your responses to the kids. You studiously avoid calling them names for goofing up or making a mistake. Instead, through discussion you help them analyze what went wrong and thereby help develop possible strategies to overcome the problem. You never forget to keep an upbeat "work smarter, not harder" attitude.

_____ **4. THERE IS NO QUESTION THAT YOU VALUE QUALITY OVER QUANTITY.** Children often become overinvolved in outside activities these days. You keep a watchful eye on your children and place reasonable limits on their extracurricular involvements. This value mandates some time for the kids to relax a bit. It also helps them gain depth in the fewer activities that remain.

_____ **5. THERE IS REINFORCEMENT OF PERSONAL COMMITMENT AND PERSEVERANCE** in spite of obstacles. In other words, one of your achievement values is that you finish what you start, or at least take it to a reasonable end point (*e.g.*, the end of a season in sports activities). You do not permit the kids to quit an activity or a project just because the going gets rough. Although they may resist, you know that it teaches them to confront obstacles, not avoid them.

_____ **6. YOU HELP THE KIDS SET ATTAINABLE GOALS FOR THEIR EFFORTS.** Often, children left to their own devices set totally unrealistic goals for themselves. Some of their objectives may be impossible (*e.g.*, a three-room treehouse). Others mistakes may result from overestimating their capabilities (*e.g.*, to build it in one day). Your input helps them to place personal effort and project reality into an attainable perspective.

_____ **7. YOU RECOGNIZE THAT COOPERATION IS OFTEN MORE IMPORTANT THAN COMPETITION.** You already know that very competitive parents sometimes teach their "win at all costs" orientation to their kids. Savvy parents know better. The adversarial relationships that are born of competitiveness often interfere with teamwork, cooperative efforts, and getting along well with others. You emphasize cooperation and working well with people instead.

_____ **8. YOU REINFORCE ADEQUATE ADVANCE PREPARATION** for meeting any personal challenge. "Anything worth doing is worth doing right" is the value behind preparation. You set the kids to thinking through what they will need to carry out a realistic plan. Then you help them get ready. You discourage them from thoughtlessly rushing into a challenging situation which may produce needless mistakes or even danger.

_____ **9. UNCONDITIONAL POSITIVE ACCEPTANCE IS ALWAYS PRESENT** when you are involved with the kids. Your children know from experience that you love them no matter what. They realize that your acceptance of them is *not* contingent on being the best or always succeeding. Because of that critical awareness, they are emotionally freed to do their best because they're not afraid to fail.

_____ **10. YOU HELP YOUR CHILD KEEP ACHIEVEMENTS IN HEALTHY PERSPECTIVE.** In other words, when your child comes out Number One or successfully meets a challenge, you communicate clearly that that does not mean that the child is better than anyone else. Success means that that child is simply more dedicated or more skilled or has tried harder. You reinforce these qualities instead of "good, better, best" hierarchies.

_____ **11. THE POSITIVE FEEDBACK YOU GIVE IS BEHAVIORALLY SPECIFIC.** Far too much of the time, criticism is quite detailed, but positive feedback is very general (*e.g.* "You played well."). To be usable, positive feedback must be behaviorally specific and that's just what you try to do. As a result, your children consistently receive from you usable information about what they did right!

_____ **12. "PERSONAL BEST" IS YOUR FRAME OF REFERENCE** in helping your child evaluate accomplishments. You avoid the trap of the perfectionist who always finds something wrong. You encourage all of your children to reach for their personal best while recognizing differences in personalities and capabilities. No matter what mistakes were made, you always find something right about what a child accomplished.

_____ **13. IN WHATEVER YOUR CHILD DOES, YOU REINFORCE PERSONAL RESPONSIBILITY** for actions taken. In other words, you don't permit your child to unfairly blame circumstances or other people for failure. In all ways, you mandate good sportsmanship and that means accepting failures gracefully. Only naive parents encourage scapegoating instead of carefully examining personal performance to spot needed areas of improvement.

_____ **14. YOU TALK TO THE KIDS ABOUT THEIR WORK CONSTANTLY,** but you do it in casual and optimistic ways. You make achieving not only a creative challenge, but you also spark enthusiasm by the way you talk about it. You tell interesting stories about yourself and you help the kids conceptualize ideas and strategies through your dialogue. As a result, they often ask questions because you make it so attractive to do so.

_____ **15. YOU BECOME A "RESOURCE DEVELOPMENT SPECIALIST" FOR YOUR CHILDREN.** If the kids don't know something, you help them find out without doing it for them. You may suggest specific books, people to call and talk to, or even particular places to visit to see how it is done. You encourage this kind of resourcefulness and outreach by the kids, and you take pride in seeing how quickly they learn to do it themselves.

_____ **16. ATTENTION TO DETAIL IS ENCOURAGED** as part of all achievement endeavors. Equipment is inspected, homework is checked, the finer points of an activity are examined. Children are notorious for global perception, but they gain an edge by attending to details. Most won't learn this skill unless it is taught. It is one of several important baseline skills that insure quality work. It also helps prevent mistakes due to omission.

On Life, Lemons, and Lemonade

Everyone has heard the now famous suggestion: "When life hands you a lemon, make lemonade!" However, the follow-up question is equally important: "Do you know how to go about it?" There's a tremendous difference between wishing and knowing exactly what to do. Healthy achievers know all about lemons and what to do with them. They've had a solid base of experience at home learning how to make good things happen and confronting adversity along the way. For years, their parents have responded in ways that helped them learn these important achievement skills. On the other hand, underachievers avoid lemons like the plague because they can't cope with the bitter taste.

In broader perspective, healthy achievement motivation is a personal asset that can enhance every part of life. Wise parents view achievement motivation in more than career terms. At its root, it is a value system that becomes a primary means for personal expression and gaining emotional fulfillment through the years. As it develops in children, it brings with it four confidence qualities that make day-to-day living easier for a lifetime.

CONFIDENCE QUALITY #1: CHANGE IS NOT THREATENING. Because there is security within, change is perceived in positive terms. And, because a healthy achiever has an inner sense of control, there is no perception of self as a victim of circumstance, of other people, or of the vicissitudes of life. This individual is capable not only of "going with the flow," but also of determining the direction of the flow most of the time.

CONFIDENCE QUALITY #2: PERSONAL GROWTH RESULTS FROM HEALTHY ACHIEVEMENT MOTIVATION. Meeting personal challenges and making things happen involve reasonable risk. The healthy achiever does not fear carefully considered risks because failure is not personally threatening. In fact, failure is seen as an opportunity to learn. As a result, healthy achievers grow personally from both their failures and their successes. It's a win-win situation.

CONFIDENCE QUALITY #3: THERE IS NO NEED FOR DEFENSIVENESS. The healthy achiever is aware of and accepts personal strengths *and* weaknesses. And, personal growth is directed to further develop strengths and to remove weaknesses or vulnerabilities. One result of this orientation is that healthy achievers, secure within, have no need to be defensive. Positive feedback is gracefully accepted. Mistakes and helpful advice are also accepted without being rejected by false pride.

CONFIDENCE QUALITY #4: SELF-ESTEEM IS INTERNALLY BASED. Healthy achievers are not emotionally driven to always win, to be Number One, or to have the most of everything to feel good about themselves. And, because self-esteem and positive acceptance are based within, there is less personal vulnerability when a failure is encountered. This quality ("I know who I am and I like who I am as a person") permits achievements to be an expression of self rather than a way to allay deep insecurity.

Now back to life and those lemons. The "I can make things happen!" attitude is a powerful quality that allows the individual at all times to make choices no matter how adverse the circumstances. As such, healthy achievement motivation is an index of deep personal strength, adaptive coping, and emotional hardiness. To a workaholic whose self-esteem is intimately tied to successful performance, a lemon is a negation of self. To an underachiever, a lemon becomes only another confirmation that life is unfair and that it's useless to try.

To the healthy achiever, a lemon is a very different story. In thinking it through, this kind of individual defines and considers options. What are the pros and cons of the proverbial lemonade stand? How about taking lemons to the customer by peddling them on the street? Perhaps there is some potential in processing them into lemon meringue pies. Maybe selling concentrate would work. Or wholesaling them to distributors. Marketing lemons to restaurants as garnishes for iced tea is yet another possibility.

Someone has said that luck is where opportunity and preparation meet. Because the healthy achiever is well-prepared, opportunities are found even within adversity. But it doesn't have to happen. It all depends on your perspective. As a wit once commented: "When opportunity knocks, most people complain about the noise!" That's characteristic of those who are insecure about meeting challenges. The healthy achiever opens the door to see the view from a different angle. Hey, anyone have some lemons? There are some real possibilities here!

Chapter 11

Games
Children Play:
Deciding Not to be
Manipulated

SCENE: Subject approached mother for food handout shortly before evening meal. Denied said snack, subject accused parent of being "bad" and of preferring other mother figures (specifically Mrs. Smith, neighbor and parent of friend). Reacting to accusations, mother provided aforementioned snack with admonition: "Just this once." Subject was observed to smile while withdrawing from scene with two cookies in possession.

RAP SHEET

NAME: Sammie Jones (alias: Sam the Smooth).
AGE: 5 years, 3 months.
OCCUPATION: Kindergarten student.
INTERESTS: Self-gratification.
MODUS OPERANDI: Inducing guilt and insecurity to control parents.
PREVIOUS CONVICTIONS: Repeat offender since age two.

You may smile at this rather whimsical description of one child's maneuvers to get his way. However, it nicely illustrates several pertinent points. First, it should be evident that Sam has already learned at his tender age to use emotional pressure (*i.e.*, to manipulate) to get what he wants from his parents. In fact, a two-year-old is certainly not too young to learn such tactics and use them effectively. Second, because Sam's maneuvers work so well (he gets the cookies), his manipulative responses are reinforced and will be used again in the future.

It should now be quite evident that if a child of two can learn to manipulate by using emotional leverage, there are certainly many more opportunities for an older child (like Sammie) or a savvy adult to do the same! Basically, a psychological game is "an unhealthy interaction in which one individual uses an emotional vulnerability in another person to arouse emotions and thereby apply emotional pressure to facilitate meeting personal needs in an inappropriate manner." Any successful game requires the involvement of at least two individuals who tacitly cooperate to produce the desired outcome: 1) an individual with an emotional vulnerability (the Pawn) and 2) another person who exploits it (the Player). Further, all games have four basic components that together define a given interaction as a game.

GAME COMPONENT #1: A "ME-ORIENTED" ATTITUDE. All individuals who play games (*i.e.*, Players), whether adults or children, are making a statement: "I want what I want whether you want to give it to me or not!" The interaction that is the game is designed to accomplish just that end.

GAME COMPONENT #2: A POWER PLAY. Games cannot work unless one individual is able to emotionally overpower another. With this kind of leverage, one individual is able to obtain something that is wanted even if the Pawn doesn't particularly want to give it.

GAME COMPONENT #3: AN EMOTIONAL VULNERABILITY. Everyone is emotionally vulnerable in one way or another. One person is a sucker for flattery. Another succumbs to a guilt trip. An emotional vulnerabilty found and exploited by a Player is part of every game.

GAME COMPONENT #4: LOSS OF PERSPECTIVE. By definition, objectivity is lost by the Pawn in any successful game. Emotional pressure produced by focusing on a vulnerability creates motivation to reduce the discomfort. A sense of right and wrong is blurred or is rationalized away.

As these destructive interactions called games occur, the person being manipulated feels used (correctly!). The person doing the manipulating is learning an emotionally inappropriate use of power that seriously compromises relationships. Given that *every individual has emotional vulnerabilities*, it is imperative that everyone be aware of them. And, when vulnerabilities can be reduced or eliminated, the individual feels better, communication is kept healthier, and relationships improve. However, to grow beyond your vulnerabilities, you must also understand psychological games in depth.

Here's a framework to help you do so.

The Anatomy of a Game

You may already have begun to realize how destructive games can be to relationships, particularly within families. You also know that the object of any game is to obtain a payoff. To get to the payoff, however, all games follow a set sequence in the interaction of the Player and the Pawn. With parenting issues, Players are almost always chidren and Pawns are one or both parents. To develop effective countermeasures to any game, you must first of all clearly understand this sequence of four basic steps. Sammie's Cookie Game is used as an example.

INTERACTION STEP #1: THE PLAYER ENGAGES IN PROVOCATIVE BEHAVIOR. In short, the Player initiates the game by behaving in ways that will surely attract the Pawn's attention. In many instances, the behavior is so blatant or outrageous that it cannot be ignored by the Pawn.

The Cookie Game: Sammie initiates the game after his mother refuses to give him the cookie. His provocative behavior is telling her she is a poor mother and that he prefers his friend's mom to her.

INTERACTION STEP #2: THE PAWN'S EMOTIONS ARE AROUSED. If provocative behaviors do not arouse the Pawn emotionally, there can be no game. Most of the time, the emotions aroused in the Pawn are quite uncomfortable. As a result, internal pressure is created by this discomfort followed by a desire to reduce it.

The Cookie Game: After Sammie's accusation, his mother begins to feel guilty and insecure in her role as a mother. Would Mrs. Smith give one to her child? Is she being unfair to Sam? Does her son really prefer Mrs. Smith? She feels bad.

INTERACTION STEP #3: THE PAWN RESPONDS IN THE MANNER DESIRED. The object of the game is to get the Player to make certain expected responses. These responses, when made, reduce the internal emotional pressure that has been created and that is now proving uncomfortable to the Pawn.

The Cookie Game: As feelings of guilt and insecurity quickly grow more intense, Sammie's mother begins to rationalize his request. Shortly, she gives in and provides the cookie, admonishing him, "Just this once."

INTERACTION STEP #4: THE PLAYER RECEIVES THE PAY-OFF WANTED. The rewards are provided by the expected responses of the Pawn. However, rewards can be either tangible, emotional, or both. When a game succeeds in providing the Player with an expected reward, it is reinforced and similar responses are more likely to be used with that person in the future.

The Cookie Game: When Sammie receives the cookie from his mother, the game is complete. She has given in despite her better judgement as a way to reduce her uncomfortable feelings. For his part, Sammie will tap her vulnerability again soon.

The Common Vulnerabilities

Too many individuals simply do not realize when they are being emotionally overpowered by others. And, there are just as many who are at least minimally aware that they are being manipulated, but have not clearly conceptualized exactly how they are being used to someone else's advantage. Because of this lack of insight, these adults find it quite difficult to reduce the personal vulnerability that permits such manipulation to take place.

When emotional vulnerabilities are surveyed, only a finite number are found. Any given individual, though, may have more than one. Of course, the more vulnerabilities that are present, the more opportunities there are for others to use these as emotional leverage. To help you pinpoint your emotional soft spots, consider the following list. Check each one that is True for you. Shhhh! Don't let anyone know what you've found. This information can definitely be used against you!

VULNERABILITY #1: YOU CAN BE MADE TO FEEL IRRATION-ALLY GUILTY. By leaps and bounds, guilt induction is the most common emotional basis for manipulation. When guilt is used, there is almost always one single issue involved: to do what is right (or giving to self) versus meeting someone else's needs. When guilt is aroused, making healthy choices is emotionally linked to personal selfishness or illegitimately denying someone else's needs. Martyrs are the masters of this kind of emotional blackmail. Gotcha!

VULNERABILITY #2: YOU FEAR CONFLICT OR ANGER. Many men and women say yes to anything if doing so will avoid an argument or a fight. This is the major vulnerability of passive and non-assertive individuals. Sometimes early family life was so filled with violent parental conflict that children learned to abhor it. Other parents so carefully hid any conflict from the kids that the children grew up with an unrealistic fantasy of what a "good relationship" (read: absolutely no conflict) is like.

VULNERABILITY #3: YOU CONSISTENTLY FALL FOR A "HARD LUCK" STORY. It's always hard to deny someone else who is in dire need or experiencing emotional pain. While some needs for help are certainly legitimate, there are individuals who learn to expertly play "woe is me." In so doing, they emotionally "hook" others into taking care of them. The key question in such situations is this: "Are my responses geared merely to reducing another's discomfort or am I responding in ways that help that person deal effectively with a problem situation and thereby gain self-sufficiency?"

VULNERABILITY #4: YOU BREAK DOWN WHEN OTHERS BREAK OUT CRYING (a.k.a. the Boo-Hoo Boondoggle). Related to the above, tears have become a favorite ploy for some to gain emotional leverage. Parents observe children turning tears off and on like a faucet. Not infrequently, there are tears for one parent but not for the other. The reason is obvious. The parent who gets the tears is vulnerable, a partner is not. Look at your responses under various "crying conditions" to see whether you are being conned. Don't forget that some adults can cry on demand, too.

VULNERABILITY #5: YOU FALL FOR FLATTERY. Little Johnny, about to be punished for a transgression, begins to profess his undying love for parents combined with bear hugs and great sloppy kisses. They melt. Johnny gets off scot-free because he's stroked his parents into submission. These same ploys are used in adult relationships with equal effect. Flattery distorts perception and creates a need to please the other person. Whoever said that "Flattery will get you everywhere" was absolutely right for those who are vulnerable.

VULNERABILITY #6: YOU HAVE A DEEP FEAR OF DISAPPROVAL. It is surprising how many otherwise bright and insightful individuals can't stand the thought that even one person in the whole world might not like them. As a result, they give in or say yes to anything to avoid the possibility of disapproval by someone else, even small children! These unrealistic and vulnerable adults have never learned that the price of their irrational needs for approval ("I want everyone to like me all the time") is loss of self-respect and of the respect of others.

VULNERABILITY #7: YOU CAN BE MADE TO FEEL INSECURE IN YOUR ROLE. This is the "role diffusion" maneuver used so effectively by certain adults and children. In a defined role (as parent, manager, or supervisor) you have been given responsibilities, prerogatives, and boundaries. Another individual, usually one who has broken rules or one who makes an unfair or unwarranted demand, makes accusations ("You don't like me!") or threats ("I'm going to report you to YOUR supervisor!"). The recipient becomes insecure in that given role and gives in. Bingo! They've been had.

VULNERABILITY #8: YOU CAN BE WORN DOWN BY NAGGING. Conventional wisdom dictates that a good way to get a job is to be so persistent that the personnel director gives it to you to get rid of you! Similarly, a child knows exactly how many "no's" a parent will deliver before giving in. The basic strategy is simple. Just bring up the subject again and again ad nauseum until the target gets so tired of hearing it they respond in the way desired. Then the game is won. The game plan is reinforced.

VULNERABILITY #9: YOU CAN'T STAND SILENCE (*a.k.a.* the Pouter's Ploy). To withdraw from even casual interaction with someone else creates painful pressure in vulnerable individuals. Any necessary responses are kept formal, clipped, and monosyllabic. As time passes (sometimes it takes a week or so), feelings of rejection grow within. The only way to deal with this power play is to avoid participating. Treat the pouter normally and put the pressure on that person to end the game by going about your business as usual.

VULNERABILITY #10: YOU CAN BE PLAYED AGAINST SOMEONE ELSE. Here's how this maneuver goes. Someone else (usually one without much power—child, subordinate, etc.) comes to you with a request. Although you disagree, to be nice you make ambiguous statements without clearly saying no. The recipient then takes your fuzzy responses, distorted in a favorable way, to someone else with power. You are reported to be in favor of the request. Given this evidence, the second individual agrees because the first person has already done so. In the wink of an eye, you've been psychologically blindsided.

VULNERABILITY #11: YOU ARE AFRAID TO BE DIFFERENT. The core dynamic here is a feeling that if you're different, then somehow you're wrong. Two facts should be considered by such individuals. First, what everyone else is doing doesn't mean it's right. Second, when your major frame of reference is other people, then you lose the capacity to clearly define and live by your own values. And, make no mistake about it. Your need to conform can be used coercively by children and adults who discover this vulnerability.

VULNERABILITY #12: YOU ARE HOOKED ON STATUS COMPETITION. Some insecure folks judge their adequacy by what their peers possess. A neighbor getting a new car triggers a need to be one-up with a better model. If the kids at school all wear designer clothes of one brand, your kids will soon be wearing an even more exclusive label. Intuitive children quickly learn to use this kind of parental insecurity to their advantage. After all, they're actually helping Dad and Mom avoid feelings of inadequacy. Right? Yes, and also helping them stay broke at the same time.

Payoffs for Game Playing

You already know that the motive for all games is for the Player to obtain a reward or payoff from the Pawn. However, it is quite easy to assume that the reward is always something tangible (*e.g.*, the cookie in The Cookie Game). This conclusion is incorrect. Of course, the payoff can be tangible, but often there is an emotional payoff as well. Or, perhaps most frequently, a successful game turns out to provide both types of benefits to the Player. And, the psychological or emotional payoffs for a game may be much less obvious than tangible ones.

To fully understand the psychological dynamics of a particular game, the more subtle emotional payoffs must be assessed along with the more obvious material rewards. While it is true that human behavior is highly complex, the psychological payoffs for games can be reduced to only four basic types. As a good rule of thumb for analyzing games, remember that virtually all games involve one or a combination of these rewards for the Player regardless of whether a tangible reward is present! These can be most easily defined in terms of certain emotional needs that are being met in inappropriate ways by the Player through a game.

Do keep in mind that these emotional payoffs are usually more important as reinforcers than are tangible rewards. And, to the extent that these needs are met through successful game playing, the more likely it is that the game will be repeated in the future. These four payoffs can easily be remembered through the acronym NARC. After you read them, test yourself by defining the psychological rewards obtained by Sammie in The Cookie Game.

EMOTIONAL PAYOFF #1: THE NEED FOR NURTURANCE. *Behavioral Message:* "Do it for me" or "Take care of me."

In this case, the Player is seeking to avoid personal responsibility by getting someone else to accept it. As others respond to the sometimes powerful emotional pull to take over, the immaturity of the Player remains. While it cannot be denied that caretaking is an essential part of parenting, emphasis must be placed on helping a child accept responsibility rather than on playing games to avoid it.

EMOTIONAL PAYOFF #2: THE NEED FOR ATTENTION. *Behavioral Message:* "Respond to me" or "I'm going to make you pay attention to me."

The ultimate intention of this game motive is to force others to pay attention to the Player whether they want to or not. Sometimes this ploy results when parents do not provide enough positive attention to a child. Then the child discovers that parents do respond to negative behavior. Or, some children have insatiable needs to monopolize parental attention. This kind of game, when successful, puts a child at the center of negative parental attention.

EMOTIONAL PAYOFF #3: THE NEED FOR REVENGE. *Behavioral Message:* "I'm going to get you back" or "I'm going to punish you for not doing what I want."

This motivation for a game is as frequently encountered as it is missed by those trying to understand a given game. The fact is that revenge games are quite common in children and adults. Success is defined by making the Pawn feel bad or creating complications that are frustrating. Children easily learn to punish their parents. For example, one common revenge game might be titled: "Let's make Dad/Mom totally lose control!"

EMOTIONAL PAYOFF #4: THE NEED FOR CONTROL. *Behavioral Message:* "I'm going to make you do what I want" or "I'm going to seize control of this situation."

Control is one of the most common motives of all for game playing. When it is present, the Player forces the Pawn to do something against better judgement, personal values, or what is right or wrong in a given situation. And, it is the feeling of loss of control in the Pawn that very frequently erodes self-esteem. It is difficult to feel good about yourself when you are frequently being emotionally controlled by a game player.

Dealing Effectively with Game Players

Psychological games are clearly destructive to everyone involved, Players *and* Pawns. The Players remain immature and Pawns continue to be exploited as long as a given game continues to be successful. On the other hand, it is also clear that any game can be stopped. It always takes at least two to play a game. The Player and the Pawn must both play their parts for the game to proceed to its end point, the payoff. However, while it takes two to play a game, a Pawn can stop a game cold by refusing to play the expected part.

To do this, the Pawn must first of all clearly understand the Interaction Steps in a given game. Then, that individual must define ways of responding that are healthier than the expected responses of the Player. Third, it helps to know some of the general aspects of game playing to strengthen personal resolve to break out of participation in one particular kind of manipulation. To provide this kind of information to game Pawns (and we are all Pawns from time to time), here are some helpful intervention ideas.

INTERVENTION IDEA #1: LOOK FOR GAME PATTERNS. In other words, games are most often played in relationships where there are ongoing, long-term interactions: for example, among coworkers and friends, between parents and children, and in marital relationships. Similar patterns of interaction can be observed to occur again and again by an astute Pawn. The reason? They are often part of a game, and they are repeated because they work!

INTERVENTION IDEA #2: USE YOUR FEELINGS AS A DIAGNOSTIC TOOL. When a game is being successfully played, afterwards you will almost always feel bad. Anger, hurt, or disappointment may be present. Or, you may be plagued by a vague sense of unease. The reason is simple: you've been had although you may not consciously understand exactly how it happened. Treat your feelings as indicative of a successful game in which you are the Pawn.

INTERVENTION IDEA #3: PINPOINT YOUR EMOTIONAL VULNERABILITIES. A game cannot be played successfully unless the Pawn has an emotional vulnerability that can be exploited. To stop a game, you must know your emotional weak points. Then, you must keep them firmly in mind. Whenever you find those particular feelings being aroused, particularly if it is by the same person, it's another sign that a game is being played.

INTERVENTION IDEA #4: DON'T DO WHAT YOU FEEL LIKE DOING. When you experience strong feelings, you will begin to lose perspective if you're not careful. It is precisely at this point that you must not do what you feel like doing. In all likelihood, *what you feel like doing is actually the response expected by the Player!* When you do the unexpected by maintaining perspective, the game cannot proceed.

INTERVENTION IDEA #5: REMAIN EMOTIONALLY CALM AT ALL TIMES. To effectively stop a game, you must not let your emotions obviously overwhelm you. It may be very difficult to avoid becoming emotionally upset. However, it is usually possible with some practice to remain calm, cool, and collected, at least on the outside. The reason is twofold: 1) obvious upsets tell the Player the game is working, and 2) getting you upset may be the object of the game in the first place!

INTERVENTION IDEA #6: DO NOT REJECT THE PLAYER. Related to staying emotionally calm, the suggestion to avoid rejecting the Player is equally important. If you lash out, name call, or attack when your feelings have become aroused, you lose in two ways. First, you have been provoked into attacking the person rather than the issues involved. Second, the Player will have even less reason to trust you to be fair and to meet personal needs in healthier ways in the future.

INTERVENTION IDEA #7: EXPECT AN INCREASE IN PROVOCATIVE BEHAVIOR. When the Pawn stops making an expected response (*i.e.,* giving in), often the disruptive behavior of the Player *increases* in frequency or intensity. The reason for this is precedent. If the Player is used to getting a payoff and then it stops, the inclination is to try harder using the same techniques. It is at this point that the Pawn must persevere. Eventually, the disruptive behavior will subside.

INTERVENTION IDEA #8: DO NOT ASSUME CONSCIOUS AWARENESS BY THE PLAYER. Most games are learned by trial and error in relationships. Children are not aware of the psychological dynamics of a game that reap an expected reward. All they have to know is: "When I do/say X, then I get what I want!" It would be easy, but clearly erroneous, to assume that all adults know when they are playing games. Some do, but many clearly do not.

INTERVENTION IDEA #9: PROVIDE THE PLAYER WITH ALTERNATIVES. Particularly with children, it is important to turn a potential game scenario into a teaching moment. Making an educated guess about the emotional payoff is the first step. Then clearly define a healthier alternative: "If you're angry with me, let's sit down and talk about it." "It wouldn't be right for me to do your homework for you, but I will be here to help you when you get stuck." Do the same for adult game players.

INTERVENTION IDEA #10: KEEP RESPONSIBILITY IN THE RIGHT PLACE. In all successful games, the Player avoids personal responsibility and/or gets the Pawn to assume responsibility. An essential guideline for stopping a game is to be very clear on who is responsible for what. Then make it a point to define those responsibilities to the player in a direct and firm, yet tactful way that reflects your concern.

INTERVENTION IDEA #11: WHEN IN DOUBT, BUY TIME. It is not uncommon for a man or woman to suspect that a game is being played. They have been made uncomfortable by the responses of a Player, but at the same time have not clearly conceptualized what is going on. The best advice is to get out of the situation for a few moments (or more) so you can think more objectively about a particular interaction. Simply say: "Give me a few minutes to think this over and I'll get back to you."

INTERVENTION IDEA #12: KEEP YOUR ABILITY TO STOP GAME PLAYING IN PERSPECTIVE. In other words, you cannot stop a Player from playing games! What you can do, though, is to stop a Player from playing a game with you. The reality is that you simply cannot control another person all the time. That child or adult can find someone else susceptible to a given game. However, by short-circuiting a game being played with you, you are doing your part to help that person grow up!

INTERVENTION IDEA #13: DON'T PLAY GAMES YOURSELF. Anyone who plays games is not being emotionally honest. And, someone who perennially plays games is not in a good position to teach others not to do so. If you are going to stop someone else from playing games with you, it would certainly make you less of a hypocrite to stop playing them yourself. After all, children often learn to play games by seeing them work time and again when parents play them with one another!

Building Character Within

The unfortunate reality that all people, no matter how mature, must accept is that no one is completely invulnerable emotionally. Consequently, no one is immune from being manipulated by a good game player. However, at this point you understand the psychology of games. You know the interaction steps for games, the kinds of payoffs being sought, and some strategies for stopping them.

Now the time has come to put into practice what you know. To begin, look at the Game Plan in Figure 1 below. It provides a useful outline for analyzing psychological games. In addition to the four steps of a game, there are places to note the emotional payoffs the player is seeking, the nature of the vulnerability that allows a game to proceed, and alternative healthier responses. You will note that for illustration, this Game Plan has been filled in for you. Analyzing a game is not as difficult as you may think. And, you will have to master this skill if you are to stop others from playing games with you.

GAME PLAN

Your Name for the Game: *Pouting Power*
Describe the Problem Situation: *Betsy, age 10, wants to ride her bicycle to a nearby shopping mall with a friend. They must ride part way on a busy highway to get there. This is a new privilege and parents say no after due consideration and explain the danger. Betsy immediately stomps out and refuses to speak to either parent.*

Analysis

Step 1: Describe the Provocative Behavior of the Player.
Withdrawal, sullen looks, refusal to communicate (or clipped monosyllabic responses), lack of cooperation.

Step 2: Define the Emotions Aroused in the Pawn.
Guilt, discomfort with child's rejection, frustration.

Step 3: Outline the Responses Expected by the Player.
To give in to demand made, to apologize for being insensitive to child's wishes.

Step 4: Specify the Payoffs for Player if Successful in Eliciting Expected Responses.
A. Tangible Benefit(s)
Gains privilege previously denied

B. Emotional Reward(s) Ranked by Importance
_____ Nurturance   _____ Attention
___1___ Revenge   ___2___ Control

Intervention

Step 5: State the Nature of Your Emotional Vulnerability.
Fear of rejection/disapproval (need to be liked).
Step 6: Define Healthier Responses to be Made in the Problem Situation.
a. *Respond to child in normal fashion/no avoidance.*
b. *Do not provide any "goodies" to make up.*
c. *Isolate child when disruptive to family members.*
d. *Offer (once) to talk about situation/make self available.*
e. *Do not badger child about need to talk.*
f. *Go about personal business as usual.*

Figure 1: Completed Analysis of a Game Plan

Now it's time to go a step further and analyze a game that you have experienced. Take a moment to think about a situation when you unwillingly gave in to someone else or where you felt used. It may have been at home with children or with a spouse. A friend may have played a game with you. You may find a good example at work. In Appendix 1 there is a blank Game Plan. Outline the game as you see it from beginning to end. Then, resolve to respond in healthier ways that prevent that other person from playing that game with you.

Again, keep in mind that the more vulnerabilities you have, the higher the probability that others will detect and exploit them in self-centered and immature ways. Perhaps the very best way to reduce your susceptibility to games is to work through your vulnerabilities. Practice doing what is right, not what is expected. You will find that many benefits will accrue as initial discomfort subsides. The process is one of regaining your integrity as a competent and responsible human being. Here's how you benefit.

INTEGRITY FACTOR #1: YOUR VALUES ARE REFLECTED IN YOUR BEHAVIOR AGAIN. When you are manipulated, you compromise doing what you know is right just to get rid of uncomfortable feelings. With reduced vulnerability, you can again stand on principle and your values are less easily negated. You will also be more consistent.

INTEGRITY FACTOR #2: YOUR SELF-ESTEEM RISES BECAUSE YOU HAVE REGAINED CONTROL. How can you feel good about yourself when others are constantly overpowering you using emotional leverage? Conversely when vulnerabilities are reduced, you regain inner control and your decisions reflect what is right. It feels good.

INTEGRITY FACTOR #3: OTHERS LEARN TO RESPECT YOU. It's interesting that those who are easily manipulated are usually well-liked, but not respected. How is respect possible when others can so easily manipulate you? By strengthening your emotional weak spots, you create the basis for respect *and* approval from others.

Make no mistake about it. When you allow others to play games with you, everyone loses. Of course, you lose because you are being used and feel bad as a result. However, if there was ever a good motivation for breaking a game, particularly games children play, it is because of the long-term detrimental effects on the Player, not the Pawn! As long as a game is successfully used, the Player remains emotionally immature and irresponsible in that area of life. To break a game, no matter how difficult, is actually the process of helping the Player grow up to be emotionally healthy, competent, and responsible.

As you eliminate game playing from family interactions, you will find that after an initial period of discomfort your relationships will change for the better. They become deeper, more honest and open, and in the long run more fulfilling for all involved. Conversely, as long as you continue to allow yourself to be emotionally manipulated, you suffer and so do your relationships. Someone who knew the score once wryly commented: "Familiarity may not breed contempt, but it sure does take the edge off admiration!" That's doubly true when your children become familiar with your vulnerabilities and you don't!

Chapter 12

Social Sensitivity and Success: "Making It" Requires Strong People Skills

"Did you notice how polite that child was? Not only to me, but to friends. Children all used to be that way, but not anymore. Not in this day and age."

"I'm really impressed with that child's manners. Those parents must be doing something right. All their kids are like that. I wonder how they did it."

"It's remarkable how well-behaved that child is. I really wish mine were more that way. Maybe someday they'll learn. I hope they do before I give up trying."

These are comments parents hear time and again about other children. Sometimes, though, positive feedback is about *their* children, and they are pleased. In fact, adults marvel at the maturity of even small children who possess good manners. This kind of positive regard is most gratifying to parents who have worked hard to teach their children the basic social skills necessary to get along well with others. On the other hand, far too many parents receive a different kind of feedback about their children.

"Those kids are just plain brats. I just can't understand why their parents don't do something about how they behave, especially in public. It's appalling."

"I love my brother, but he has two of the rudest kids I've ever seen. I've told him about it many times, but it hasn't done one bit of good."

"I don't even want my children around those two. After my kids visit, they come home with atrocious manners just from being around them."

Now let's take a quantum leap to adulthood for these last children, growing up in solid middle-class families, but without the advantage of being taught good manners and basic social skills. Though many are quite bright, they have problems because of these deficient areas. Here are some familiar scenarios easily found in every community. Each is accompanied by a statement of the price tag for not being sensitive to others as an adult.

ROLFF'S PROBLEM: While bright and motivated, Rolff was allowed to have his own way all through childhood. Never corrected by his parents, as an adult it's catching up to him. His relationships with his wife and children have been steadily deteriorating for years. His rude putdowns, his tactless remarks, and his general insensitivity to the emotional needs of his family are the cause of his distant relationships. His wife has withdrawn from him so she won't be hurt any more. The kids go out of their way to avoid him. Rolff doesn't understand what is wrong even after his wife leaves him.

The Price Tag: Isolation from loved ones, absence of warm and fulfilling relationships, and, ultimately, loneliness.

CHARLOTTE'S PROBLEM: An up-and-coming young professional in a growing company, Charlotte was on the fast track to the top. She worked diligently in her specialty as a computer "trouble shooter." Then she was promoted to a management position. Over time, her insensitive and often sarcastic way of responding to her subordinates caused problems. Before long, a bad morale problem in her office resulted in Charlotte's being one of the first to be "let go" in a reorganization. She was hurt and angry because without question she "knew her stuff."

The Price Tag: Career advancement is seriously compromised beyond midlevel where people-oriented management skills outweigh technical expertise.

KEN'S PROBLEM: A well-trained physician in a small city, Ken was technically competent, but had a brusque, sometimes abrasive, bedside manner and spent little time with his patients. While he was the only practitioner of his specialty in the area, things were fine. Then a youngster, just out of residency training, moved to town and set up practice. Ken quickly found that his patients were steadily deserting him in favor of the newcomer. The new physician, clearly not as experienced, took time to talk empathically with each patient. Feeling that their fears and concerns were understood, they kept coming back.

The Price Tag: Loss of professional standing in the community and the serious deterioration of a once-thriving practice.

While many lament the absence of good manners in a "me" oriented society, the fact remains that politeness and sensitivity to the needs of others remain important assets on the road to success. Basic social skills involve the ability to transcend the essential impulsiveness, self-centeredness, and pleasure orientation of children. As such, the presence of such skills and their consistent use are an important criteria of emotional maturity. It is a sad commentary on current social values to see the numbers of achieving men and women who simply neglect to teach their children good manners.

Good Manners Are Functional

While emphasizing the importance of good manners as crucial to success and the good life, it is instructive to separate these skills from etiquette. To do that, you must first understand that good manners and etiquette are composed of both form *and* function. The difference lies in the balance. In etiquette, the emphasis is on *form*. For example, the rituals, the ceremonial aspects of human interaction, the details of the "proper" ways to do things are paramount. On the other hand, the emphasis in manners is on *function*. These are the more basic skills useful in getting along well with others and in day-to-day living.

To illustrate this difference, the rules of etiquette dictate *which* fork to use in what sequence during a meal. In good manners, the emphasis is on using *one* fork consistently and correctly. In a nutshell, etiquette is simply advanced manners in which form becomes ever more dominant over function. While the details of etiquette are undoubtedly good to know, politeness and sensitivity to others are an absolute must no matter where you are or what your station in life. And, good manners must be learned before the details of etiquette can make sense.

In broader perspective, basic good manners has four important functional values to individuals and to society. And, good manners are becoming ever more important as population increases and living and working conditions become more crowded.

FUNCTIONAL VALUE #1: GOOD MANNERS ORDER HUMAN INTERACTIONS AND PREVENT CONFLICT. *Examples:* Saying "excuse me" when accidentally bumping into someone else. Not pushing into a formed line. Observing the "rules of the road" helps to avoid accidents when driving. Manners are, quite simply, the rules of the road for social interactions. In a nutshell, basic manners, understood and used by all, help human interactions go more smoothly and aid in preventing misunderstandings.

FUNCTIONAL VALUE #2: GOOD MANNERS HELP PROTECT THE HEALTH OF EVERYONE. *Examples:* Washing your hands before eating or handling food. Averting your head and covering your mouth when you cough. These aspects of good manners come under the general heading of good personal hygiene. They reflect an understanding of disease and how to prevent potential health problems for yourself and for others. As such, these kinds of good manners not only protect the individual, but also society as a whole.

FUNCTIONAL VALUE #3: GOOD MANNERS CONVEY RESPECT FOR OTHERS' RIGHTS. *Examples:* Avoiding loud and boisterous behavior in a restaurant. Asking permission to use someone else's property. Everyone has rights, legally speaking. However, in a much more informal way, everyone has personal rights that must be respected through use of good manners. Strong social skills reflect a sensitivity to the rights of others and willingness to respect the prerogatives that each individual, whether adult or child, possesses.

FUNCTIONAL VALUE #4: GOOD MANNERS REFLECT CARING ABOUT OTHERS AND HOW THEY FEEL. *Examples:* Apologizing for an insensitive remark. Directly expressing appreciation for gifts. Being insensitive to others really means putting personal wishes first while ignoring the emotional needs of others. This selfish orientation is the antithesis of good manners in a child or an adult. Solid social skills require first of all awareness of others' feelings and then an appropriate response to them.

The Social Sensitivity Training Scale

Parents often wonder how well they are doing in helping their children learn politeness and social sensitivity. While teaching good manners to children is frustrating at best, parents can check to find out whether they are placing proper emphasis on these critical skills. In the following Social Sensitivity Training Scale, answer each statement True or False as it pertains to your responses to your children *most* of the time. The more of these statements you answer True, the more consistent and comprehensive your manners training is likely to be. Statements answered False should be used to pinpoint areas where your manners training needs strengthening.

T   F

___ ___ 1. As parents, we insist that our children treat us with respect at all times.

Rationale: Children who do not learn to treat their elders with respect have no reason to treat anyone else with respect, either.

___ ___ 2. If our child mistreats a friend, we see that all parties get together to talk it out and have our child apologize if necessary.

Rationale: The ability to discuss problems and admit a wrong is an essential ingredient in all healthy relationships.

___ ___ 3. At the dinner table in our home, good manners are about the same as when eating out at a restaurant.

Rationale: Good manners are good manners everywhere. There is no reason for a manners "double standard" to develop.

___ ___ 4. From time to time, in areas of defined weakness in the kids, we have them practice key social skills with us.

Rationale: Good manners and social sensitivity do not come easily or automatically. Persistence, direct training, and practice are necessary.

___ ___ 5. In our marital relationship, and with the children, we consistently model good manners in how we respond to one another.

Rationale: Children who experience good manners from adults and who observe these skills used throughout their development find them easier to learn and adopt themselves.

___ ___ 6. We give our children plenty of specific and positive feedback on the good manners they display.

Rationale: Children usually get plenty of negative feedback. Behaviorally, specific positive feedback is even more important in helping the kids learn appropriate social skills.

___ ___ 7. As parents, we insist that our social values be respected by friends of our children who come to visit or play.

Rationale: Household norms and rules must be consistent whether others are present or not.

___ ___ 8. When our children experience a relationship problem, we take the time to help them try to understand their feelings and those of others involved.

Rationale: Talking about social rights, wrongs, and grey areas helps to develop a child's sensitivity to social situations and to refine judgement about proper ways to respond.

_____ _____ 9. As parents, when we goof in good manners or sensitivity to others, we can admit it and talk about what happened with the kids.

Rationale: Adults who are able to admit fallibility help the kids learn that everyone makes mistakes and deserves forgiveness.

_____ _____ 10. We regularly chat with teachers and parents of our children's friends about the manners and social skills of our children.

Rationale: There are often great disparities in a child's manners in different social situations. Outside feedback helps parents teach a child to be more consistent in use of good manners.

The Age Eight Checklist

For social skills to be well-learned by children, they must be made an integral part of family life from birth until that child leaves home. In families where this teaching process has been consistent, by age eight, or roughly third grade, a child should have grasped the basic elements of good manners. For example, by this age a child should have a reasonable understanding of what is expected in specific social situations. Further, a child should have available basic social skills and a rudimentary awareness of others' rights and feelings. At age eight, though, it is to be expected that there will be many slip-ups, mistakes, and gaps in use of good manners.

It is legitimate to ask what skills a child of about eight should have grasped (even if used inconsistently). The Age Eight Checklist is composed of twenty-five basic skills which a third grader should be aware of when relating to others. It can be used as an overall guide for parents to assess their child's social sensitivity and maturity. It can also be used to spot parenting blindspots, as well as specific areas of difficulty with particular children. As a way to begin, check each of your children on the following social skills.

_____ 1. Does not interrupt others who are conversing to make a comment or a request.

_____ 2. Is able to introduce parents to others or self to others.

_____ 3. Answers the telephone in a polite fashion.

_____ 4. When appropriate, sincerely apologizes when wrong and graciously accepts an apology.

_____ 5. Routinely says "please" and "thank you" in interactions with others.

_____ 6. Regularly "checks in" with parents when away from home and plans change.

_____ 7. Refrains from slamming doors and screaming when angry and upset.

_____ 8. Politely acknowledges being spoken to by others, particularly adults, but also peers.

_____ 9. Avoids pushing ahead of others in line or pushing others away to get ahead.

_____ 10. When eating, uses utensils in a reasonable and proper way.

_____ 11. Acknowledges gifts verbally or through a thank you note.

_____ 12. Expresses appreciation to a friend's parents after a visit, even for play.

_____ 13. Does not try to talk with mouth full.

_____ 14. Asks to be excused from the dinner table.

_____ 15. Respects furnishings at home and at friends' homes.

_____ 16. Turns head and covers mouth when coughing or sneezing.

_____ 17. Says "excuse me" or "I'm sorry" when a social blunder is made.

_____ 18. Holds a door open for others, particularly adults or the elderly, but also peers.

_____ 19. Accepts a "no" from an adult gracefully.

_____ 20. Does not chew gum or chews with mouth closed, without snapping or cracking.

_____ 21. In new or unknown situations, requests permission to proceed from those in charge.

_____ 22. Remains quiet in special situations to avoid bothering others (i.e., the movies).

_____ 23. Does not resort to name calling or putdowns when angry or upset.

_____ 24. Consistently seeks permission before using someone else's property.

_____ 25. Returns borrowed items within a short period of time and without being repeatedly asked.

The Manners Mandate

Ask virtually any parent: "What have been your experiences teaching your children good manners?" The answers come back quickly:
"One of the most frustrating things I've ever tried to do."
"Sometimes I just feel like giving up."
"No matter what I do, it just doesn't seem to take."
"See this grey hair? That's what happened."
Very typical answers by men and women who have been there. While the teaching process is most difficult, good manners clearly is one of the most crucial ingredients in the Hidden Curriculum of Success. And, without question, teaching social sensitivity to children is well worth it in the long run. For everyone. In fact, it is not going too far to state that good manners is a "hard asset" on the road to success.

To help parents maintain their resolve and focus their efforts a bit more effectively, it is necessary to be aware of the rationale for teaching good manners. It's simple. It's the Manners Mandate that parents must keep firmly in mind at all times.

THE MANNERS MANDATE: TEACHING GOOD MANNERS IS THE PROCESS OF HELPING A CHILD LEARN ACCEPTED SOCIAL RESPONSES THAT WILL DETERMINE THE QUALITY OF THAT CHILD'S RELATIONSHIPS FOR A LIFETIME.
In fact, there is no other forum within which the qualities that make relationships healthy can be more consistently and effectively taught than through manners training. However, to teach these crucial social skills well, parents must understand that there are several specific areas of learning that together determine the capacity for good manners. Each of these specific areas must be addressed by parents. A major deficit in even one of these four components will have serious consequences on social savvy and the quality of later relationships.

INGREDIENT #1: AN AWARENESS OF OTHER PEOPLE. A child is essentially impulsive and interested solely in the pursuit of personal pleasure without regard for others. For good manners to develop, it is necessary for parents to help a child to develop an *awareness* of other people close by who may be affected by personal behavior. While a subtle skill, the awareness of others in the immediate vicinity is the necessary foundation of good manners.

INGREDIENT #2: AN UNDERSTANDING OF PERSONAL NEEDS AND EMOTIONS. This is basically "action-impact" learning. It involves teaching a child about others' basic rights. It also entails communicating to a child an understanding of the feelings of other people as they are affected by personal behavior. The number of adults who have remained quite immature in this important area of social learning is truly surprising.

INGREDIENT #3: AN ARRAY OF SPECIFIC SOCIAL SKILLS. The most obvious component of good manners is behavioral, that is, saying or doing the right things at the right time. However, these skills, though basic, do not come naturally or easily. Building on people awareness and on an understanding of others' rights and feelings, parents must then begin to teach their children specifically how to respond in particular social situations.

INGREDIENT #4: THE COMMITMENT TO DOING WHAT'S RIGHT. Unless a child is willing to do what's right rather than what's easy, knowing what good manners is all about will be to no avail. It's difficult to apologize to someone else. It's easy to leave without taking the time to say "thank you" for the hospitality. Taking time and facing emotionally difficult situations directly is the essence of commitment; it's also the capstone of good manners.

Tips for Teaching Good Manners

At this point, it's time to outline some additional aspects of teaching good manners to make this rather long, arduous process easier and more effective. Don't forget that in teaching good manners, you must first of all have sound knowledge yourself of good human relations. Further, some aspects of teaching social sensitivity and politeness can easily add to frustration if parents do not understand that teaching manners is a long-term developmental learning process. Here are some basic teaching concepts for good manners that may help to keep your commitment high.

TEACHING CONCEPT #1: THE GROUND RULE IS TO REMIND AND INSIST *AD NAUSEUM*. For children to learn all the essential ingredients for good manners takes many years. During these long years, parents become extremely weary of reminding children about what is right and insisting that good manners be used. While it often seems that all is for naught, do not give up. Learning is taking place, albeit slowly, and constant reminders are critical to the process.

TEACHING CONCEPT #2: PERIODIC BACKSLIDING IS PAR FOR THE COURSE. Your child goes to camp for a week or ten days and comes home to act as if manners were unheard of, much less practiced. To see this happen is most disappointing to parents. It takes time and effort to help that child regain skills sometimes lost by even a weekend away. However, as time passes and your child gets older, reversing a backslide becomes much easier as long as good manners are consistently practiced at home.

TEACHING CONCEPT #3: DIFFERENT CHILDREN MAY HAVE DIFFERENT MANNERS PROBLEMS. Johnny may have trouble with his temper and not calling others names, while Jane just can't seem to learn to say "please" and "thank you." And, as children grow, they may exhibit manners problems that they didn't have earlier. For example, a child who is polite at nine may backtalk and act disrespectfully toward parents at fifteen. Throughout their children's development, parents must fine tune their manners training to reflect the current needs of each child.

TEACHING CONCEPT #4: POSITIVE FEEDBACK IS ABSOLUTELY ESSENTIAL. Busy parents easily slip into the bad habit of taking good manners for granted and then scolding children for bad manners. A much better strategy is to make sure that you con-- sistently comment on and reward good manners. Remember that especially during the early years, because a child wants to please you, your positive comments on good manners powerfully reinforce those responses. Do be as specific as possible so a child knows exactly what behaviors are being rewarded.

TEACHING CONCEPT #5: DON'T NEGLECT PRACTICE. To teach good manners, training must extend to actual practice if learning is to be complete. Have your child pick up the telephone and practice answering it correctly. Or role play introductions. When one child has wronged another, don't say "apologize next time." Instead, have your child apologize directly to that other child right now. This kind of practice helps a child translate understanding into direct experience.

TEACHING CONCEPT #6: CHILDREN LEARN BY OBSERVING ADULT MODELS. Make no mistake about it. Children carefully observe their parents for eighteen years before leaving home. And, they often imitate the positive as well as the negative responses they see. Further, the parents' marital relationship becomes the framework on which children construct adult relationships, sometimes with disastrous results. The bottom line is that you must model good manners.

TEACHING CONCEPT #7: "MAKE HAY WHILE THE SUN SHINES." The best time to teach a child good manners and social sensitivity roughly corresponds to the elementary school years. From about five or six to about twelve, a child is responsive to parents' input and is able to understand good manners (although does not practice them consistently!). Wise parents place emphasis on learning basic social skills during these years before the tumultuous changes of early adolescence begin.

Manners Are a Must

One point already made is worth stating again: the presence of good manners is one of the best signals of effective parenting and the growing personal maturity of a child. And, it is quite clear that politeness and social sensitivity are not only the building blocks of good relationships, but also a crucial ingredient of later success in a career. As with all seven components of the Second Curriculum, good manners gradually taught all through the course of development come easy later in life. Conversely, trying to learn even the rudiments of good manners as an adult is tremendously difficult.

The reality is that when parents neglect to teach their children good manners, everyone suffers, even parents. All too frequently, good manners are simply not made part of the value system in solid middle-class families. Sadly, some parents have simply not learned good manners themselves. Others are just naive in terms of what skills are needed to get along well in the world. Still other parents give up trying because they are overwhelmed with work responsibilities, and good manners don't seem to be "taking" in the kids.

Related to the neglect of teaching good manners in many families is another phenomenon. In at least some families, unstated, but negative agreements about manners develop. Implicitly understood by parents and children, these "silent contracts" sound ridiculous when spoken aloud. Nevertheless, it is not uncommon to find them alive and well within parent-child relationships. Here are the three most important variations of this kind of manners tradeoff. Eliminate each and every one of them you detect in your family.

TRADEOFF #1: "AS LONG AS YOU KEEP YOUR GRADES UP, YOU CAN TREAT US AND EVERYONE ELSE BADLY AND WE

WON'T SAY MUCH ABOUT IT." In households where this contract is found, parents obviously put grades above all else. Often, they naively believe that grades and/or technical skills are most important to ultimate success. Nothing could be further from the truth. *Parents and children* who buy this erroneous idea usually discover its fallacious nature the hard way later in life.

TRADEOFF #2: "AS LONG AS YOU DON'T ABUSE US, YOU CAN TREAT EVERYONE ELSE LIKE DIRT." In this case, parents need acceptance by their children so badly that no one else outside the family matters. Such parents often find to their chagrin that in the long term they get neither respect nor positive regard from the kids. If children are taught to be polite only to people they need, then when parents are no longer needed, they are treated just as badly as everyone else.

TRADEOFF #3: "AS LONG AS YOU MIND YOUR MANNERS IN PUBLIC WHERE IT REFLECTS ON US, YOU CAN FORGET ABOUT THEM AT HOME." Here, parents are overconcerned about their public image. When impressing other people becomes more important than promoting healthy values within the home, trouble is usually brewing. This kind of family hides significant problems while projecting the "perfect marriage and family" to the community. The image eventually collapses beneath the weight of its own deceit.

Parents typically don't set out to create these kinds of tradeoffs. Over the course of time, they subtly develop and become ingrained. However, the longer they are present, the more difficult it is to reverse them. Parents who suspect that such an implicit contract is present with their children must take two necessary steps to correct the problem. First, to accept that *good manners must never become a negotiable commodity at any time.* Second, insist on having it all: good grades *and* good manners, good manners *and* respect for parents, good manners at home *and* in public.

A final word. Don't forget that neglecting to teach your children good manners may backfire on you. As the old saying goes, "What goes 'round comes 'round." Those parents who do not thoroughly teach their children basic social skills often suffer for a lifetime at the hands of rude, selfish, and emotionally insensitive kids who never learned anything different growing up!

Despite the rather impersonal social values so commonly encountered these days, good manners and social sensitivity will never cease to be vital for a successful life. Do yourself a favor and keep this area of teaching at the very top of your parenting priorities. No matter how frustrating the process, you'll be glad for a lifetime that you did. So will the kids. But, it's up to you and your resolve. This ditty says it all in a nutshell:

"The difference between those who do
And those who don't,
Is those who will
And those who won't!"

That's the sum of it. You do or you don't. You will or you won't. And, what goes 'round comes 'round . . . to you!

Chapter 13

Nickels and Dimes and Dollars and Sense: Savvy Parents Begin Economic Education Early

Perhaps you've heard about the two busy achievers who were chatting. One, waxing philosophically, commented: "You know, money is the root of all evil." The other, with a bit of tongue-in-cheek, replied: "Yeah, I know. I've been rooting for it for years!"

Between the extremes represented by these two individuals, there is a tremendous psychological distance in how money is valued. Since money is the major medium of exchange and using money well is steadily becoming more sophisticated, it should not be surprising that teaching children how to relate to money in positive ways is an extremely important area of parenting. This economic education, done wisely, goes a long way toward helping prepare children for later success. Or, without perspective, parents can teach values about money during childhood that contribute heavily to later adult irresponsibility, lack of achievement, and low self-esteem. For example, look at some typical scenarios occurring every day in communities across the country.

DOWNSIDE SCENARIO #1: Just sixteen, John has a brand new car to drive to school. All his life, he has had everything he has ever asked for—the best clothes, abundant spending money, the latest fad items. On the other hand, he is definitely not a good student. From experience, he knows that his parents will always take care of him. Certainly not wealthy, they are constantly broke keeping up with his needs as they attempt to give him an advantage compared to his peers.

DOWNSIDE SCENARIO #2: Barbara, now in her midtwenties, started at the top. In fact, her parents paved the way for her with their hard earned money all along. Finally graduating from a second-rate college with poor grades, she was immediately made manager of the first branch office of her parents' rental car agency. Though earning a decent salary, she was constantly in debt, with her parents continually bailing her out of financial jams. And, no matter what, she never let her social life interfere with work!

Perhaps you can relate to these two well-cared-for, but unfortunate young people. They were psychologically done in by well-meaning parents who wanted to provide them every advantage. For the sake of contrast, let's take a look at two more positive scenarios.

UPSIDE SCENARIO #1: Mollie was raised in a hardworking family of more than modest means. However, from day one she earned whatever she received. She had regular chores around the house and did odd jobs for neighbors from an early age. To be sure, her parents were helpful financially, but from grade school on she was made to create and live within a budget. She became a consistent achiever and graduated from college not only with good grades, but with money in the bank to start her career.

UPSIDE SCENARIO #2: Dan's dad was the owner of a small company he founded. He always wanted Dan to take over when he reached retirement age, and Dan was most willing. He literally worked his way up from the bottom, beginning as a stockboy. It was not until after college that he moved much beyond minimum wage in terms of salary. And, he was given no bonuses or perks because he was the boss's son. He eventually took over the company as a well-respected and financially competent administrator.

The contrast between these two sets of young people is stark. Each had caring parents who wanted to do their best for their children, but these parents went about it in dramatically different ways. Much of the difference can be accounted for in the money values that were communicated to the children during their course of development. These values are exceptionally powerful in determining the later achievement motivation, life satisfaction, and emotional well-being of children.

However, the misuses of money these days are not only common, but are also easy traps. And, financial mismanagement occurs frequently among bright and talented men and women who are successful at work, but whose life after work is highly stressful because of chronic money problems. Several cultural factors make this a most seductive area in which problems can develop both in adults and in kids.

CULTURAL FACTOR #1: EASY CREDIT IS READILY AVAILABLE. Practically anyone can get a loan these days. Credit cards are often sent without request, and the typical American adult averages six or seven in a wallet or purse. Finance companies and banks incessantly advertise their easy loan policies. Getting your hands on someone else's money to spend presents very little problem these days.

CULTURAL FACTOR #2: A HIGHLY MATERIALISTIC VALUE SYSTEM IS IN PLACE. More than ever before, families have a wealth of material goods within their financial reach. Furthermore, advertisers often seek to link a feeling of adequacy or success to use of their products. Cars, homes, electronic gadgets, clothes, and adult toys all become necessary visual proofs of success. Adults and children fall for this ploy in droves.

CULTURAL FACTOR #3: THE NEED FOR INSTANT GRATIFICATION. When you wanted something in years gone by, practically the only way you could get it was by careful saving. "I want it now!" has rapidly become the dominant ethic in recent years. Instant gratification—without the need to sacrifice or save—has virtually become a way of life for many. Although the piper must be paid later, having it all *right now* is more important.

A wise person once commented that society does a good job teaching people how to make a good living. However, it often fails miserably to teach people how to "live good." Nowhere does this statement have more validity than in the ways that people manage (or mismanage) their money. The good life becomes an impossible dream if financial obligations are out of control or you are living beyond your means. In addition to increasing stress within the family, money problems also erode the crucial sense of control that individuals need to maintain positive self-esteem. And, of course, for better or for worse, children learn how to deal with money from their parents.

Parental Mistakes with Money

Perhaps only credit counselors and mental health professionals fully realize how many otherwise talented men and women experience problems stemming from misuse of money. And, anyone who studies this fascinating area of human behavior will quickly encounter a number of recurring patterns that produce financial problems. Driving each of these spending patterns is an emotional issue that must be addressed if the problem is to be permanently resolved. When such a problem is worked out, that individual matures and a chronic source of family conflict is eliminated.

Here are seven emotionally-rooted money mistakes frequently found in those who make a good living, but who perennially experience money-related family problems. Each is presented with a capsulized case history and discussion. Don't forget that these patterns, often seen in parents, had their roots in childhood experiences and how *their* parents dealt with money. Make it a point not to pass the same kinds of problems on to your kids!

MONEY MISTAKE #1: LOVE IS DEFINED IN MATERIALISTIC TERMS. John and Amy had had financial problems since early in their marriage. Although their income was quite adequate, they were constantly in debt and couldn't save a bit of money. Amy came from a family that was emotionally distant, but when she was a child, material things were lavished on her. That was how "love" was expressed in her family. Then she married John, who was somewhat reserved. Whenever Amy felt neglected and unloved, she experienced an immediate and powerful need to make a major purchase. It represented caring even if she purchased it for herself. So buy she did—to the extent that family finances were a disaster.

Defining love and caring in materialistic terms is becoming more of a problem these days. Busy parents give children things instead of time. Adults do the same to one another. The difficulty with this materialistic definition of caring is twofold: 1) it is shallow and not emotionally fulfilling in the long run and 2) meeting the need to be loved materialistically becomes more expensive as time passes. To bring family finances under control, it is necessary for each partner to learn self-acceptance and how to build true intimacy in their relationship. That's just what John and Amy did, but only after serious marital conflict and one separation.

MONEY MISTAKE #2: SPENDING TO COPE WITH ANXIETY OR DEPRESSION. Max, always high-strung, had had problems with anxiety and tension since adolescence. As an adult, even minor problems could set off a downer for him. Over the years, though, he found a way to cope. When he became upset, he headed for the nearest shopping center and put his plastic to work. Unfortunately, this strategy did help to temporarily reduce his tension. Inevitably, though, another problem soon came up. His home was filled with possessions he didn't need or enjoy. And, his pocketbook was always empty as the result of his maladaptive way of dealing with stress. Needless to say, his family also suffered from Max's response to tension.

Max had fallen prey to the classic "shopaholic syndrome," which is psychologically similar to overeating as a response to anxiety or tension. After giving in to the urge, the depressed state is replaced by a short-lived sense of well-being. However, such a strategy is no solution to the problem. The response is reinforced by temporary relief and repeated whenever uncomfortable feelings arise. And, the resulting money problems grow with time. Max began to do much better emotionally and financially when he learned to keep minor frustrations in perspective and learned to use exercise as a way to reduce daily tensions.

MONEY MISTAKE #3: THE FUTURE-ORIENTED ENTREPRE-NEUR. Jim was a builder. He had spent virtually his entire adult life building for his future and that of his family. Not only did he work hard, he consistently invested money in stocks, bonds, rental properties, and other tangible assets. His strong savings orientation came from his parents, who had lived through the desperate times of the Great Depression. However, every time Jim even came close to being on top of things financially, he took it upon himself to make another investment using the credit available to him. As a consequence, the family had a very good income, but couldn't enjoy life because of constant financial pressure. The good life was always somewhere in the future.

This very common spending pattern results from a positive value carried too far. In contrast to many patterns of financial mismanagement, money invested for the future is certainly well spent. This orientation backfires, though, when it creates so much financial pressure that enjoying life today becomes impossible. If Jim doesn't break this habit, at retirement he may look back with regret at the good times with his family that he didn't experience. Jim and those like him must get beyond the "more is always better" and the "someday" philosophies. While it's always prudent to prepare financially for the future, the core question is simple: "When does the future begin?" The correct answer is today.

MONEY MISTAKE #4: BECOMING OBSESSED WITH MONEY.
Tommy, from an impoverished home, had to struggle most of his life. Finally, he made it. However, there were problems with his wife and kids. Virtually every conversation quickly turned to a discussion of money: How much does it cost? Who is paying for it? Where is the money coming from? Isn't everyone irresponsible with money these days? Are the kids ever going to learn anything about the value of money? *Ad nauseum.* Everyone turned off because of Tommy's obsession with money. And, although making a good living, he couldn't enjoy anything himself because of his never-ending concerns about cost.

The cue here is that every conversation with a spouse, children, or even friends turns into money talk, often ending with a heated argument. True, sometimes there are excessive financial demands made by family members. However, at the root of this problem is an outright parental obsession with money. Often such an individual cannot use money to enhance quality of life, preferring to hoard it instead. Frequently, this is done secretively, and in many instances a spouse doesn't even know where the money is or even how much is being made! Further, everyone in the family is constantly made to feel guilty about money and its use. The usual result is that everyone withdraws and avoids the "money monger."

MONEY MISTAKE #5: USING POSSESSIONS TO DEFINE SELF-WORTH. Patty was a young woman who grew up in a family in which both parents were workaholics. Her mother and father both gauged their self-worth by the size of their home, the labels on their clothes, the people they knew at the country club, the exotic vacations they could afford, and the money they had in the bank. Patty and her brother grew up with the same need to define their adequacy externally. Now Pat and her husband Sam, who has the same needs, keep themselves deep in debt trying to feel good about themselves through the purchase of ever more expensive possessions. As time has passed, the financial strain has became almost unbearable.

The crux of the problem here arises from the answer to one pertinent question: "Is your self-esteem based within you or on external factors?" If you can't define yourself as acceptable based on who you are as a person, then you are vulnerable because all the externals on which your self-esteem depends can be taken from you. You can lose a job, your money, possessions, even your friends. In a nutshell, the one who defines adequacy externally is faced with a double whammy: 1) the increasing expense of supporting personal adequacy and 2) the lack of internally based self-esteem necessary to deal with life's inevitable setbacks and failures.

MONEY MISTAKE #6: OVERSPENDING AS A PUNITIVE MEASURE. Evelyn grew up in a close and affectionate home. She was also an only child who was somewhat dependent and craved attention. Interestingly enough, she met and married Andy, a man who withdrew when he was tense or tired. His work required that he be away several days a week. For her part, Evelyn needed closeness—physical and emotional—when she was tired and upset. If Andy withdrew when she needed him, she became angry. And when Andy left for his next business trip, she would tuck her credit cards and checkbook in her purse and go to town. Literally and figuratively. When Andy returned, he was faced with bills to pay as penance for not being as responsive and affectionate as Evelyn wanted him to be.

Finding within spending patterns a need to punish another person is not difficult. Often, children who are showered with material things, but not responded to emotionally, learn to indirectly punish parents by putting on them the financial burden of their very expensive tastes. Parents can punish one another the same way for not adequately meeting emotional needs. Punitive spending, though, is usually destructive to all involved because it becomes habitual. Furthermore, it often makes a positive emotional bond even more difficult to establish. Evelyn and Andy nearly divorced before they came to terms with their problem.

MONEY MISTAKE #7: USING MONEY TO CONTROL OTHER PEOPLE. All through his life, Mike was at the mercy of his very dominating father. The father's philosophy was simple: "There are two ways to do anything—my way and the wrong way!" Every time Mike made a decision on his own, he was threatened with a financial cutoff if it wasn't the "right" decision. When Mike tried to emotionally break away from the family, the same thing happened. The father's ploy was to keep all his children and his wife, Mary, financially dependent. He then used that dependency to control them. Mike and his sister eventually broke away and made it on their own, but the rift with their father never really healed. One brother stayed around home, dependent and resentful. So did Mary.

The message here is a simple one: "You can do whatever you want as long as you do what I want. If you rebel . . . nothing!" At the root of this problem is an individual so insecure and mistrusting that money is used to dominate others. And, it inevitably creates a power struggle between two individuals and a relationship contaminated by deep anger. The individual being controlled by money—adult or child—has a no-win choice. One option is to break away from the financial controls and make it on your own. Often this is emotionally and financially difficult. On the other hand, the individual can succumb and passively accept someone else's control. However, under these circumstances, true autonomy and high self-esteem are not usually possible. Either choice breeds resentment. In this sad but common situation, everyone loses.

Teaching Money Management to Children

Teaching children sound money management skills requires that parents have internalized healthy values about money and its uses themselves. Since money is an economic necessity, direct teaching of healthy values that underlie its use cannot be neglected or abandoned. Parents should keep two facts firmly in mind. First, they are teaching values about money whether they consciously set out to do so or not. Second, the values within the family that govern use of money reveal its soul. It is far better to teach positive money values consciously and directly than to let unhealthy values about money govern your life, diminish your parenting effectiveness, or be left to chance for the children to learn.

Here are some basic money management skills that can be directly taught to children through aware parenting. These basic strategies, when implemented in a positive and supportive way, help children develop a healthy relationship to money. It goes without saying that the earlier this kind of training is started by parents, the easier it is for the kids to learn.

MONEY MANAGEMENT #1: NEGOTIATE A REASONABLE CHORE-ALLOWANCE RELATIONSHIP. A weekly allowance is really the "baseline salary" for work completed against which a child must balance spending. Parent and child should talk annually about the amount of allowance, what expenses must be covered by it, and the responsibilities it entails. The chores and the allowance should be commensurate with the child's age. An appropriate allowance should cover defined needs, if managed well, but not many extras.

MONEY MANAGEMENT #2: USE A PARENTAL MATCHING SYSTEM AS AN INCENTIVE. Many items that children want these days are beyond their earning capacity. However, parents can still help a child learn money management by matching on a one-to-one basis the funds a child earns, receives as gifts, or saves. Through this process, achievement motivation is learned, initiative is preserved, and the desired reward is gained through personal effort.

MONEY MANAGEMENT #3: INSIST THAT A CERTAIN PER-CENTAGE OF INCOME BE SAVED. The ability to save money is essential to work toward long-term goals and to provide for future security. Insisting that a child save a percentage of earnings in a personal passbook account is an excellent basis for developing this skill. Immediately spending every cent received is a bad practice, but children will consistently do just that unless parents teach otherwise.

MONEY MANAGEMENT #4: A CHILD SHOULD OPERATE EX-CLUSIVELY ON A CASH BASIS. Childhood is no place to begin relying on any kind of credit. Purchases should be made with money in hand that has been earned or saved. Letting a child use a credit card (or worse yet, giving the child one) or borrowing money against future allowances or earnings teaches the child that you can always get what you want without prior sacrifice or work by "charging" it. Do not teach your child this negative value.

MONEY MANAGEMENT #5: WITHIN LIMITS, PERMIT YOUR CHILD TO MAKE FINANCIAL DECISIONS. Parents should insist they be consulted on any sizeable purchase by a child and that they also retain veto power. Beyond that, the child should be free to make reasonable decisions about use of personal money. Once a decision is made, however, the child *must* accept the consequences: "If you spend your money on 'X,' you won't have any money for 'Y.'" Reinforc-ing this reality helps a child learn to make more reasoned choices about purchases.

MONEY MANAGEMENT #6: DO NOT PAY A CHILD IN ADVANCE FOR ANYTHING. Hopefully, as parents, you would not pay another adult in advance for work not started or left unfinished. Payment comes only after satisfactory completion. That's the way the world works, and that is the way you should deal with your children. Particularly with children, but also with adults, the incentive to do quality work or even to finish it is destroyed if they receive payment prematurely.

MONEY MANAGEMENT #7: A CHILD SHOULD PAY FOR

ABUSED OR MALICIOUSLY DAMAGED PROPERTY. All children must learn a sense of personal responsibility for both their own property and that of others. When property is willfully damaged, lost, or impaired through negligence, a child should (within reason) be held financially accountable. It helps to teach both responsibility and the necessary cause-effect relationship that enables a child to adapt to the real world later.

MONEY MANAGEMENT #8: IF YOU MAKE A CONTRACT WITH YOUR CHILD, PAY OFF. You give your child an allowance, but when it's time to pay up, you default or delay. You child conscientiously does an odd job for you, and the same thing happens. Once in a while, a shortage is understandable. However, when not paying on time becomes a consistent parental habit, then it undermines your child's incentive to work and to work well. This is one reason why children readily work for neighbors who pay immediately and not for parents who don't!

MONEY MANAGEMENT #9: MAKE THE USE OF MONEY A VERY CONCRETE EXPERIENCE. Well-meaning parents often directly deposit gifts or a child's earned money into a passbook account. The rationale is that it is thereby "kept safe" by parents. A better strategy is to let your children handle and use money. Take your child to the bank to make a passbook deposit. Let a child hand money to a cashier for a purchase and receive change. Back up these experiences with explanations about how the financial system works and how to deal with it responsibly.

MONEY MANAGEMENT #10: RESPECT YOUR CHILD'S MONEY AT ALL TIMES. Parents who do not manage their money well often surreptitiously raid a child's piggy bank or covertly withdraw funds from a trust account. This is gross disrespect of a child's money. If parents must borrow from a child, it should be with permission and with a specific time to repay the money. Then repayment should be made directly to the child. This communicates to the child that debts must be taken seriously and dealt with responsibly.

MONEY MANAGEMENT #11: TEACH YOUR CHILD COMPARISON SHOPPING. With a wide variety of goods available, an informed consumer typically makes the best purchases. Especially with big items, parents can help a child gather information about and examine various models before making a purchase. As a bonus, learning to consistently comparison shop is also an excellent hedge against the impulse buying that is such a self-defeating habit in children and adults. This positive habit saves a lot of money in the long run.

MONEY MANAGEMENT #12: PLACE EMPHASIS ON FUNCTION RATHER THAN ON STATUS. If you are what you wear, drive, or have in your billfold, you are probably going to be broke most of the time making the purchases to bolster your self-esteem. Instead, help your children place priorities on the usability of a product and whether its purchase will fit a personal budget. Habitually buying for status value alone usually leads to financial mismanagement. It also promotes emotional immaturity and a very shallow orientation to life.

MONEY MANAGEMENT #13: REINFORCE GOOD MONEY MANAGEMENT WITH PERSONAL PRAISE. There is no question that parental support for demonstrating positive money habits is important to a child. Your positive responses not only reinforce, but motivate a child to do it even more. Studies have shown that tangible rewards alone are not enough to create good feelings and learn necessary skills. Personal support and consistent positive feedback is necessary. However, don't forget to consistently express unconditional love for your children, too.

Money and Quality of Life

There can be little question that how you, as parents, handle money within the family significantly influences the future of your children. It is also a fact that money management skills are an important ingredient in the Hidden Curriculum of Success for which parents bear primary responsibility. These critical skills far transcend good grades in terms of potential influence on achievement motivation and quality of life during adulthood. Aware parents realize this and carefully structure how money is handled during the developmental years to insure that their children have solid money management skills in place by the time they leave home.

Extending the implications of these skills just a bit, it is well-known that money simply cannot buy happiness. In your own community, there are certainly unhappy and depressed millionaires. Nearby, there are also many individuals who, comparatively, earn quite modest incomes, but whose quality of life is very rich. The difference frequently lies in whether healthy achievement motivation and sound money management skills are present. A successful money manager once made a comment that nicely underscores this point:

"It's not how much money you earn that makes the difference. It's how much you have left over that counts!"

The bottom line is that there are some very basic and powerful benefits that accrue from parental teaching of healthy values about use of money. These skills will significantly and positively influence virtually every area of your child's life as an adult. There are four baseline benefits of importance.

BASELINE BENEFIT #1: THE CAREER INFLUENCE. If an adult works only to keep up with a huge debt burden, there can be little emotional gratification from a career. Personal fulfillment is replaced by the need for intense work just to keep up with bills. By training a child in sound money management skills early, later in life career growth continues because the panicked, driven quality that stems from accounts unpaid and creditors unsatisfied is eliminated.

BASELINE BENEFIT #2: THE HOME INFLUENCE. A child taught solid money management skills at home is able to live within a budget, insure future security, and have some left over to enjoy life. The entire family benefits because quality of life is only then possible. No matter what their income is, families with these skills live within their means and manage to have lots of good times along the way, too.

BASELINE BENEFIT #3: THE EMOTIONAL INFLUENCE. A healthy achiever with sound money management skills is more secure and personally in control from within. As a result, such an individual is not as vulnerable to financial setbacks. And, because there is sound financial management, stress levels remain much lower than in individuals without these skills. If you're not in control of your spending, you're not in control. Period.

BASELINE BENEFIT #4: THE PARENTING INFLUENCE. Your children are observing and learning from how they see you dealing with money during all the developmental years. Helping your children learn sound financial management will aid them in being better parents and in more adequately providing for their families someday. And, they won't be as likely to pass questionable money habits along to *their* children.

Now you know why making a good living and "living good" are two different things. An adequate income can lead to the good life, or it can easily make you and those you care about most absolutely miserable. It may be far past time for you to closely examine just what you are directly and indirectly teaching your children about money management. There's a tremendous incentive to begin economic education for your children early. In a real sense, you will be teaching them how to live the good life for a lifetime.

One last point. In its most practical form, economic education for children boils down to how often you open your wallet and for what reasons. An amusing takeoff on the Seven Dwarfs' song now appears on bumper stickers everywhere: "I owe. I owe. So it's off to work I go!" Fine. Most of us do just that. The real questions are how much do you owe and why. Important questions to consider for you now and for the kids later.

Chapter 14

Your Fears and the Kids' Careers: Helping to Develop a Positive Relationship to Work

In their parenting, concerned mothers and fathers strive to do their very best for their children. They want the kids to grow up to be economically successful and competent to take their place in the world as responsible citizens. In other words, these parents want their children to be achievers just like they are. On the other hand, parents are also well aware that not everyone is "making it" these days. In fact, a good case could be made that it's steadily getting tougher to reach the "good life" and the American Dream.

However, behind parents' efforts also lies fear. Fear that a child won't make it. Fear that career mistakes will be made. Fear that a child's choice of work will not reflect family values. Some of these apprehensions are expressed openly. Others are communicated indirectly. All significantly affect a child's self-esteem, relationship with parents, and ultimately, personal fulfillment in life. The problem is that parents' career fears often subvert true guidance of their children by using subtle and not so subtle forms of career control.

Let's look at one example of what might happen when a parent imposes personal needs on a child's career choices from an early age. Let's assume that two parents own a retail outlet with several branches in nearby cities. Parents are the third generation of the family to own the business; hopefully, one of the kids will make the fourth. Over the years, parents have made it abundantly clear that their first child is to take over. This pressure allows for three possible outcomes.

POSSIBILITY #1: A CHILD'S INTERESTS AND PARENTS' WISHES COINCIDE. In such circumstances, there is very little problem. A child accepts a parent's career choice and finds both success and fulfillment. The relationship with parents usually remains strong, although it is sometimes difficult for parents to "let go" and allow their child to assume full operational control.

POSSIBILITY #2: A CHILD ACCEPTS PARENTS' WISHES TO PLEASE THEM. In this instance, a child puts aside and denies personal fulfillment because parental approval is so important. Though the child gains approval from the parent, personal interests and aptitudes may lie elsewhere. Often this kind of emotionally pressured choice leads to an adult who makes a good living, but who is personally dissatisfied with work.

POSSIBILITY #3: A CHILD REBELS AGAINST PARENTS' WISHES AND CHOOSES SOMETHING ELSE. Here a child must sacrifice parental approval to make a personal career choice. And, after doing so, the child must then live with the reality that parents are disappointed or that family standards have not been met. A feeling of failure often ensues, endangering the child's self-esteem even though the career choice may be very satisfying.

In order to circumvent these kinds of problems, parents must become aware of their personal prejudices about careers and systematically remove them from their parenting. Then, these same parents must learn to reinforce in their children qualities that not only are essential for success, but that also preserve the kids' freedom of choice about work. Let's consider each of these two interrelated parenting issues in turn.

Removing Personal Biases

Typically, parental biases about careers and the reasons for them cannot be clearly conceptualized by a child until later in life. However, all through the developmental years, the biases are felt by the child as parents make statements about various careers. In many direct and indirect ways, parents manage to communicate what is acceptable and what is not about a life's work. This evaluative communication may powerfully and negatively influence career choices and directions in a child.

These kinds of problems are compounded by parents who are not aware of their biases or who deliberately reinforce them to meet personal needs or to allay their fears. The net result is that a child's freedom to choose is narrowed. Here are some common prejudicial attitudes communicated by parents. Included is a statement of the emotional block created by each one. Take the time to examine what you say to your children about the world of work. Then strive to remove each and every bias that you find.

PREJUDICIAL ATTITUDE #1: THE MANDATE TO CONTINUE FAMILY TRADITIONS.

Verbal Message: "There is nothing in this world that would make us feel better than if you would carry on the family business/career line. You will be the fourth generation to do so."

Emotional Programming: "If you don't follow in your father's/mother's footsteps, you will not only fail us, but all the generations that have preceded you as well!"

Seen frequently in parents with strong dynastic ambitions, these messages place a heavy burden on a child to continue an intergenerational career line whether or not the child has the interest or aptitude for it. These kinds of messages are more often than not directed to a first child who feels the strongest need to achieve in ways that generate parental approval. However, this kind of parental pressure limits a child's career options to just one! It can easily stifle motivation and inhibit development of personal potential.

PREJUDICIAL ATTITUDE #2: CONSTANTLY COMPARING ONE CHILD TO ANOTHER CHILD.

Verbal Message: "Why don't you be more like your brother/sister? You know that it's the only way that you're going to get anywhere in this world."

Emotional Programming: "We really admire your brother/sister, but you're a disappointment to us because you're not doing the same things."

Parents often make such comparative statements in a misguided attempt to motivate a child. However, what is really being communicated is a failure message that not only diminishes that child's self-esteem, but also narrows career choices to lines of work that generally correspond to an older sibling's direction. Further, such statements create a competitive relationship between children that may result in sibling discord lasting a lifetime. These messages fail to recognize a child's personal strengths because parents see one child only in relation to another. In a nutshell, comparisons are a painful putdown that parents must avoid.

PREJUDICIAL ATTITUDE #3: FOCUSING EXCLUSIVELY ON MONETARY CONSIDERATIONS.

Verbal Message: "You really should become a doctor or lawyer. They make lots of money and can buy whatever they want."

Emotional Programming: "The only way to be happy is make lots of money so you can buy and own lots of material things."

Many parents who have worked themselves up from humble beginnings view career choices only in terms of money and the security it can buy. Other parents have learned to gauge their self-worth solely by material possessions ("I am what I make or own"). However, happiness and real success do not necessarily require great amounts of wealth. For a career to be fulfilling, it must satisfy emotional needs and reflect personal interests and aptitudes. Far too many competent men and women who make a good living have discovered the hard way that personal fulfillment doesn't stem from high income.

PREJUDICIAL ATTITUDE #4: WORK OPTIONS ARE BASED ON SEXUAL STEREOTYPES.

Verbal Messages: "You really don't want to become a nurse. Real men just don't do that." "Becoming a management specialist may be all right, but most of the women executives I know just aren't very feminine at all."

Emotional Programming: "If your work choice isn't appropriate for your sex, your entire identity as a man/woman becomes suspect."

These kinds of statements reflect sexual stereotyping that was quite prevalent in years gone by. However, they are simply not relevant today as career options for both sexes have widened considerably. Certainly women have broken many barriers as they have entered traditionally masculine professions. However, and less obviously perhaps, men have also broken many barriers by entering traditionally feminine professions. The resultant benefits have been great for men, for women, and for their employers. Parents do their children a great favor by removing personal prejudices based on old-fashioned sexual stereotypes.

PREJUDICIAL ATTITUDE #5: USING CLASS SNOBBERY TO NARROW WORK CHOICES.

Verbal Message: "Everyone in our family has always gone to college and become a professional. Going into construction work simply isn't acceptable."

Emotional Programming: "You are automatically a failure if you choose a career that isn't up to (or beyond) family status standards."

Families who make distinctions of this type are basically snobs. And, they impose their elitist attitudes on the children. Often this is covered by worries that "lower status" occupations will not provide a good living for the children. However, deep down it is usually the parents' public image that is of concern. "What will people think of us as parents if you do that?" is their fear. These insecure parents fail to realize that with initiative and vision, a person can advance and make a very good living in virtually any kind of work. It's a shame that such superficial status standards are allowed to interfere with children's well-being and personal fulfillment for a lifetime.

PREJUDICIAL ATTITUDE#6: PARENTS STRIVE TO KEEP CHILDREN'S CAREER ASPIRATIONS LOW.

Verbal Message: "You can never become a pilot. It's just too hard. Besides, getting financial aid is really tough these days. Pick something easier instead."

Emotional Programming: "As your parents, we really don't believe that you can do it, so don't even try. It's better not to try than to try and fail."

These kinds of messages come from parents who feel very inadequate themselves. Perhaps they've failed to reach their own career goals. Sometimes their perceptions of the world have become jaded and cynical. Occasionally, the intent of these "no confidence" messages is to protect a child from failure. In all instances, however, this kind of communication is emotionally limiting. A child, to be able to reach and risk, must have consistent encouragement and support. Children who receive these kinds of negative messages become insecure; this in turn can diminish motivation to achieve. The result is that career choices are limited because many options have been ruled out by parents who equate challenge with automatic failure.

PREJUDICIAL ATTITUDE #7: DIRECTLY ATTACKING A CHILD'S CHOICES.

Verbal Message: "There is absolutely no way you're going to become an artist. Artists can't support themselves, and besides, you live in a fantasy world."

Emotional Programming: "You aren't capable of choosing your life's work for yourself, and you'd better listen if you don't want to make terrible mistakes."

For reasons of their own, parents may directly reject a child's career choices. Such an attack frequently precipitates a power struggle with a child (particularly an adolescent). Parents take an adamant position and the child does likewise. To assert independence, a child may rebel against parental dictates. To circumvent this unfortunate circumstance, it's better to support a child in a career choice as long as time and energy is being directed into developing it. Without a parent to rebel against, a child is better able to determine if it is a correct choice or not!

The Effort-Reward Relationship and Work

Now it's time to discuss the world of work. Parents who have struggled and sacrificed to make it to the good life are often highly ambivalent about making their children work. For some, a child working brings back painful memories of early deprivation or painful poverty. Other parents rationalize giving the kids everything with letting them enjoy life before the heavy responsibilities of adult life must be accepted. Still others find that they are not emotionally strong enough to withhold materially from their children when they clearly have it to give. To them, it is selfish not to share parental bounty with the kids.

All of these reasons for permitting children to escape work during development are well-intentioned. However, all of these reasons also have a powerful inhibiting effect on the development of children into responsible and competent adults. Emerging research findings support the belief that adults who worked during the growing years are consistently happier, better adjusted, and more successful than adults who were denied such experiences during development.

"Working" in the sense meant here is not sending children to work at an early age to help support the family as was often the case during the Great Depression. Work by the kids is just not a survival issue for most families these days. Rather, it must be justified as a necessary experience to help a child mature emotionally and to develop critical skills required for a successful career. Work, simply defined, is "personal effort directed toward achieving a specific goal during which focus is dominated by the rewards, tangible and intangible, expected at successful task completion."

The next question interested parents ask is: "What kind of work can a child do?" In fact, there are a number of different kinds of work that a child can experience with great personal benefit. Provided with parental support and encouragement, each kind of work has its own benefits and opportunities to learn the ways of the world. Here are the five basic kinds of work that a well-rounded child has experienced by the time adult self-sufficiency is expected. Each carries with it unique learning opportunities and experiences.

WORK MODALITY #1: HOUSEHOLD CHORES. *Examples:* setting/clearing the table, keeping a bedroom clean, taking out the trash.

These kinds of regular chores are the baseline work experiences for a child, beginning early in life and continuing unabated until the child leaves home. *All children* should participate in the maintenance of the home in this way. The children should be paid a regular allowance weekly for successful completion of their work. On the other hand, the allowance should be withheld or the child "docked" a portion of it for unsatisfactory or incomplete work. The chores and the allowance should be commensurate with age and the child's degree of responsibility. At a very basic level, this is the child's first "salaried" position.

Note: It can be legitimately argued that a child should not only have assigned household chores, but should complete them with no expectation of monetary reward. Such work is seen by some parents as a personal contribution to the family as a whole. Through such experiences, a child learns to give altruistically for the common good, not personal gain. A sizeable number of families choose this option. However, while altruistic values are learned, children sometimes resist because direct, immediate rewards are not available.

WORK MODALITY #2: OCCASIONAL ODD JOBS. *Examples:* mowing a neighbor's lawn, babysitting, cleaning out the attic/garage.

This kind of employment, whether for a neighbor or the family, involves specific, nonregular tasks for which set payment is agreed upon and paid at completion. This is the first type of work a child may complete for someone else. The reward (payment) is also more immediate than an allowance received at the end of the week. Parents can do a great deal to provide a child with such opportunities, or they can encourage seeking odd jobs in the neighborhood. The work is circumscribed enough to give a sense of personal accomplishment, which of course is reinforced by the earnings. Odd jobs are the child's first exposure to "contract" work with some opportunity for negotiation of price.

WORK MODALITY #3: ENTREPRENEURIAL ENDEAVORS. *Examples:* collecting pop bottles for return, digging worms to sell as fishing bait, recycling aluminum cans, selling scout items.

The essence of entrepreneurial work is to put energy into an endeavor with no guarantee of reward. This type of work teaches persistence, faith in personal effort, and development of the positive attitudes that make an earning project successful. This kind of experience is extremely valuable, but does require some parental guidance and encouragement so that a child does not become excessively discouraged or needlessly fail. It is in this kind of project that ingenuity, people skills, and personal effort are directly tested and developed. "Entreprenuerial endeavors" expose the child to work based on self-trust with a reasoned risk of failure.

WORK MODALITY #4: PART-TIME WAGE WORK. *Examples:* bagging groceries, stocking shelves in a retail outlet, bussing tables in a restaurant.

Although usually not well-paying or prestigious, earning an hourly wage is usually an adolescent's first real job. It is formalized work experience in which responsibility and initiative are required, and good work habits (or lack of them) will quickly make a difference. It is early testing of all that has been learned previously and is especially valuable during high school or college. Parents, however, must be cautious so that such a position does not take needed time away from an adequate family life, from schoolwork requirements, or from necessary social experiences. "Part-time wage work" requires definite expectations for performance (like an allowance), but evaluation is done by sometimes more critical supervisors who are nonfamily representatives of the real world.

WORK MODALITY #5: CAREER-PATH APPRENTICESHIP. *Examples:* becoming a veterinarian's assistant, working as a helper in an accountant's office, finding summer work with the city engineer's office.

An important variation of wage work is found in jobs that allow a youngster to "get the feel" of a particular career possibility by actually working it in. Viewed from a distance, a given line of work may be idealized as glamorous and filled with interesting experiences every minute of every day. However, from the inside, the daily frustrations along with "hands-on" dirty work and record keeping quickly bring that career path into more realistic perspective. Some youngsters are reinforced in their dedication to a particular kind of work through such experiences. Others are motivated to seek something else. For all, a "career-path apprenticeship" is a valuable opportunity to learn about self and to directly test a career possibility.

Part-time Wage Work: Some Cautions

There is little doubt that work during the course of development toward adulthood provides a context for learning important life skills relevant to the workplace. And, spending money earned is an added bonus. Further, learning possibilities are increased when teens find part-time positions in the "real world" of the adult marketplace. However, the benefits may not be all positive. Witness these high school students.

—Art works in a fast food restaurant twenty-five hours a week and sometimes more. Recently, his grades have dropped because he doesn't have time to study, and his teachers complain that he falls asleep in class.

—Working for almost two years, Jane has saved diligently for a car. Now all the money she makes goes for gas, insurance, clothes, and having a good time. She never saves a dime, and her parents wonder what she is really learning from work experiences.

—Tim works at a car wash several evenings a week and most weekends. His parents, though, never see most of the money he makes. The reality is that he's been using virtually all of it for some time now to buy drugs to use when partying with friends.

—Jenny has a "part-time" job that has been causing her parents some consternation. While she is conscientious, works hard, and saves her money, she has virtually no time for the social life that her parents deem very important at her age.

It is unfortunate that some parents never see beyond the work that their adolescent is doing to the underlying issues. However, for savvy parents, a key question involves how much time an adolescent is spending at work. A related question is whether this time is detracting from other important adolescent experiences that are necessary for mature development. A third question parents must assess is the reason an adolescent is working. Is it only to support a good time (or drugs) rather than saving toward long-term goals?

Again, while it is a good experience for adolescents to "get their feet wet" in the real world, parents must remain vigilant and, if necessary, limit these activities in the best interests of their adolescent's long-term development. As an aid to parents of adolescents who work, here are four sound guidelines that help keep a teen's work experiences within healthy limits.

WORK GUIDELINE #1: THE NUMBER OF HOURS WORKED MUST BE LIMITED. An excellent work boundary is that a part-time job while in high school should require no more than ten or twelve hours a week. And, that position should not involve late evenings that could interfere with schoolwork. An after school position for a few hours several times a week, or on Saturdays, is ideal. Beware of work hours that creep upward with time.

WORK GUIDELINE #2: STRUCTURE THE SPENDING PATTERNS OF YOUR ADOLESCENT. A young man or woman who is spending every cent to have a good time or to support superficial needs (a new car, more clothes, etc.) is not learning maximally from a work experience. Insisting that at least some money be saved or reasonably budgeted is necessary for effective money management and for the attainment of long-term goals.

WORK GUIDELINE #3: MONITOR HOW YOUR ADOLESCENT'S MONEY IS BEING SPENT. This suggestion certainly does not mean that parents must know where every dime of a teen's money goes. However, adolescents are not known for their mature judgement. Knowing about how much is being earned and in general where it is going makes good parental sense (witness Tim). Do not permit your adolescent to be evasive because "It's my money and where I spend it is none of your business."

WORK GUIDELINE #4: WORK MUST NOT REPLACE FAMILY TIME OR OTHER NECESSARY ADOLESCENT EXPERIENCES. It's a given that teens want their "independence." As a result, work may provide a convenient excuse to spend more time away from the family. Further, work may completely negate social experiences (dating, dances, a party at a friend's house) that are important to adolescent development. When they allow their teen to accept part-time work, parents must not allow healthy developmental priorities to slip away.

Two final cautions about working adolescents are now in order. First, parents must remain aware that the academic demands of high schools are increasing. A part-time job that takes too many hours a week adds stress to an already demanding lifestyle. This stress, along with lack of opportunity for a satisfactory social and family life, may contribute to a drift toward truancy or alcohol and/or drug use as a means to cope. These are dangerous and completely unnecessary response patterns for a teen to develop. Parents must remain especially vigilant in these regards and put their foot down before such problems have a chance to develop.

Parents must also be aware that when a teen is making too much money, income may be used as an excuse for precocious independence. "I don't have to listen to you, I have my own money!" is their response to parental input or discipline. Often, successful outside work and money in a pocket promotes outright defiance of any parental attempt to discuss important issues. And, this occurs despite the fact that a teen is living at home and not emotionally or economically self-sufficient at all.

When parents accept this grossly fallacious adolescent argument, teens may begin to drift away from the protective guidance of parents or other concerned adults. As this happens, an adolescent becomes more vulnerable to serious problems because true emotional maturity is not yet developed. To insure that adolescents stay closer to home and retain healthy family ties during the growing years, it is often necessary to not only limit the number of hours worked, but also to reduce the amount of money a teen has to spend without supervision! And, as with most other problems, this one is much easier to prevent than to reverse once it has developed.

Beyond Your Fears

Parents these days instinctively understand that making a good living requires more training, motivation, and savvy than ever before. Jobs at or near minimum wage abound. However, the days when you can live well on such income are virtually gone. These realities are the wellsprings of parents' fears. And, because they care, concerned and frightened parents are prone to impose their "wisdom" on the kids in ways that are positive in intent, but negative in result.

Do keep in mind that a child's interests are usually not stable during the growing years. In fact, it is somewhat unusual for a child to seize upon a particular career at an early age and never waver. Scuba diver, nurse, pilot, engineer, astronaut, and president may all strike a child's fancy over the years. Along with relevant work experiences, each of these interests also becomes an opportunity for parents to provide pertinent information, relevant learning experiences, and consistent encouragement. The positive message that must be communicated is simple: anything is possible with hard work and dedication.

Further, each of a child's passing fancies may meaningfully contribute to fulfillment later in life. For a few children, an early interest may evolve directly into a successful career. For example, Mike's early interest in coin collection led to his own business selling collectibles, including coins. Other children may find that an early interest evolves into a satisfying adult avocation. Angela's early aspiration to become a golf pro turned into a fulfilling adult leisure activity. For still others, such involvements may help a child more clearly define true interests. At one point in her life, Wylene was deeply interested in nursing as a career. However, experiences as a candy striper helped her realize that nursing wasn't for her.

In the end, secure parents trust their children to make reasonable career choices for themselves. Parents who grant their children true freedom of choice in a life's work have overcome their fears. And, they have learned to trust their parenting skills. By so doing they have freed their children to develop personal potential without emotional blocks or unnecessary psychological barriers.

However, this parental stance does not mean that parents have abandoned guidance for their children. Rather, it requires that parents recognize the sometimes fine line between supportive guidance and coercive control. Parents should feel good about providing information, encouragement, and background support *as long as children demonstrate initiative and are putting energy into developing a particular area of interest.* However, it is a danger sign when parents are expected to take the lead, financially and emotionally, rather than follow the initiative of a motivated child. Under these conditions, wise parents do not allow themselves to be taken in by a child's whims.

Now you know that effectively helping your child find a satisfying life's work goes far beyond imposing what you as a parent think is right. But, it's also more than blind luck, too—unless, of course, luck is defined as the point where opportunity and preparation meet. It's amazing how many "lucky" opportunities a child will encounter when actively pursuing personal interests. From a related perspective, it is also true that "success begins when you define the difference between motion and direction." The point? Parents of Healthy Achievers help their kids get lucky by actively promoting each child's directions, not their own!

Chapter 15

The Perils of Puberty for Parents: Understanding Your Early Adolescent

Here's a riddle that conscientious parents who thought they were doing all the right things for years are suddenly forced to ponder.

> *"What's up and down and all around?*
> *With easy smile but quick to frown.*
> *Wants you. Needs you. Can't admit.*
> *No time to talk. Gotta split.*
> *Loves one moment. Rebels the next.*
> *Confusion reigns. Adults perplexed!"*

The answer, of course, is your emerging early adolescent. The changes have come incredibly fast. Almost overnight, in fact. From the relative tranquility of the elementary school years has emerged a highly verbal young man or woman who is daily demanding "personal rights" from you in no uncertain terms. Adultlike in appearance, the emotional immaturity driving the fight for freedom and independence is difficult for concerned parents to handle. These parents have already been through the "terrible two's." In retrospect, they realize that that was no more than a mild training ground for the "trying teens." While *they're* trying to grow up, they're trying *your* patience!

Now, almost without warning, these parents find that they're square in the middle of unexpected turmoil. In the face of it, parents usually harbor personal doubts about their ability to guide their teen well through this confusing and particularly trying phase of development. They must realize that the erratic behavior and constant changes in their teen are probably par for the course. In fact, the inconsistencies and contradictions of this age group are quite normal. What these parents have on their hands, though, suddenly and precipitously, is absolutely adolescence! And, they've begun to experience the perils of puberty for parents. Now let's look in for a moment on a school-sponsored program on this very topic.

In the large auditorium, concerned parents wait for the program to begin. The speaker appears to talk about the problems of parenting in the eighties, especially the parenting of teens. The talk begins with a question to the audience: "How many of you would choose to live your adolescent years over if you had the chance?" Relatively few hands are raised, and some of those waver indecisively. For just a few, the adolescent years are some of the best. The majority, however, are happy to have reached adulthood and put those emotionally difficult years behind them.

Then a second question: "How many of you would choose to live your adolescent years over if you had to do it in this day and age?" This time, practically no hands are raised. The fact is that in any era, early adolescence is a most problematic time of life. On the other hand, there is ample evidence that this critical period of growth and change for young people is steadily becoming more difficult to negotiate emotionally. Caring parents seem to sense this, and they are afraid for their children. Sadly, their intuitive awareness is quite accurate. The simpler world of their youth has irrevocably changed.

Yet, in the midst of the sometimes confusing and ever changing social environment characteristic of this decade still resides the remarkably enduring Basic Adolescent. Understanding the changes that occur and the typical behaviors of a young man or woman growing up regardless of time or place provides a reassuring backdrop of information for parents. It also provides the basis for the necessarily changed relationship with a child who is rapidly growing physically and emotionally. Armed with such understanding, parents can better cope with the many issues that are presented by the changes in their adolescent. At times, they can even manage a knowing smile at the many "typical" reactions they observe.

Parents who have survived the perils of puberty themselves know, though, that dealing with one or more adolescents is not fun and games by a long shot. Looking after the kids is relatively easy when they are small, dependent, and their whole world is the immediate neighborhood. Three parent apprehensions, however, are forced into the forefront of consciousness by the onset of puberty. Then they are fueled daily by powerful adolescent strivings for independence.

PARENT APPREHENSION #1: "MY ADOLESCENT WILL DO THE SAME THINGS I DID WHEN I WAS YOUNG." With the wisdom of their years, parents look back at their adolescent antics with a bit of amusement tempered by a fair share of "Only by the grace of God . . ." feelings. These now mature parents cringe at the thought of their children taking the same kinds of chances.

PARENT APPREHENSION #2: "THE WORLD MY TEEN MUST LIVE IN IS MUCH MORE DANGEROUS THAN IT WAS YEARS AGO." This absolutely valid fear is constantly reinforced by public awareness of high suicide rates in adolescents, life-threatening sexually-transmitted diseases, and the easy availability of drugs. Mistakes and missteps can be much more serious these days than in the past.

PARENT APPREHENSION #3: "MY CHILD NOW HAS A PRIVATE LIFE THAT I CAN'T DIRECTLY CONTROL ANYMORE." A reality is that teens force parents to trust them. Adolescence brings more mobility and much more time spent outside the sphere of direct family influence. Parents are forced to "let go" and hope that their teen will handle unknown and possibly dangerous situations well.

With the first signs of impending puberty, the drama of early adolescence begins to relentlessly unfold. At the same time, responsible parents struggle to safeguard their teen's present and future. This is made immensely more difficult as an adolescent precociously lays claim to all adult prerogatives and privileges. In the background, a chosen peer group powerfully influences a child to do its immature bidding. Peers, parents, and puberty all interact to produce the conflict-laden Adolescent Triangle. It's normal, but it sure isn't easy.

The complex relationships of the Adolescent Triangle have been a perplexing part of family life for centuries. It is incumbent upon parents to understand the unfolding developmental processes being experienced by their growing teen. Only then can they effectively modify their parenting relationship to their child-cum-adult in ways that will promote healthy growth toward maturity. And, they must persevere without thanks in the face of active resistance by their teen. To set the stage for effective parental coping, here's an overview of the normal changes that occur during early adolescence.

The Stages of Adolescence

If a typical individual is asked where adolescence begins and ends, the immediate response is "the teen years." Implicit in this response is the assumption that when the early twenties are reached, adolescence has ended and the individual has become an adult. Nothing could be further from the truth! True, in the past there has been an easy biological marker for the beginning of the adolescent years: puberty. And, in generations past, young men and women became financially and emotionally self-sufficient shortly after leaving home in their late teens.

However, these days, the beginning and ending of adolescence have both become more diffuse and consequently more difficult to define clearly. On one hand, there is often seen a precocious beginning of adolescence that may predate overt signs of puberty. Children begin to act like adolescents before physical changes even begin! At the other end of this growth period, the difficulty is obvious. How do you define when a chid has become a true adult? The best way is to use *emotional* maturity as a gauge rather than more obvious, but often misleading criteria like finishing school, earning a living, marrying, or becoming a parent.

In short, adolescence in this society at present encompasses a time span of approximately twenty years! For almost two decades young people struggle to become emotionally mature adults. There are three basic stages of the adolescent experience as it exists today. However, for parents and children, the most critical and by far the most dangerous is the first.

STAGE I: EARLY ADOLESCENCE (THE RISE OF TRIBAL LOY-ALTIES). *Age Span:* late 10 or 11 through 17 years. In other words, this most tumultuous stage of growth begins in late fifth or sixth grade and typically ends about the senior year of high school. During this time, your child joins a "tribe" of peers that is highly separated from the adult world. The peer group (tribe) clearly defines itself as a distinct subculture struggling for identity with dress codes, language codes, defined meeting places, and powerfully enforced inclusion criteria.

During these most difficult years for parent and for child, the most pronounced changes of puberty occur. The core struggle of the child is to become "independent" and that means emotionally separating from parents and forging a new "adult" identity. Initial attempts are awkward and emotionally naive. In three key areas, here's what the Early Adolescent is like.

A. Relationship To Parents. Suspicious and distrustful. Begins to actively push parents away and resists their attempts to give advice. Lives in a secretive world dominated by peers. Rebelling, pushing limits, and constantly testing parental resolve are characteristic.

B. Relationships With Peers. Emotionally intense "puppy love" emerges with members of the opposite sex, accompanied by "best friends" relationships with peers of the same sex. Relationships are often highly superficial with undue emphasis placed on status considerations: participation in sports, attractiveness, belonging to an "in" group.

C. Relationship To Career/Future. Highly unrealistic in terms of the expectations of the adult world. Sees making a good living and the training required to do so as easy and "no problem." Money made working is often spent on status items such as cars, clothes, or on just having a good time. The future is far away.

STAGE II: MIDDLE ADOLESCENCE (TESTING ADULT REALITIES). *Age Span:* about 18 through age 23 or early 24. Beginning late in the high school years, a new awareness with a subtle accompanying fear begins to grow within the adolescent. "It's almost over. Soon, I'll have to face the world on my own." A personal future and the hard realities it entails can no longer be completely denied. Shortly after high school, this young adult typically leaves home to attend college or technical school, to join the service, or to enter the work force.

While on their own, but still basically protected by parents, Middle Adolescents are actively engaged in testing self against the "real world" in ways not possible while living at home. More personal accountability is required, and some difficult lessons are learned. These sometimes painful experiences help the Middle Adolescent learn the ways of the world, but many signs of immaturity remain. In more specific terms, here is what's happening.

A. Relationship To Parents. Improved but still problematic at times. Middle adolescents still aren't really ready to be completely open with parents, but they are less defensive. During visits home, intense conflicts with parents still erupt about lifestyle, career decisions, or taking responsibility.

B. Relationships With Peers. Frequent visits home may be more to see the "old gang" from high school than to see parents. Good buddies remain at home, but new friends are being made in a work or school setting. A deeper capacity for caring is manifested in more mature relationships with both sexes.

C. Relationship To Career/Future. The economics of self-support and making a good living are steadily becoming more reality-oriented. Sights may be lowered and changes in career direction are common. Meeting new challenges successfully brings a growing sense of confidence and self-sufficiency.

STAGE III: LATE ADOLESCENCE (JOINING UP). *Age Span:* late 23 or 24 to about 30 years. By the midtwenties, early career experimentation has ended as has protective parental involvement. The Late Adolescent is usually financially self-sufficient and remains quite social. Life is simple because there is minimal community involvement, little property needing upkeep, and an income adequate to meet basic needs. The Late Adolescent years are often remembered as good ones filled with hard work and many good times.

At first glance, the Late Adolescent may appear to be fully adult, but this perception is deceptive. Significant adjustments to the adult world are still being made, but are less obvious. Many insecurities in relationships and at work continue to be faced and resolved. Spurred by growing commitment to creating a personal niche in the adult world, changes in the direction of true adult maturity continue. Here's how.

A. Relationship To Parents. Over twenty years, the Late Adolescent has come full circle. Now emotionally self-sufficient, this young man or woman can form a closer relationship with parents. Mutual respect and acceptance grows. The Late Adolescent begins to understand parenting behaviors that were resisted earlier.

B. Relationships With Peers. Most high school chums have been left behind and are seen only occasionally. A new group of work-related peers has been solidly established. Love relationships are more mature with increased capacity for give-and-take. Commitment to a shared future and to a family grows.

C. Relationship To Career/Future. Active striving toward "the good life" and personal goals intensifies. At work, there is a continuing need to prove competency and get ahead. At home, a more settled lifestyle that is characteristic of the middle-class mainstream slowly evolves. Limited community involvement is seen.

Early Adolescent Attitudes

While adolescents struggle for nearly two decades to attain emotional maturity, the period of Early Adolescence is clearly the most striking. It is during this critical five or six years that the growing young adult is most vulnerable to major mistakes. It is emotional, intense, painful, and confusing. It is also a time remembered by parents as the most trying on their ability to cope.

Because the vulnerability of parents and their children is never so high as during Early Adolescence, it is well to define some of the characteristics of the normal teen during these years. Here are listed fifteen of the most common adolescent attitudes that make life difficult for parents and children, but which are quite typical in this age group. **Note:** "Teen" in this discussion refers specifically to Early Adolescence.

ADOLESCENT ATTITUDE #1: CONFORMITY WITHIN NON-CONFORMITY. The early adolescent attempts to separate from parents by questioning or even bluntly rejecting their values and standards of behavior. Paradoxically, at the same time, an extremely strong tendency to blindly conform to peer group standards emerges. It is very important to be accepted as "one of the gang" by peers while need for parental approval diminishes.

ADOLESCENT ATTITUDE #2: OPEN COMMUNICATION WITH ADULTS DIMINISHES. The early adolescent doesn't like to be questioned by parents or other adults. In fact, the more direct questions that are asked, the more likely it is that a teen will begin responding with vague and noninformative answers. Key parts of events may be conveniently "forgotten" as a personal life outside the family is protected from parental intrusion.

ADOLESCENT ATTITUDE #3: WITHDRAWAL FROM FAMILY TIMES TOGETHER. With the advent of puberty, there is increasing resistance to participation in family experiences. The teen would much rather stay home to be "available" in the neighborhood just in case something might happen. Or, that adolescent will want to spend time with friends doing absolutely nothing in lieu of a fun outing with the family.

ADOLESCENT ATTITUDE #4: ACCEPTABILITY IS LINKED TO EXTERNALS. With the approach of puberty, parents begin to notice a change in how their child gauges self-worth. In short, personal adequacy is measured by possession of just the right clothes, by an

BEYOND THE CORNUCOPIA KIDS

"in" group of friends, and by fad items that are an accepted part of teen culture at any given time. Parents are badgered to distraction to finance these externally-oriented "acceptance" needs.

ADOLESCENT ATTITUDE #5: SPENDING MORE TIME ALONE. Parents quickly find out that their teens are very social with frequent outings with friends, constant telephone calls, and time spent in one another's homes. Ironically, however, early adolescents also like to spend considerable time by themselves. Teens will retreat for hours to a bedroom and tell parents in no uncertain terms to respect their "privacy" and let them alone.

ADOLESCENT ATTITUDE #6: A KNOW-IT-ALL PSEUDOSO-PHISTICATION. Attempts by parents to give helpful guidance are often rebuffed by adolescents. Any parental input is met with a weary "I already know that" retort. In reality, most teens' information about topics important to health and well-being is incomplete, full of distortions, and at times, patently false. What teens actually know and what they tell you they understand are vastly different.

ADOLESCENT ATTITUDE #7: RAPID EMOTIONAL CHANGES. One of the most difficult aspects of early adolescence for parents to cope with is rapid shifts in mood. One minute a teen is on top of the world and full of exuberant optimism. Within minutes, that same teen can be sullen, withdrawn, or even "down in the dumps" depressed. The emotional triggers for such changes are unclear, unpredictable, and quite puzzling to parents.

ADOLESCENT ATTITUDE #8: INSTABILITY IN PEER RELA-TIONSHIPS. Early adolescent relationships are marked by intensity and constant change. Overnight, a best friend may become a mortal enemy because of a real or imagined betrayal. Rivalries quickly emerge and just as quickly dissipate. Fickle switches in loyalties are frequently triggered by the incessant gossiping about one another that is so characteristic of teen culture.

ADOLESCENT ATTITUDE #9: SOMATIC SENSITIVITY. In other words, a teen's rapidly changing body becomes intensely interesting and a cause for great concern. Frequently, an early adolescent will become obsessed with and highly distraught about a perceived "major physical deformity" (an asymmetrical nose, not quite right ears, two pimples). Physical development is assessed against a highly unrealistic ideal with consequent doubts and personal insecurity.

ADOLESCENT ATTITUDE #10: PERSONAL GROOMING TAKES A SPECTACULAR UPTURN. To parents' astonishment, a preadolescent somewhat lackadaisical about personal hygiene and appearance suddenly changes dramatically. Practically overnight that teen turns into a young man or woman who spends hours grooming and checking the mirror. Every detail of personal appearance must be letter perfect before appearing in public. **Note:** To parents' chagrin, concerns about neatness and a good appearance definitely do not extend to a teen's bedroom which often remains a perpetual mess!

ADOLESCENT ATTITUDE #11: EMOTIONAL CRUELTY TO ONE ANOTHER. Parents often become very disturbed by the insensitivity with which members of this age group treat one another. Malicious gossip, hurtful teasing, and negatively descriptive nicknames, not to mention capricious rejection by a peer group, abound despite parental attempts to intervene. This is a major reason why early adolescence is a time of such great emotional pain for so many.

ADOLESCENT ATTITUDE #12: A HIGHLY PRESENT-ORIENTED EXISTENCE. Parents often learn the hard way that seriously discussing "the future" with an early adolescent is often an exercise in futility. An early adolescent's perception of a wonderful career is still quite unrealistic. Conflict results when an unready and unconcerned teen insists on continuing a day-to-day, pleasure-oriented way of life while parental fears mount.

ADOLESCENT ATTITUDE #13: A RICH FANTASY LIFE DEVELOPS. The adolescent's inner world is filled with hopes and dreams come true: meeting knights in shining armor, achieving great things, easily making lots of money, living a life of freedom and fun without much personal effort, living happily ever after. Such dreams are an important emotional buffer for a teen who has slowly begun to come to grips with the harsh realities of the real world.

ADOLESCENT ATTITUDE #14: THERE IS A STRONG NEED FOR "INDEPENDENCE." Translation: "I can make my own decisions by myself. Don't try to control me. I'm not a kid, you know!" Teens take it as an insult to their perceived "maturity" to have their decisions questioned. Or, to have to ask for parental permission about anything. Frequently, this leads to clever ways of circumventing established rules or making decisions without parental knowledge.

ADOLESCENT ATTITUDE #15: A PROCLIVITY FOR EXPERIMENTATION. With a new body and new feelings, the early adolescent develops a sometimes reckless impulsivity. Covertly experimenting with forbidden "grown-up" behaviors (smoking, drugs, sex) becomes quite attractive to more than a few teens. This attempt to be "cool" and all grown-up, as well as to satisfy curiosity, are at the core of parents' very realistic worries about teenage sons and daughters.

The Emotional Arousal of Parents

It is a given that early adolescence is difficult for parents. On first thought, the reason is assumed to be the erratic and challenging behavior of their teens. While this is certainly so, at a deeper emotional level, the onset of adolescence in a child arouses strong and often confusing feelings in parents. As long as their child is clearly a child, these emotions remain weak or lie dormant within. However, once puberty begins, a myriad of powerful feelings well to the surface in parents.

In many respects, a child's puberty forces parents to actively deal with emotional issues that promote their own growth and development if handled well. It is as important for parents to understand their suddenly aroused feelings as it is for them to understand what is happening emotionally within their teen.

AROUSED EMOTION #1: UNADULTERATED FEAR. It would not be going too far to say that the parents of teens live with fear and constant worry. "What's happened now?" "What am I going to find out about next?" A child's world is quite small. At puberty, it suddenly expands and the teen is gone much of the time. This occurs at the same time that a teen becomes evasive about what is going on in his or her world. Fears intensify.

AROUSED EMOTION #2: A DEEP SENSE OF HELPLESSNESS. Parents grow very uncomfortable as they watch their teen experience all the pain and turmoil that early adolescence usually brings. Because adolescents perceive adults not to be able to really understand, parents may be pushed away when problems occur. The kids don't realize how helpless parents feel when they see their child emotionally suffering, but are relegated to the sidelines unable to actively help.

AROUSED EMOTION #3: HIGH LEVELS OF FRUSTRATION. It's a fact of life that many of the behaviors of an early adolescent trigger parental anger. One of a teen's strongest emotional needs is to emotionally separate. This need is expressed by constantly confronting parents verbally, violating rules, and pushing limits right to the brink. This entirely normal adolescent response pattern takes its toll on parents who are already very busy, highly stressed, and tired.

AROUSED EMOTION #4: A GROWING AWARENESS OF LOSS.
With the onset of puberty, parents are forced to recognize that in just
a few short years, their teen will be going into the world, gone forever
as part of the nuclear family. The undeniable reality that "our little
girl/boy is growing up" triggers this deepening sense of loss in parents that is compounded by the withdrawal of a teen from family life.
Often this nostalgic awareness is overwhelmed by fleeting wishes
that their child hurry up and grow up so parents can have some peace
of mind!

AROUSED EMOTION #5: PERSONAL HURT. Parents of teens
struggle to do their very best to guide and protect their children.
However, during these years, very little in the way of thanks is
forthcoming. In fact, parents' efforts are often highly resented, often
being labeled old-fashioned, Victorian, or "old fogies" completely out
of touch with reality. Angry confrontations are the norm. Sullen
withdrawal is an everyday occurrence. Continued rejection and hurt
feelings make it difficult for parents to continue giving their personal
best to an unappreciative teen.

Precocious Behavior and Deeper Needs

In recent years, much has been written about the changing nature
of growing up in America. Some authorities emphasize the fact that
teens these days are exposed to so much more at an earlier age than
their parents. Others who study this special group find that beyond
the surface precociousness of teens, attaining emotional maturity is
steadily becoming a more prolonged and difficult process than ever
before. The reality that parents must understand is that these seem-
ingly divergent points of view are both absolutely valid and in no way
contradict one another.

To be effective, parents must not be fooled by the easily misleading
pseudo-sophistication of teens and instead respond to the deeper and
more complex developmental issues that lie beneath this surface
veneer. To be of maximum aid in promoting healthy growth toward
maturity, parents must make sure that their responses reflect three
important teen needs.

TEEN NEED #1: "DEPTH PERCEPTION" BY PARENTS. Basically, parents must be able to accurately see beyond the often erratic
surface behaviors of an adolescent to the real issues that simply can't
be articulated by a teen. Then parents must respond in caring ways to

those deeper emotional needs despite protests, confrontations, and denials.

TEEN NEED #2: CONSISTENCY OF PARENTAL RESPONSES. Teens are notorious for their inconsistency. One of the most important needs of teens during these years of turmoil is to have parents who are steady and consistent. Such parents become a stabilizing influence and a center of strength that help a teen cope much more effectively with rapid change in every part of life.

TEEN NEED #3: STRENGTH OF PARENTAL CONVICTION. At no other time during the entire child-rearing process must parents be surer of their values. Teens focus tremendous pressure on parents to convince them they are wrong or that their values are irrelevant in the here and now. Far too often, the kids are allowed to succeed in compromising solid parental values to the detriment of the family and to themselves.

In the end, one of the most emotionally rigorous tasks that parents face during the adolescent years is to keep doing what is right with little positive feedback and without becoming too insecure. And, after all is said and done and those difficult years are over, most teens do mature to join the ranks of responsible adults. With all your adolescent shenanigans, you did, didn't you? If you parent well during these critical formative years, you will be rewarded. But not now. It will happen only years later when your adult son or daughter thanks you directly for all your sacrifices despite the problems they caused you growing up.

In the meantime, exasperation becomes part of daily life. Change greets you every morning. The unexpected is part of every day. You go to bed at night wondering whether you can keep your sanity until it ends. As a personal statement, one frustrated parent put up a sign in the kitchen: "NOTICE TO ALL TEENS! If you are tired of being hassled by unreasonable parents, NOW IS THE TIME FOR ACTION. Leave home and pay your own way WHILE YOU STILL KNOW EVERYTHING!" It's very trying to keep your composure with a fourteen- or fifteen-year-old who already knows more than you do and who doesn't hesitate to tell you so.

The bottom line is that these days puberty has perils for parents and for the children in grown-up bodies who are in their charge. And, adolescence is no time to cut corners and take the easy way out of the problems that teens will inevitably bring your way. Perhaps it was a wise parent who once remarked that, "A shortcut is often the quickest way to get somewhere you weren't going!" When dealing with adolescents, the best road usually turns out to be the one more difficult for parents. In the long run, this is also the path that eventually turns out to be the most rewarding. Shortcuts too often lead to dead ends. Or dangerous precipices. Sometimes to places you never expected to visit.

Chapter 16

In the Eye of the Hurricane: Providing Healthy "Protective Custody" for Your Teen

The excitement of individuals seeing one another once again masks a subtle tension that pervades the room. Laughter erupts spontaneously midst the hustle-bustle of movement. Beneath the veneer of cordiality, those present are watching, assessing, evaluating. The group is mixed. There are doctors, lawyers, homemakers, businessmen and women, plumbers, and factory hands. It is a twentieth high school reunion, an adult rite eagerly anticipated by some, dreaded by others. Old friends, acquaintances, even mortal enemies from the "good old days" are greeted good naturedly this special evening.

In the room, small groups spontaneously form around festive tables to recount favorite stories about youthful escapades. Snatches of conversation reflect present camaraderie and old memories.

"Do you remember that time when we were down by the lake at midnight and . . .?"

"Boy, was your dad ever mad when he happened to come home early and found us . . . ."

"How about that time when we were in ninth grade and you and I . . .?"

"Will you ever forget the look on that teacher's face when she found . . .?"

"I never thought that we'd ever live to tell about it that time when we . . . ."

These are the living legends of high school, some now more fable than fact, but always fun to relive with friends. They help keep memories of the heady days of early adolescence alive and well. The world was new. There was no future. Adventures were everywhere. It's a time past, remembered nostalgically for the good times, with lingering pain for insecurities and disappointments experienced.

And, so it is with reunions. But gathered in this room after all these years are also parents. In their late thirties, former high school chums now find themselves coping, as *their* parents did, with adolescent children. Throughout the evening, with clocklike regularity, conversations turn to teens. Hopes and fears are expressed: "I don't want *our* kids to do what *we* did! I'd worry to death. We want good kids, and kids today just don't know what it's all about!" Deep down, though, these parents already know that some things don't change with the years. One of them is that teens *will* be teens.

Early adolescents are growing very rapidly emotionally, socially, and, of course, physically. Their world is confusing and unstable, and that makes effective parenting quite frustrating. Add the present dangers that weren't there when parents were growing up, and a volatile mix of strong emotions and parental protectiveness emerges. Part of the problem lies in differences in perspective that lead to ongoing tension in relationships with parents. Here's what this psychologically touchy "hassle factor" is all about.

WHAT PARENTS SEE GOING ON. From the relative tranquility of childhood has suddenly emerged a physically larger, psychologically stronger, but still emotionally immature young adult. And, this young man or woman, more mobile and not as communicative as before, is stoutly demanding new privileges, complete freedom of choice, and personal rights all loudly and in no uncertain terms. Because parents are rightly fearful of teens' lack of experience and perspective, they resist lifting limits.

THE VIEWPOINT OF ADOLESCENTS. With their new "adult perspective" on life and living, teens develop a rather acute sensitivity to being "controlled." They see themselves striving for their "independence" from the domination of too-restrictive parents who are holding them back. And, teens, bless their naive hearts, resist (as they have from time immemorial) what they perceive to be the old-fashioned, out of touch, completely unreasonable, and dictatorial control of parents.

WHAT'S REALLY GOING ON. At this age, early adolescents are beginning to actively separate emotionally from their parents. Although they do not realize it, their "rebellion" is actually a way to begin establishing an adult identity quite different from the childish dependency of earlier years. The psychological questions are "What is you (parents)" and "What is me (young adult)." As the process of separation continues through testing, challenge, and resistance to adult dictates, more emotional autonomy gradually develops.

However uncomfortable for parents *and* teens, all of the above is entirely normal during the early adolescent years. The fact is that during the teen years, parents must psychologically walk a fine line if they are to be helpful to an emotionally vulnerable young man or woman frantically struggling for autonomy and independence from them! On one hand, they must give more responsibility to a physically maturing and now mobile teen who just yesterday was a dependent child. On the other hand, they must also provide enough structure to give that adolescent personal security and to insure a modicum of safety.

In short, the task of parents during these critical years is to provide healthy protective custody in ways that teens can accept (albeit grudgingly) and emotionally respect. It's not easy at all. During these unstable years, parents must retain perspective when their emotions may be overwhelming. They must remain strong even when they are tired and vulnerable. Depth of understanding must remain when change is occurring daily. And, parents must hold onto sound values despite intense pressure to give in to teen demands. The trick is to remain calm and even thrive during these hectic times when parents must live in the eye of the hurricane. Here are some tips to help you learn to do just that.

The Limits of Control

Now, here's a riddle for you to ponder for a moment: "What does a man who escapes from jail and a working woman who wins a lottery and then becomes an alcoholic have in common?"

Perhaps your initial reaction is that this is a rather strange question to think about in a discussion of adolescence. Then, as you give the two situations more thought, you might seize on the idea of freedom. In fact, the escapee has gained freedom and so has the lottery winner. She has been given tremendous economic freedom practically overnight by virtue of her winnings. With this perception you are getting closer, but you've got to push a bit farther.

The core issue is the effects of external limits on the functioning of individuals. And, this is also the bridge that connects these two adults with those who are attempting to parent their adolescents well. It strikes at the heart of a question that all parents of teens wrestle with constantly: "What are reasonable limits that will provide my teen with enough 'independence' to grow toward maturity without being lax or so controlling to the point of inviting serious trouble?"

To get at some of the answers, let's go back to our escapee and lottery winner. Before making his break, Dan had become a pro at cleverly circumventing all of the prison rules without being caught and punished. Further, he wasn't about to give in to forced confinement. He carefully watched for a weakness in the security system and finally escaped from his guards. For him, although emotionally immature to begin with, the prison "limits" were too strict. And, the confining nature of those very limits forced him to become very manipulative and sneaky and to resort to subterfuge to get his way. He was successful. There was no way to negotiate with the authorities to allow him more freedom in exchange for personal responsibility.

Molly, the big winner, was different. Hard-working and quite responsible, she had always been limited (as have most of us) by her income. She worked diligently all her life until that fateful day when she suddenly became rich overnight. Initially, she thought that her problems were over. In fact, they were only beginning. Within a year, she had quit her job (why should she work?), had started associating with a very fast crowd, and was well on her way to significant problems with drug abuse and alcoholism. The problem? Molly was given too much freedom too fast. And, as many who quickly become very affluent find out the hard way, it can lead to big trouble.

Perhaps you already see some interrelationships among these two individuals, your adolescents, and the limits they need. You find yourself astraddle the balance beam. Too many limits for your teen will force that child to become crafty and develop manipulative ways to circumvent your rules. And, the price tag for too many restrictions is to reinforce evading personal responsibility rather than accepting it. On the other hand, parents of teens often find (as did Molly) that too much freedom too fast is also dangerous. Gradually gaining freedom allows for the continuous adjustments that are necessary as "control" from external sources (parents) is transferred to internal resources (self).

The best guideline is that a reasonable balance between too much freedom too soon and too little independence too late for your teen must be created and constantly monitored by parents, and then adjusted as necessary. The desired end point of this process is to maximize the probability that a teen will grow toward emotional maturity and personal responsibility while minimizing the risk of serious problems. While there are no pat answers to implementing this process, there are some basic guidelines that do help.

GUIDELINE #1: DO NOT USE THE "SENIORITY SYSTEM." In industry, "perks" and privileges are often granted automatically on the basis of how many years you've been with the company, but not necessarily on competence or demonstrated responsibility. As a result, individuals in such organizations don't have to actively earn new privileges. They just have to live long enough! Translated to parenting teens, this is not a great idea. Instead, grant your adolescent new privileges based on maturity and *demonstrated* responsibility, not on how long that young man or woman has been with the family. Each child is different in terms of how much responsibility can be handled and when.

GUIDELINE #2: "JUDGEMENT CALLS" ARE THE NAME OF THE GAME. As you gradually extend more freedom, your teen will in most instances want even more—much more than you're willing to give! Somewhere between the unrealistic demands of your adolescent and your need to hold on tight for that teen's safety is the happy medium. But, you can't ever be completely sure that what you've okayed is exactly right. When granting privileges to your growing youth, you're continually breaking new territory, and you must therefore use your judgement, backed up by common sense.

GUIDELINE #3: USE THE "LIGHT LEASH" AS A GAUGE. The best way to assess whether you are in the healthy middle ground in terms of limits is to look for a modicum of ongoing tension between parents and a teen. This healthy level of limits, the "light leash," produces a somewhat uncomfortable, but tolerable tension. It lies somewhere between the outright rebellion of a too-short, too-tight leash and the dangerous freedom of no restraints at all. You will have to adjust the reins continually for the right tension.

GUIDELINE #4: "NEGOTIATE, DON'T MANDATE." Your adolescent, with rapidly growing mind, body, and emotions, desperately wants to be treated as an adult. Although remaining emotionally immature, it is helpful to begin directly negotiating limits with your child from time to time. Sitting down to talk about new privileges and responsibilities is far better than unilaterally setting rules and inviting rebellion or having your child attempt to directly wrest control away from you in a power struggle.

GUIDELINE #5: BEWARE OF "SERIAL EXCEPTIONS." An insidious problem for parents is to frequently grant well-rationalized exceptions to set ground rules for behavior. The danger is that *if this is done too much, then the exception becomes the rule* for that teen. Granted, parents must be reasonably flexible and respond to extenuating circumstances. However, be sure that your adolescent doesn't learn to manufacture these circumstances for you to gain the easy "just this once" exception from you.

GUIDELINE #6: WATCH FOR "REVERSED REWARDS." Albert, in eighth grade, was suspended from school for continual misbehavior. Albert received his reward when his parents decided that these three days would provide a wonderful time for a skiing trip! Or, Nan found that the only time that she got to really talk to her parents was when she was in trouble. When she was good, she was virtually ignored. The moral? Parents of children in general and teens in particular must be very conscious of what they are rewarding if they want their limits to be respected!

Maladaptive Parenting Styles

As teens grow in size, how parents relate to them must, of necessity, change. The parent-child relationship, as it evolves, can remain healthy and open or it can quickly become quite problematic. And, it is difficult for parents to keep these relationships emotionally strong as teens rapidly grow in the power to confront, to persuade, and to deceive. When a parent-child relationship grows in unhealthy directions, it almost always spells trouble for that adolescent and for parents.

There are five maladaptive kinds of response patterns that easily develop between parents and a teen. It is much easier to prevent these kinds of relationship problems from developing than to reverse them once established. Guard against each and every one of them.

RELATIONSHIP DISTORTION #1: THE DODGE CITY POWER TRIP. *Tipoff:* Constant ultimatums or threats given to a teen to obey . . . or else!

This destructive relationship problem results from attempts by frustrated parents to overpower a teen with their authority. However, this response style usually degenerates into a power struggle with constant confrontrations between a teen and one or both parents. As time passes, the ante in the ultimatums goes up as does adolescent defiance. The parent-teen relationship steadily degenerates to become more abusive to all involved. Parental pride and teen ego-involvement complicate matters. No one wins. Everyone is emotionally damaged.

Skew Correction: Bite your tongue and don't give "or else" ultimatums. An excellent hedge is also to spend more quality time with your teen and to talk a lot during good times together so there is an established basis for discussing problems when they occur.

RELATIONSHIP DISTORTION #2: THE "IF YOU CAN'T LICK 'EM, JOIN 'EM" COPOUT. *Tipoff:* Adopting the dress, language, mannerisms, and friends of a teenage son or daughter.

The essence of this skew is excessive parental identification with an adolescent. Many adults (now parents) have unresolved emotional issues left over from their own teen years. As their child reaches adolescence, these issues surface. Parents may attempt to resolve them by reliving their own teen years with the kids. Or, parents may try to become closer to their teen by attempting to become just like them. Whatever the reason, the net result is: 1) a parent winds up looking foolish, and 2) the ability to parent effectively is sorely compromised.

Skew Correction: It is entirely possible to be friends with teens without becoming one of them. Practice being an understanding and open parent while retaining enough distance to effectively guide and set limits for your teen.

RELATIONSHIP DISTORTION #3: YE OLDE OSTRICH MANEUVER. *Tipoff:* Refusing to acknowledge or confront a teen problem despite ample evidence that a problem is present.

It's very easy for busy parents to develop tremendous blinders with their teens. What is seen or sensed is simply not emotionally acknowledged. Sometimes, clear evidence of a problem contradicts parents' image of their teen. In other instances, to confront a problem means having to deal with it, and that's too threatening. This kind of denial permits parents to maintain the pretense that nothing is wrong. In the meantime, the problem usually gets worse and eventually blows up in parents' faces.

Skew Correction: Parents must assume that every teen is vulnerable and that significant problems can easily develop. Then, remain alert and make it a point to confront problems early when any evidence that trouble is brewing is found.

RELATIONSHIP DISTORTION #4: THE DO-DON'T DOUBLE MESSAGE. *Tipoff:* Expressing subtle, but obvious pride in a teen's escapades while overtly admonishing that same adolescent to "behave."

This problem might also be termed the "chip off the old block" syndrome. Here, a teen receives a mixed message: 1) "What you're doing is OK. I did the same thing when I was young," and 2) "Don't do that because it's wrong." The problem occurs when the teen (accurately) senses that the overt message to shape up doesn't carry much conviction. At the same time, the subtly expressed pride of a parent, also accurately sensed by that same teen, encourages more of the same. Then parents complain when their adolescent gets into trouble although in fact problem behaviors are being systematically (although subtly) reinforced.

Skew Correction: Consistency in communicating parental values is the key to resolving this problem. For heaven's sake, don't brag about or express admiration for your teen's acting out behavior. Doing so not only confuses a teen, but also represents an unhealthy form of parent-child identification on your part.

RELATIONSHIP DISTORTION #5: THE BEST FRIEND AND CONFIDANTE ROLE DIFFUSION. *Tipoff:* Excessively sharing personal problems or marital issues with a teenage son or daughter.

It is seductively easy for an unhappy, lonely, or single parent to develop this kind of "confidante" relationship with a teen. However, problems are usually the result. Teens are just not emotionally ready to be burdened with adult problems. Often they weigh very heavily on that youngster. Sometimes a teen even feels a burden of responsibility to make things better. The teen loses. Worse yet, a parent loses because the ability to parent well is compromised by this emotionally unfair relationship.

Skew Correction: As an adult, create primary relationships with other adults. If you are struggling to resolve personal issues, make it a point to get appropriate help. With your adolescent, make sure you create and respect a clear line between acknowledging a personal problem and burdening a teen with it.

Guidelines for Parenting Teens

Parents intuitively realize that the early adolescent years are disproportionately influential in shaping adjustment to the later responsibilities of adulthood. Patterns set during the teen years often last a lifetime. Parents want to make sure that as many of these ways of relating and coping as possible are positive. While recognizing that no two teens are exactly alike, a number of sound parenting guidelines, when used consistently, are helpful.

Here are a dozen suggestions to use as a diagnostic checklist. As a first step, make sure that your adolescent understands every one by making them an integral and ongoing part of your family value system. Then, where you find parenting weaknesses, make it a point to strengthen your responses in that particular area.

_____ **TEEN GUIDELINE #1: INSIST ON MEETING YOUR CHILD'S FRIENDS.** When a teen gets into trouble, more often than not it is found that parents have had little or no contact with their child's peer group. Assume that it means trouble if: 1) you know friends' names, but have never seen or met them; 2) your child insists on always going to meet friends somewhere else; or 3) your teen and friends never spend time at your home. Make it a clear mandate for yourself to personally meet all of your teen's friends and have them spend at least some time together at your place. It's one of the best preventive measures possible.

_____ **TEEN GUIDELINE #2: GET TO KNOW THE PARENTS OF YOUR TEEN'S FRIENDS.** There are several very sound reasons for this suggestion. First, it's nice to know others who are experiencing the same parenting issues that you are with your teen. Second, when you get to know those parents (at least on the telephone), you already have a relationship and it's easier to call if you sense trouble or if there's a problem. Third, you get a sense of how effectively these other parents parent. This last kind of information helps you better protect your teen if other parents' responses are found lacking.

_____ **TEEN GUIDELINE #3: DON'T HESITATE TO CHECK ARRANGEMENTS WITH PARENTS OF YOUR TEEN'S FRIENDS.** Most teens attempt to pull a fast one at least once by saying they are going to a friend's house and then going somewhere else. This kind of deceit should be confronted early and not permitted to become a pattern. Savvy parents spot-check such arrangements and invite friends' parents to do the same. Especially beware when the frequency and/or regularity of such time away develops into a pattern. It's also a mighty good idea to insist that your teen call and check with you if there is any change in plans.

____ TEEN GUIDELINE #4: STAY IN TOUCH WITH THE SCHOOL AND YOUR CHILD'S TEACHERS. At no other time is the possibility of problems at school higher than during early adolescence. Dramatic changes in academic performance often occur. There may be relationship or authority problems at school that sometimes don't show up at home because teens hide them or refuse to discuss them. Teachers often have insight into a teen's behavior that helps parents to become more aware and to prevent emerging problems from getting worse. Effective parents *make time* to talk with teachers regularly during these crucial formative years.

____ TEEN GUIDELINE #5: INSIST ON REASONABLE FAMILY TIME TOGETHER. It is natural for a teen to want to spend more time with friends in lieu of the family. However, responsible parents don't let a teen completely abandon or withdraw from the family. Although it may be resisted, some quality time with the family is necessary for healthy emotional development to take place. An alternative acceptable to most teens is to have a friend come along on family outings. The families of friends may then reciprocate and everyone is satisfied. It is not a good sign when an adolescent is allowed to spend no time with anyone's family.

____ TEEN GUIDELINE #6: EDUCATE YOURSELF AND YOUR TEEN. The "If they don't know about it, they won't do it" approach to parenting teens is a prescription for problems. The fact is that your teen will become educated in one of two ways: 1) through parents who provide sound and up-to-date information, or 2) from peers who disseminate distortions, myths, and completely erroneous information. With educated awareness, teens are in a much better position to make responsible choices. And, it is primarily the parents' responsibilty to inform (not preach). With failure to do so, teens will inevitably educate one another with sometimes disastrous results.

____ TEEN GUIDELINE #7: DON'T ASK SO MANY QUESTIONS. Teens develop a tremendous sensitivity about privacy and their independence. If there is one thing an early adolescent dislikes, it's to be constantly questioned by parents about thoughts, feelings, actions, or plans. When there are too many questions, teen responses become short and evasive. Sometimes, this triggers more questions by parents, and a vicious circle begins. The best antidote is to learn to casually converse with your adolescent without rapid-fire intrusive questioning. Patience and good listening skills are absolutely crucial when communicating with teens.

____ **TEEN GUIDELINE #8: DEVELOP A SUPPORT GROUP FOR TEEN PARENTING.** Parents these days may not be close to neighbors, and teens are more mobile than ever before. As a consequence, parents are increasingly isolated and sometimes have no friends or forum to express concerns about how to respond to teen issues. The sense of aloneness can be even more acute among single parents. It is most helpful for parents during the adolescent years in particular to seek out a parenting support group. In recent years, more of these groups have formed through churches and under the auspices of PTO/PTA organizations. Find one or start one in your community.

____ **TEEN GUIDELINE #9: IF YOU SUSPECT TROUBLE, FOLLOW UP IMMEDIATELY.** This suggestion should definitely not be interpreted to mean jumping to unwarranted conclusions or confronting a teen with unsubstantiated accusations. However, it does mean that parents must remain vigilant, sensitive, and aware of what is going on with their teens. Knowing what to look for as far as emotional problems and drug use also helps. If you suspect your teen is in trouble, seek more information and then calmly bring your concerns to your son or daughter. Angry, irrational confrontations usually don't work, but an informed and mature approach just might.

____ **TEEN GUIDELINE #10: CONSTANTLY ENCOURAGE AND POSITIVELY REINFORCE YOUR TEEN.** Early adolescents are no longer children, but they aren't adults, either. A teen's adult identity is just forming during these critical years, and it is tender and vulnerable. Despite a tough exterior, personal insecurity remains quite high. It is a time when positive feedback, reassurance, and encouragement from caring parents can make all the difference in the world. Too often, frustrated parents become excessively critical of their teen because of the problems and erratic behavior so characteristic of this age. No matter how you feel, try to reinforce the positive. You and your teen will come out ahead.

____ **TEEN GUIDELINE #11: ALLOW YOUR TEEN TO BE DIFFERENT WITHIN LIMITS.** There is a twofold thrust to this suggestion. First, your teen *will* adopt different language, dress, and behaviors as part of the separation process. This is healthy and must be accepted within reasonable limits. Second, because early adolescence is a time when teens are struggling to define personal values and directions, some freedom to do so is necessary. Frightened parents who prematurely overreact to newfound career possibilities (not going to college, becoming a rock star) often inadvertently reinforce that option. An accepting openness and patience helps immeasurably, especially when it is communicated by secure parents who don't feel that a teen has to "conform" and be exactly like them.

___ **TEEN GUIDELINE #12: DO NOT IMPOSE YOUR SOLUTIONS ON ALL TEEN PROBLEMS.** Your teen is becoming more emotionally self-sufficient and wants to deal with problems in a more independent way. If parents insist on taking over and imposing their will or solutions on every problem, everyone loses. An adolescent does not learn judgement that way and may even become more evasive and private. Or, power struggles with parents can erupt. Instead, create a relationship with your teen in which there is freedom to talk over problems openly. As a parent, help to define options and consequences, but let your teen make the final decision (your teen will anyway). This way, you keep the relationship open, and your teen will feel better about returning to you for needed advice.

Letting Go Responsibly

Deep within the center of every hurricane is the eye. In this area, there is relative calm despite the intensity of the storm that swirls around it. This is an excellent way to conceptualize the relationship of effective parents to their children during the tumultuous adolescent years. At puberty, a teen becomes inexorably swept up in the swift winds of change. To help themselves and their child, parents must remain calm and aware in the eye of the hurricane.

It almost goes without saying that during this time, a healthy sense of humor is one of the best coping skills possible for parents. However, a good sense of humor requires perspective and the ability to sort out what is typical and what signals real trouble in your teen. Witness the knowing parent who confided to another: "I know how to help you understand your teen. Just keep in mind the six M's of early adolescence: Moody, Mouthy, Messy, Me, Money, and Monosyllables!" How true and how frustrating. It's precisely this ability to smile, though, that helps so much during these trying years.

For your teen, there is little question that growing up these days is more emotionally treacherous and fraught with dangers than ever. And, a difficult emotional reality is that early adolescence is a time of "letting go" for parents. For emerging young adults, it's an age of many firsts: a first date, a new driver's license, awareness of emerging sexuality, the first prom, evenings out alone, a first real job. The list goes on. Vivid memories of their own adolescent experiences are evoked in parents with each new step a teen makes toward independence. The memories are bittersweet because each signals the undeniable reality that "our little boy (or girl)" is really growing up.

As old memories and the new independence of teens conspire to make life an emotional roller coaster for parents, there are several parenting "givens" that, once accepted, go far toward making these trying years easier.

PARENTING GIVEN #1: THE HEALTHIER YOUR INVOLVEMENT DURING THE PRETEEN YEARS, THE EASIER IT IS TO EFFECTIVELY PARENT DURING ADOLESCENCE. In other words, don't wait until puberty when your child is bigger than you and very mobile to begin to teach values, to spend quality time together, and to implement discipline. It doesn't work. Teens who have consistently experienced a solid family life and effective parenting from day one find early adolescence emotionally easier and so do their parents.

PARENTAL GIVEN #2: ONE CHILD WILL GIVE YOU MUCH MORE TROUBLE THAN ANY OF THE REST. Personality, placement in sibling order, and individual emotional needs may conspire to make the adolescent years immensely more difficult for one child than for another. It is with this child that parents must be even more sensitive, patient, and strong because their sensitivity, patience, and strength will be sorely tested.

PARENTING GIVEN #3: YOUR VALUES DO MAKE A DIFFERENCE ALTHOUGH THEY ARE RESISTED. You must understand how very important you and your value system are to a teen experiencing confusing changes and intense emotions. You will be resisted and that's normal, so positive feedback won't be forthcoming. Over the long haul, your understanding and strength of conviction during these years will influence your teen more significantly than you may ever know.

In a nutshell, neither parents nor teens ever forget the experiences of early adolescence. To handle it well requires that you as a parent possess personal security, a sound value system, and sensitive understanding of the inner turmoil taking place within your growing children. With tongue-in-cheek, a parent who had been through it all commented that on the average, a parent can expect somewhere in the neighborhood of 35 to 40 minutes of peace of mind during a child's teen years. That statement is blatantly untrue. Why, with energy and commitment, you can easily expand that time to upwards of two hours! Enough tongue-in-cheek. But, it sure seems that way sometimes . . . .

Chapter 17

Helping the Troubled Teen: Understanding Adolescent Depression and Its Consequences

FACT: The teen years have steadily become a more emotionally tumultuous period of development.

FACT: Adolescence is immensely more dangerous these days because of life-threatening drugs and incurable sexually-transmitted diseases.

FACT: The social and academic pressures on young adults to succeed is steadily becoming more intense.

FACT: The emotional immaturity lurking beneath a thin veneer of pseudoindependence of teens makes them vulnerable to inappropriate ways of solving life problems.

FACT: Premature sexual involvements and drug use are increasingly drifting to ever younger age groups.

FACT: The incidence of adolescent suicide has increased more than three hundred percent in the last thirty years.

Awareness of completed suicides, suicide attempts, and "cluster suicides" in young people are now stamped indelibly in the national consciousness. These frightening trends have been growing for years, yet are still not completely understood. And, no prospect concerns parents more than an adolescent son or daughter who has become suicidal. While this disturbing aspect of adolescent development has received the most publicity, it is only a reflection of a wider problem. This problem, easily missed, is that of teen depression and its consequences.

The early teen years (which are the ones when adolescents are most vulnerable to serious crises) are best characterized by constant change. Physical maturation, emotional volatility, social change, new roles, and an unformed adult identity all converge to make the years from twelve to eighteen a most confusing time of life. Teens must learn to cope with new feelings, a new body, new relationships, and new responsibilities. And, this must be done without an adult frame of reference or a base of experience coping with the problems that rapid change brings.

Parents are often prone to perceive a teenage son's or daughter's experience from an adult frame of reference. The reality is that a teen is not an emotionally stable, mature adult. Parents frequently forget their own experiences growing up, along with the problems they encountered. To really understand their growing son or daughter, it's helpful for parents to remember their own teen years and to be able to shift into seeing the world from an adolescent perspective. Further, it is also essential for parents to understand that there are four qualities (sometimes known as the Four I's of adolescence) present in teens that often lead to irrational solutions to problems.

1. IDEALISM. First, a teen's view of the world has all the qualities of romantic idealism. This includes vision of knights in shining armor, heroes and heroines, and living "happily ever after." The problem is that this romanticism often dramatically clashes with the emotional realities of adolescent experience.

2. INTENSITY. Most parents are quite aware that a teen's moods are changeable, daily ranging from exuberant highs to the lowest of lows. What is less obvious is that these intense feelings may be triggered by issues that seem quite minor or even inconsequential to an adult. The highs may be great, but the depths of despair can be overwhelming.

3. IMMEDIACY. Most early adolescents live almost entirely in the present. The future and the responsibilities of true adulthood seem far away. And, because they are still emotionally immature, their ability to delay gratification is underdeveloped. They want what they want "right now."

4. IMPULSIVITY. Impulsivity, part of the essential spontaneity of adolescence, is what makes early teens delightful. But it's also frightening to parents because with inadequately developed internal controls, teens act on feelings without considering dangerous consequences.

Put these four characteristics of adolescence together with today's stresses and pressures of growing up. Then add the dangers that have only come on the scene in recent years and the results are twofold: 1) teens who are more emotionally vulnerable than ever before, and 2) parents are less sure how to help their teen negotiate this most difficult time of life in healthy ways. Parents feel that they have just gotten used to their youngster during the relatively calm elementary school years. Then, with the onset of early adolescence, everything suddenly changes. The necessary adjustment in parenting style is a shock to unprepared parents.

By definition, early adolescence is always stressful on parents *and* teens. With understanding and perspective, though, parents can make these years easier on themselves and better for the teens struggling to reach adulthood. However, sometimes an adolescent encounters significant problems. One of the major perils of puberty for parents is dealing effectively with a troubled teen. Parents often find it difficult to assess the seriousness of adolescent problems because of ongoing changes in their teen and the often diminished candor so characteristic of this age.

The Depressive Signs

You already know that a young adult is prone not only to romanticism, but also to deep feelings, both positive and negative. During the course of adolescent development, aware parents develop an understanding of how each of their children functions emotionally. While one teen in a family may cope well with normal adolescent problems, another may not. It is parental awareness of baseline day-to-day "normality" for a particular child that becomes the backdrop for detecting serious teen problems. Parents must be very observant during these years. And, they must know what to look for to spot emotional trouble.

The fact is that there are any number of emotional issues, some social and others psychological in nature, that create significant vulnerabilities in teens. And, because these early adolescents have no adult base of experiences to deal adaptively with problems, their immature ways of coping often make the situation worse, not better. Add to this situation the fact that teens, especially those who are experiencing severe problems, may be reluctant (or outright resistant) to talking about them with adults. The result is an emotionally trying, psychologically difficult, immensely frustrating, and sometimes dangerous situation for parents to deal with.

However, it helps if parents understand that the core of most serious emotional problems in teens is adolescent depression. And, there is a well-known behavioral pattern that reasonably accurately reflects this all too common depressive state. To protect their children, parents must be able to recognize the presence of this behavioral pattern as assessed against the "normal" responses of a given teen. There are ten signals that a teen is experiencing significant emotional problems. The more of them observed in a teen and the longer they persist, the more dangerous the situation may be.

BEHAVIORAL SIGNAL #1: SIGNIFICANT CHANGE IN SLEEP PATTERNS. An active adolescent may suddenly begin to sleep very long hours. Fourteen to sixteen hours is not unusual. And when up, the teen exhibits pronounced lethargy and lack of willingness to be involved in usual activities. Do recognize, however, that at least a few teens may respond in just the opposite way. They begin to suffer from chronic insomnia or hyperactivity.

BEHAVIORAL SIGNAL #2: GRADES SUDDENLY BEGIN TO DETERIORATE. Many preadolescents do quite well in school. However, when puberty sets in, grades may begin a rather dramatic decline. However, most adolescents usually show at least some concern and incentive to improve on them. The teen in trouble reacts differently. With the precipitous drop in grades there is often absolutely no interest in improving them. Along with a completely disinterested attitude, there is often associated an outright resistance to any parental attempts to help.

BEHAVIORAL SIGNAL #3: INTEREST IN PERSONAL GROOMING FADES. Early teens are known for their vanity. When they leave the house, every hair must be in place. Clothes must be correct. It is important to "fit in" with the best image possible. When parents notice a growing lack of interest in personal appearance, it may signal a significant drop in self-esteem. In addition, personal hygiene is frequently neglected.

BEHAVIORAL SIGNAL #4: THERE ARE MORE "ACCIDENTS" THAN USUAL. A teen beginning to experience significant emotional trouble (or who may be involved in drug use) may have many more "accidents" than usual. That's because depression or drug use both may diminish alertness. These accidents are almost always covered by legitimate-sounding excuses where parents are concerned. However, it is the number of personal injuries, car accidents, tickets, or other problems encountered by a teen that should cue alert parents.

BEHAVIORAL SIGNAL #5: THERE IS A PROLONGED DE-PRESSIVE STATE. Parents of teens find out very quickly that they experience frequent highs and lows. Change is the norm, though, as one mood, however intense, soon gives way to another. Parents must watch for a teen who gets way down and stays down for weeks or months at a time. Such a situation may be even more serious if there is no clear or apparent reason for the down feelings.

BEHAVIORAL SIGNAL #6: EVIDENCE OF ALCOHOL/DRUG ABUSE. Adolescents are interested in experimentation, and drugs are readily available in most locales. In fact, these days, drug use may begin as early as elementary school in some areas. As with adults, adolescents often turn to drugs or alcohol to cope with personal problems. On the other hand, do keep in mind that drug and alcohol abuse may be a *cause* of adolescent depression. And, as with any kind of drug use, impulse control is lowered. This is an especially danger-ous situation for an already depressed teen.

BEHAVIORAL SIGNAL #7: EXTREME EMOTIONAL WITH-DRAWAL OCCURS. Let's face it, most teens do grow somewhat more distant from parents during early adolescence as they struggle for independence. However, a frequently encountered sign of a severe teen problem is unusual and prolonged withdrawal from friends, normal teen activities, *and* parents. Sometimes associated with such withdrawal is an outbreak of highly aggressive conflict with parents and peers.

BEHAVIORAL SIGNAL #8: MARKED CHANGE IN PHYSICAL APPEARANCE. In depressed adults, eating may increase or decrease with consequent weight loss or gain. The same is true for teens. Alert parents can often spot this signal as it is manifested in eating behavior and in body weight. And, depressed adolescents may look different in another way. As in adults, clinically depressed teens develop a strained, almost haunted look about them. This look is especially apparent in their eyes.

BEHAVIORAL SIGNAL #9: A RECENT LOSS OR SERIES OF LOSSES. To an adult, an early adolescent who "breaks up" or who experiences the loss of a best friend who moves away may be no big thing. Losses are a part of life that must be accepted. However, to a teen, it may be catastrophic in the depths of despair it can bring. Several significant losses, or disappointments in relationships, in a short period of time may overwhelm ability to cope. Parents must be aware of the significance of such events from the teen's perspective, not their own.

BEHAVIORAL SIGNAL #10: OVERT SIGNS OF SUICIDE. There is a prevalent myth that anyone who talks about suicide won't do it. The facts show that those who commit suicide, or who make serious attempts, usually communicate their intentions beforehand. Many teens who are contemplating suicide are often willing to talk about it, especially if asked directly. Also, watch for other danger signals: giving away prized possessions, a sudden intense interest in religion (or afterlife), or signs of a suicide attempt (cuts on wrist).

Parental Blinders

After a teen pregnancy, a serious drug problem develops, a school expulsion or charges of delinquency, or an attempted or completed suicide, shocked parents are often jolted into recognizing that their teen had been experiencing problems for some time. Sometimes for months, even years. And, as the saying goes, hindsight is usually twenty-twenty. However, often the problem of detecting teen problems early is complicated by the fact that many parents develop emotional blocks that prevent recognition of the problems. These parents often realize too late that problems steadily worsened behind the scenes until they suddenly burst forth with startling clarity.

A pertinent question is why parents didn't recognize the signs and do something about a growing teen problem in the beginning. In parents' defense, while virtually always present, the telltale signs are often quite subtle and easily missed. And, they're even easier to miss if parents don't know what to look for. Further, most of the time, teens do not clearly communicate the magnitude of the problems they may be experiencing. On the other hand, parents frequently have blind spots that compound the recognition problem. Here are five of the most common. To protect your teen, make sure you don't fall into any of these traps.

PARENTAL BLINDER #1: YOU TOO EASILY ACCEPT A TEEN'S DENIALS. *Mindset:* "He/she says everthing's okay." Because teens strive for independence and because teens are ambivalent about parental authority, parents cannot rely on a teen to volunteer information about serious problems, even life-threatening ones. Teens' fears of parental response reinforce reluctance. Instead, parents must understand this adolescent trait and not take a teen's denials at face value when what they see with their own eyes contradicts such statements!

PARENTAL BLINDER #2: YOU NEED TO MAINTAIN A SUC-CESSFUL COMMUNITY IMAGE. *Mindset:* "What would everyone think of us if our teen had serious problems?" This attitude is one of the paramount determinants of denial in parents: refusal to recognize and/or deal with teen problems because of fear of damage to personal or community image. In such households, everything seems to be fine publicly, but within them, parents are desperately trying to suppress a myriad of problems. Energy that could be used to solve the problems is used for bolstering a public image instead.

PARENTAL BLINDER #3: YOU FEEL OVERWHELMED BY WORK RESPONSIBILITIES. *Mindset:* "I have so much to do that I just don't have time for the children anymore." This mindset is usually found in parents who have let priorities become distorted over the years. Parents do get busier, but they then make the mistake of putting work far above relationships with the kids and spouse on the priority list. The net result is very busy parents who progressively emotionally lose touch with loved ones, while they more than adequately provide for physical needs.

PARENTAL BLINDER #4: YOU DISMISS TEEN PROBLEMS AS "NORMAL" FOR ALL ADOLESCENTS. *Mindset:* "All teens have problems during these growing years, and they all get through it." Such an attitude does have an element of truth. All teens do have ups and downs during adolescence. However, two aspects of the teen experience have changed. First, it's steadily becoming more difficult to emotionally negotiate these crucial years. Second, the dangers to which teens are highly vulnerable these days are more serious than at any time in history.

PARENTAL BLINDER #5: YOU DEFENSIVELY REJECT HELP-FUL FEEDBACK FROM OTHERS. *Mindset:* "My child isn't like that and wouldn't do such things!" Kids in general and teens in particular are often highly skilled at relating one way at home and another in public. And, a parent with this kind of mindset is prone to ignore concerned feedback from other parents and teachers, even from a teen's friends. Sometimes the problem is compounded by a parent's perception that others don't like their child or are just picking on him or her to make life difficult.

What Parents Can Do

While negative changes in a teen's basic life patterns do not necessarily signal imminent suicide, they almost always do reflect growing emotional problems. As such, these changes must not be easily dismissed or rationalized away. The core problem may vary: alcohol or drug abuse, deep feelings of rejection (teens can be very cruel to one another), unhealthy sexual involvement, or "running with the wrong crowd." And, a teen problem in one area can often lead to other destructive involvements with worsening emotional problems as the usual consequence.

With all the social changes occurring these days, it is easy for parents to feel very insecure and unsure of themselves when dealing with teens and their needs. This problem is exacerbated because parents often have few outlets to talk about their feelings with other concerned parents (or professionals). To provide parents with specific suggestions when they suspect a serious teen problem, here are ten parental responses that have proven to be helpful under these potentially life-threatening conditions.

As with anything else, teen problems are easier to reverse early than when fully developed and where there is more potential for tragedy. Don't feel self-conscious about following these suggestions. It's easier to follow them and be found wrong than to ignore signs and find yourself full of regret later.

PARENTAL RESPONSE #1: DON'T PANIC AND OVERREACT. Calm, cool awareness is the byword here. A parent who emotionally overreacts signals to a teen: "You can't handle my problems." The result is usually even more reluctance to communicate. Deal with facts as much as possible. Losing your temper about a teen problem is extremely detrimental. Above all what is needed under such circumstances is to communicate calm concern so that your teen will not defensively withdraw from you when you are needed most!

PARENTAL RESPONSE #2: CHECK OBSERVED CHANGES WITH OTHER ADULT SOURCES. A parent who suspects serious emotional trouble in a teen should quietly and unobtrusively seek corroborating information. Often it is helpful to approach a teen's teachers, parents of your teen's friends, or other significant adults. Again, calm concern is the most helpful way to approach the subject. The input of others who have signficant contact with your teen will help put your thoughts or suspicions into perspective.

PARENTAL RESPONSE #3: BECOME MORE OBSERVANT AND LISTEN MORE CAREFULLY. Once you suspect a problem is developing, begin to observe your teen's behavior for cues. This does not mean to sneak around, to snoop, or to invade your teen's privacy except under the most extreme conditions. Most of the time it means to keep your eyes and ears open. Keep in mind that teens in trouble are usually defensive and aren't going to tell you much. It will be up to you to keep an extra eye out for trouble so that you can short circuit it before it becomes dangerous.

PARENTAL RESPONSE #4: KEEP LINES OF COMMUNICATION OPEN. It's exceptionally important to regularly take the time to talk with your teen. And, it's important to do this when things are going well. Trying to open communication when there is trouble, after ignoring opportunities to do so for years, just doesn't wash. And, usually your teen will tell you so in no uncertain terms! Don't forget that it is the lack of caring communication and a solid relationship with parents that is often one of the principle causes of teen problems in the first place.

PARENTAL RESPONSE #5: WHEN YOU'RE REASONABLY SURE OF A PROBLEM, MAKE A DIRECT INQUIRY. Once there is reasonable evidence of a problem, even if it is circumstantial, it's a good idea to ask your teen directly about it. It is essential that this be done at a good time for you both, when neither is angry or upset. Make your point directly, while at the same time expressing your deep concern and your willingness to help. This is good advice even if you think a teen is suicidal. Adults and teens rarely volunteer information about suicidal intent. However, they will often talk openly about their feelings or thoughts about ending it all if asked directly in a caring way.

PARENTAL RESPONSE #6: AVOID REINFORCING NEGATIVE FEELINGS IN YOUR TEEN. It is almost axiomatic that teens in trouble often suffer from low self-esteem. At the same time, parents' initial responses may be to do and say things that are personally rejecting to a teen. Alternately, they may make an adolescent feel guilty about having problems, or they may communicate a deep sense of disappointment. This is exactly what a teen doesn't need. Instead, while staying with the facts, try to communicate caring, loving concern, and your willingness to help and be there no matter what.

PARENTAL RESPONSE #7: FIRMLY REMOVE OPPORTUNITIES FOR PROBLEMS. When a teen becomes deeply depressed, whatever the cause, anything can happen. Under these circumstances, knowledgeable parents begin to take precautions. Time spent with friends suspected to be part of the problem should be reduced or eliminated altogether. Any means for suicide (guns, poisons, medications) must be removed from the home. A teen under these circumstances should not be driving alone, especially at night. Social activities should be chaperoned. Friends should be invited to the house rather than a teen going out. If possible, personally transport your teen to school and home, particularly if your child has been riding with friends you don't know well.

PARENTAL RESPONSE #8: EDUCATE YOURSELF ABOUT TEEN PROBLEMS. You're undoubtedly aware that a teen's social environment these days is more complex and stressful than in the past. Because of this, it is necessary for parents to educate themselves. They must understand the confusing changes that are rapidly taking place biologically, emotionally, and socially in their adolescent. Then, these same parents must obtain specific knowledge about drug and alcohol use, sexually-transmitted diseases, teen sexuality and its determinants, and teen depression and suicide.

PARENTAL RESPONSE #9: MOBILIZE PROFESSIONAL SUPPORT AS NECESSARY. When a teen is seriously depressed, professional intervention is often necessary. At the very time they are in dire need of help, many adolescents actively resist it. They fear a peer group's reactions or being labeled "crazy" or as having problems. Parents should not permit a teen's protests to override common sense. On the other hand, it is a rare situation where resolving a serious teen depression does not involve parents, directly or indirectly. As a result, parents must be active participants in any therapy or counseling provided for a teen.

PARENTAL RESPONSE #10: FOLLOW THROUGH ON A PROBLEM. Parents who face a serious teen problem are often reassured when things begin to go better. That could be a mistake. It is well-known that suicidal individuals (teens and adults) often seem to be better just before they act. In other instances, a teen may simply have become better at hiding a problem or conning parents. It is a wise parent who continues to closely watch a teen after things seem to get better. Keep in mind that a vulnerability to a particular problem may remain and that it is positive parental involvement that may prevent a relapse!

PARENTAL RESPONSE #11: MODEL HEALTHY COPING FOR

YOUR TEEN. One key ingredient in many teen problems is lack of closeness and support at home. Sadly, many such young men and women grow to adulthood without the opportunity to observe close at hand a healthy relationship between adults. One of the major preventive measures for parents is to model for their children over the years an upbeat orientation to life, positive ways to resolve conflicts, and closeness and intimacy in a relationship. And, parents who have these qualities in their relationships are better able to cope when problems do come.

PARENTAL RESPONSE #12: RESPOND TO TEENS' NEEDS, NOT TO THEIR WISHES. It is very important that parents not be deceived by a teen's physical development. While the teens are approaching adulthood biologically, their emotional development usually lags far behind. They continue to have many needs that more resemble those of a child than an adult. However, teens often deny their need for support and guidance by adults and in their place they substitute a shallow pseudoindependence. It is critical for parents to "see through" this adolescent facade to the real needs beneath and then meet those needs. And, they must do so without thanks or in the face of active resistance by a son or daughter.

PARENTAL RESPONSE #13: HELP DEVELOP SCHOOL AWARENESS AND PREVENTIVE PROGRAMS. Where one teen is having a problem, it is likely that others are having similar ones. The school may be the only common denominator and as such must play a key part in education and prevention of significant adolescent problems. However, school officials (like parents) have been known to deny that there are any "problems" in their school. Concerned parents can voice their concerns to school officials and help initiate programs helpful not only for parents, but also for the students in those schools.

The Rocky Road to Adulthood

At no time in history have the teen years been more emotionally complicated. And, at no time in history has early adolescence been more dangerous. Greater mobility and precocious independence, growing academic pressure, easy drug availability, life-threatening sexually-transmitted diseases, the decline of family and community support systems, not to mention the dramatic increase in adolescent suicide, all combine to make the storms and stresses of the teen years a time of deep concern for parents.

Unfortunately, there are few signs that growing up healthy and emotionally strong will become easier in the near future. And, teens *will* be teens no matter when or where they grow up. This means that parents must be more savvy and responsive than ever before to help their teens emotionally navigate the rocky road of adolescence leading to mature adulthood. A commitment to knowing and growing with your children through the perils of puberty is certainly the wisest path for all involved parents.

Problems in the teen years are certainly not unusual these days. And, geographically, there is little immunity. They are occurring everywhere, even in rural areas that were once isolated enough to escape them. Further, it is a cause for great concern that significant problems (drug use, promiscuous sexual involvements) seem to be drifting down to ever-younger ages. These trends are, for the most part, independent of socio-economic status of parents. Teens at every level of intelligence become victims. And, such problems are even independent of other siblings. One child in a family may have serious difficulties while the others breeze through the adolescent years with a minimum of conflict.

The most significant countermeasures to prevent problems must come from parents. And, these measures are best begun long before the trials and tribulations of adolescence begin. Input to your children all along is a powerful buffer against the often traumatic changes and experiences of the teen years. Here are three of the most potent countermeasures that you as a parent can take.

COUNTERMEASURE #1: HEALTHY INVOLVEMENT. Many parents mistakenly assume that when children become more self-sufficient, they need less time from parents. Nothing could be further from the truth. As the kids grow, certainly they can dress themselves and make a sandwich. But, they need more time and attention and emotional nourishment from you during these years when life becomes very confusing.

COUNTERMEASURE #2: EDUCATION AND INFORMATION. How sad it is to see so many parents who leave all drug and sex education to the schools (and sometimes the schools don't have effective programs). Or, once adolescence is reached, uncomfortable parents provide the perfunctory "drug rap" or a one-shot "birds and bees talk." It is better to talk to your children openly with accurate information about these issues all during the preadolescent years.

COUNTERMEASURE #3: PARENTAL OUTREACH. Teen problems these days are often exacerbated because many middle-class parents in particular are so busy and so isolated from one another. There are no opportunities to talk over concerns and check perceptions. To counter this unfortunate social trend, parents must make it a point to develop friendships with other parents (parents of your teen's friends, for instance) or even to begin a parent support group through your church or school.

In the end, it is virtually impossible to totally insulate an emerging young adult from all dangerous situations and serious problems. What you can do, however, is to provide the very best environment possible for your teen during these hectic growth years when vulnerability is so very high. And, you must do so in a healthy fashion with accurate knowledge backed up by sound parental values. Children who know that they are loved no matter what and who know that parents will always be there for them usually cope well. These young adults are psychologically hardy. Why? Because these parents have consistently put energy into *their* "home work" before their children ever reached puberty!

Some years ago, a public service message about suicide prevention stated a simple truth: "Suicidal people don't want to die; they just want to stop the pain." The same could be said for teens involved in drug use, or an adolescent who becomes prematurely involved sexually to feel closeness and caring. A young man or woman with low self-esteem who winds up in court is no exception, either. The bottom line should be clear. To the extent that caring parents respond in ways that meet basic emotional needs of their children, they help ease the pain of adolescence. And, by easing the pain of the teen years, they help prevent their growing children from taking drastic and highly inappropriate measures to do the same thing!

Chapter 18

Environmental Enrichment at Home: Family Life Is a Learning Experience

These days, there is little doubt that long years of training are required to gain the skills necessary for success in the work world. And, new learning to supplement an already established base of knowledge is constantly required. On the other hand, while concerned parents are quite aware of these realities, they often tend to completely miss other important sources of learning. In fact, parents too frequently subscribe to a basic myth: that is, the only valid learning for children these days stems from experiences that are carefully structured and then evaluated by adults. And, increasingly, such experiences occur outside the home.

Savvy parents know that this belief is quite erroneous. The fact is that learning by children at home in completely unstructured circumstances is taking place all the time. Actively and passively. Directly and indirectly. Knowledge may be subtly absorbed or learned in obvious circumstances. Like it or not, your children are learning as much from you at home as they are learning at school. And, this learning is extremely important to a child's adjustment later in life. It's also a fact that much of what your children are learning from you may not be exactly what you intended!

Unfortunately, it is only much later in life that children are able to look back at their family life and clearly articulate whether those experiences were a help or hindrance in adult life. Parents frequently give sound advice to their children throughout the developmental years. However, this "do as I say" instructional mode of teaching is *not* where most learning at home takes place. Rather, it is what a child directly experiences and observes in the family during the developmental years that is the source of most home-based learning. Who you are as a person and how you relate at home teaches a child about life, about relationships, and about values. The bottom line is simple, but easy to miss. *Children, when they become adults, will behave in ways highly reminiscent of what they directly experienced during childhood!*

Perhaps an example of the power of this subtle form of learning at home would be apropos. It is a rare child who, at some point during the developmental years, does not label treatment by a parent as totally unfair, perhaps even tyrannical. As a result of this perceived "oppression," the child or adolescent makes a deeply felt personal oath. Sometimes it is stated directly to a parent; sometimes the vow takes the form of a silent commitment. Regardless, the basic content is exactly the same: "When I become a parent, I will never, ever do to my children what you are doing to me. No way will it ever happen!"

The child grows through adolescence and becomes an adult. Sooner or later, this emerging adult marries and has children. Life inevitably becomes more complicated and intense. Then the surprise. That very same child, now a parent, hears the very same words coming out of his or her mouth that is the absolute antithesis of what he or she vowed never to say or do many years before! And, to that new parent's amazement, these words are often stated in an identical context and in the very same tone of voice that a parent used many years before. So much for the vow "never to do that to my children." Déjà vu! While most parents experience this phenomenon now and then, it is startling, years later, to hear one of your own parents speaking through your mouth.

The fact is that during the developmental years, learning from family experiences was taking place in ways that neither you as a child nor your parents were fully aware of at the time. The message here is very simple. It is up to you as parents to maximize the potential for positive learning at home by creating an intellectually and emotionally enriching family life environment for your children. However, the learning that takes place at home during these crucial developmental years is easily misleading to parents who often tend to use formal academic education as their focus for what a child needs to learn on the road to success. In fact, there are four deceptive qualities about family life as a learning experience that are quite different from school-based teaching. Parents must not be misled by any of them.

DECEPTIVE QUALITY #1: THERE IS NO FORMALIZED TEACH-ING OR EVALUATION. Parents often miss how much learning is taking place at home because the teaching isn't structured, formally taught, or evaluated as it is in school. And, there are no regular progress reports. It is the soundness of parental values and trust in the appropriateness of parenting that become the major criteria against which family-based learning must be assessed. That's harder than looking at a report card.

DECEPTIVE QUALITY #2: LEARNING IS TAKING PLACE CON-STANTLY. In the family environment, every day, weekends included, is a "school day" as far as learning is concerned. There are no holidays or vacations. The reason is simple. The primary way that children are learning from you is through their experiences with you day in and day out. This kind of learning is ongoing and ceaseless throughout all the developmental years.

DECEPTIVE QUALITY #3: THE RESULTS OF THIS LEARNING MAY NOT SHOW UP FOR YEARS. In contrast to formal education where learning can be demonstrated immediately (*e.g.* reciting a multiplication table), the learning that takes place at home often "goes underground" for many years. In fact, parents may lament during adolescence in particular that no parental values are being learned. However, what has actually been learned years earlier emerges in its full and powerful influence when that child is an adult and has started a family.

DECEPTIVE QUALITY #4: LEARNING DURING CHILDHOOD MAY BE EITHER POSITIVE OR NEGATIVE. It's a fact that positive and negative learning at home may occur with equal efficiency. And, because home-based learning is so indirect and may be suppressed for years, the results of what was learned in the family during child-hood may not show up until that child becomes a parent many years later. Of course, it follows that the healthier home-based learning is, the better that child will be able to cope with pressures, problems, and relationships as an adult.

Now, to put this kind of home-based learning into proper perspec-tive, it is necessary to peek inside the homes of some typical middle-class American families. Barbara, Ron, and Connie, all in middle school, reside in the same small, semirural community some twenty miles from a larger metropolitan area. In fact, all three live on the same street and know one another at school. Their parents are economically successful, and they each live in a well-kept home.

However, while their experiences at school are all rather similar, significant differences emerge when what goes on at home is examined. These differences reflect the diversity of home learning environments, created by parents, that can adversely affect children during the developmental years.

BARBARA'S PARENTS: At Barbara's place no one ever does much of anything. Everyone sticks around the house. The television set is always on and there are virtually no magazines or other reading materials to be seen. In fact, Barbara's parents rarely read anything at all. She and her brother have plenty of playthings, but there is little in the way of family "adventures" outside the home. Community functions are almost totally ignored. What Barbara notices most is her parents' immediate distrust of anything new. She hears constant diatribes about social changes and how much better things were when her parents were young.

RON'S PARENTS: Overwhelmed by all they have to do and get done, Ron's parents are literally too pooped to pop. They used to go out regularly and even had a solid family life together. Not for the past few years, though. Now even though they spend a lot of time at home, they spend little quality time together. Homelife, characterized by his parents' constant irritability, conveys the message: "Stay away from me. Don't ask for anything. I already have too much to do!" Although well-educated, his parents are simply too tired to take advantage of interesting events in the community or to share much in the way of family experiences.

CONNIE'S PARENTS: There is constant pressure at Connie's house. She is taken to structured "enrichment" activities almost every day after school where she is pushed to learn and to refine skills. Her competitive parents encourage this in her as they constantly compete with one another and with their colleagues at work. Even when she is playing, they strive to be active "teachers" who become very frustrated when Connie just wants to have fun without necessarily "learning" from the experience. If she doesn't learn, her frustrated parents see the experience as time wasted. All she wants is to have some unpressured free time for herself.

In each of these homes, well-meaning parents are doing their best to provide for their children. However, in long-range perspective, they have failed to provide an environment where family life is emotionally fulfilling and where home-based learning by children is maximized. Although each family is surely "getting by" on a day-to-day basis, the children are just as surely being adversely affected by their day-to-day experiences within that home. The effects of these kinds of home environments will not show up for years—that is, until the kids become adults themselves.

Three Common Family Styles

Few, if any, parents set out to deliberately provide a poor-quality family life for their children. However, sometimes parents do so inadvertently by making erroneous assumptions about children's needs or about adult competency. The reality is that a sound family life that meets both the emotional *and* intellectual needs of children is required for adult success. It is quite easy for parents who are successful themselves to get off the track. And, since parents set the tone for the quality of the home life, it is up to them to make needed changes.

Barbara, Ron, and Connie are really being short-changed at home although they don't realize it at their tender ages. Because they are not adults, their immature perspectives prevent them from making positive changes by themselves. And, because they are still children, they have little capacity to conceptualize the issues and suggest needed changes to their parents. To reiterate the basic point, it's up to parents to see the big picture and to make family life fulfilling emotionally and intellectually for everyone.

Now let's examine a bit more closely what's going on inside the homes of our subjects. Although these three sets of parents are probably not going to radically change their basic lifestyles, it is entirely possible for each of them to realign some of the family life activities to more adequately meet the emotional needs of their children and at the same time better prepare them for the future. Here is a synopsis of each of the three narrowly-based family styles with some facts and a fallacy statement for each.

BARBARA'S PARENTS: A PROBLEM OF EXPOSURE. Here the problem is basically one of environmental sterility. Barbara's parents are small town people who started a business early in life and made it successful through years of hard work and sacrifice. Although not exactly deprived growing up, neither could afford college. In this respect, they are truly a self-made couple. They have spent all of their lives living and working in their small town where they are respected. However, they have little interest in the outside world and in fact find change of any kind difficult to cope with. They do not subscribe to a newspaper nor do they read anything else. In fact, they rarely travel outside the county, and local cultural events are of no interest.

Although they certainly want Barbara to make it, they naively think that the rules of the success game have stayed exactly the same over the past three decades. Perhaps in terms of solid work habits they are right. More likely, though, this kind of blanket assumption may ultimately make attaining the good life more difficult for their daughter. Although there is a loving home life, Barbara is simply not being exposed in a positive way to the big world that exists outside her small home town. It's a world that she will not be able to avoid facing in the future. Barbara's parents need first to remove a basic fallacy from their thinking and then to accept some pertinent facts.

The Fallacy: That parents living in a small town in a basically rural area can ignore or hide from the world at large and that exposure to it is really not necessary for success.

The Facts:

1. Even small towns are growing. With growth come new problems as people with different life experiences, values, and ways of doing things move in.

2. While the basic work skills required for success do not change, there has been a steady increase in the level of intellectual and emotional sophistication required to "make it."

3. Parents can give their children a tremendous head start in coping with social change and lifestyle complexity by exposing them to it early and consistently so they learn to respond effectively to such situations.

RON'S PARENTS: A PROBLEM OF BURNOUT. Although well-educated and successful, Ron's parents are certainly not living the good life these days. Each with a strong work ethic and both with careers, his parents have become totally and completely overwhelmed with their responsibilities at work and at home. They are experiencing stress symptoms; they are irritable all the time and have little energy to do anything except go to work, come home exhausted, and then work some more. Although they used to create adventures for themselves and enjoy life, in recent years they have given up leisure activities, cultural events, getting away from it all, and even friendships.

Needless to say, Ron is feeling the effects of his parents burned-out way of living. He is given many things materially, but at the same time is neglected emotionally. The discipline at home is not what it should be, and he gets away with a lot because his parents simply don't have the energy to provide adequate discipline and positive emotional support. Without realizing it, Ron is growing up an emotionally deprived child despite the fact that he has virtually everything he wants. Home for him is little more than a place to eat and sleep. And, unfortunately, it's the same for his parents who don't feel close to one another these days, either.

The Fallacy: That children will grow up to be successful if provided with material wealth in spite of a lack of parental closeness and a fulfilling family life.

The Facts:

1. Children need consistent, high-quality emotional nourishment from parents to grow into adults with personal confidence and high self-esteem.

2. In a rapidly changing external world, it is necessary for children to base personal security within themselves. And, internal security comes from a stable family life and high-quality, shared experiences with parents.

3. For children to learn healthy relationship skills, it is necessary to observe use of them between parents and to consistently experience them directly in interactions with parents.

CONNIE'S PARENTS: A PROBLEM OF ACHIEVEMENT INTENSITY (*a.k.a.* the Hothouse Effect). Highly successful and workaholics by nature, Connie's parents are competitive pushers. They each have a strong personal need to be constantly meeting challenges and reaching goals to feel good about themselves. However, when they stop, they quickly begin feeling anxious and guilty so they keep on going. What is important in their lives is to "get ahead." More is always better is their philosophy. And, they have been getting ahead for years. In the meantime, they've forgotten how to relax and live the good life. And, to a one, leisure activities are intensely competitive and goal-oriented.

Her parents' style is definitely affecting Connie. She has been pushed to achieve since early childhood. She is positively reinforced only for being the best, and perfection is the standard. After school, she is taken to achievement-oriented "enrichment" activities that her parents euphemistically refer to as play. Recently, however, she has been suffering from stress. In fact, at her early age she is already burning out. It has gone so far that she has been turning off to learning at school. All she wants is some love and some free time for herself. It seems that her parents can't relate to her in any way except as pushy instructors.

The Fallacy: That to gain a competitive edge, children must be constantly pushed from early childhood on to get ahead. It's up to parents to make sure that a child's progress is as accelerated as possible.

The Facts:

1. Children are naturally inquisitive and put forth great energy learning on their own if given the freedom to do so without adults taking over to insure that "appropriate learning" takes place.

2. The motives for excessively pushing young children (*i.e.*, Hothousing) is more often to meet parents' competitive needs than as a response to the developmental requirements of a child.

3. To preserve an interest in learning and to remain emotionally healthy, children need plenty of free time just to be kids and to do all the things kids do without interference by adults.

The Family Adaptive Development Scale

As a means for parents to assess the quality of the environment at home within which children live, the Family Adaptive Development Scale (FADS) has been created. This Index reflects the basic values and emotional health of parents as well as the opportunities for children to learn at home. As a parent, read each one of these statements, each with an explanation and a rationale, and then check "X" or "O" depending on whether it is present at home. The more "X's" you have marked, the healthier your home environment tends to be. Do keep in mind that FADS reflects important informal learning experiences that are a natural part of family life, not formally structured and graded educational experiences.

____ **1. TELEVISION WATCHING BY CHILDREN IS CAREFULLY CONTROLLED BY PARENTS.**

In other words, the TV set is definitely *not* on all the time. Neither is it being chronically and indiscriminately watched by children *or* parents. By mandating carefully-controlled and limited TV viewing time at home, parents encourage their children to involve themselves in other interesting activities and in quality interactions among family members.

____ 2. PARENTS HELP CHILDREN KEEP ABREAST OF WORLD EVENTS AND HOW THEY AFFECT CONTEMPORARY LIFE.

In the home, there is discussion about what happens in the world because parents are aware and they care. And, they take pains to talk to the children about current events. The kids are encouraged to ask questions, and parents take the time to provide informed answers about current events and their implications. Over time, such informal conversations about current events help the kids gain a deeper understanding of the world around them.

____ 3. THE CHILDREN REGULARLY OBSERVE PARENTS READING FOR PLEASURE AND ARE ENCOURAGED TO DO THE SAME.

It is quite difficult for parents who do not read for pleasure to meaningfully encourage their children to do the same. Reading for interest or personal pleasure is one of the most important life skills of all. However, it is also one of the life skills most easily missed in a television-dominated era. And, don't forget that children who enjoy reading as adults most often were read to by parents when they were young.

____ 4. INTERESTING AND STIMULATING BOOKS AND MAGAZINES ARE AVAILABLE TO CHILDREN AROUND THE HOUSE.

It is difficult to encourage reading if there is nothing to read at home. In homes where there is a solid stimulation ethic, parents subscribe to newspapers, high quality magazines, and have interesting books and resource materials around the house at all times. Children are encouraged to pick them up and browse through them and observe parents doing the same.

____ 5. YOUR CHILDREN VISIT THE LOCAL LIBRARY REGULARLY AND KNOW HOW TO USE IT.

Clearly, one of the most important resources in any community is the library. As a center for information storage and other educational activities, children must be exposed to its resources early in order to feel good about it later in life. Aware parents make regular visits to the the library with their children. In fact, visits to the the library often become the focus for inexpensive, but fulfilling family outings.

____ 6. FAMILY VACATIONS INCLUDE VISITS TO MUSEUMS OR OTHER EDUCATIONAL ACTIVITIES.

A zoo, a museum, a special festivity, or a celebration each provides experiences that are important to children. Parents who show an interest stimulate the kids' interests as well. Children learn through exposure especially when parents relate what is being seen to other experiences. However, don't overdo this to the point where a vacation is no fun at all!

_____ 7. YOU TAKE GREAT PAINS TO USE CORRECT GRAMMAR WHEN YOU CONVERSE AND CONSISTENTLY CORRECT THE CHILDREN.

It is a sad reality that many otherwise bright and talented individuals do not advance in their careers simply because they have not mastered the basics of the English language. Parents who consistently use correct grammar help children to hear basic mistakes and eliminate them. An adult who uses incorrect grammar in speech carries a subtle, but powerful liability into the marketplace.

_____ 8. YOU TAKE THE TIME TO REGULARLY TALK TO YOUR CHILDREN ABOUT YOUR EXPERIENCES AND THEIR ACTIVITIES.

In a nutshell, the kids like to talk to you because you regularly make the time for conversations. And, you make it interesting. You aren't constantly trying to teach them something. You know how to relate in an easy and comfortable way that helps children absorb information. One interesting result is that you learn *from* the children as well as getting to know them.

_____ 9. YOU MODEL HEALTHY INTIMACY IN YOUR RELATIONSHIPS.

When you are relating to the kids, you are very comfortable with emotional closeness and with sharing your feelings. Further, the children daily observe your affectionate responses to your spouse. You often say "I love you" and regular bear hugs are the norm for you. The kids know how to be close because you're modeling it for them every day.

_____ 10. YOU ENCOURAGE CHILDREN IN THEIR NATURAL CREATIVITY AROUND THE HOUSE.

Children have a natural tendency to make things. Just as naturally, they tend to make a mess while doing so. You are able as a parent to see the big picture and reward this kind of trial-and-error learning instead of only responding to the sometimes frustrating results. In fact, sometimes you participate with the kids in "piddlin' around" experiments that are fun and different.

_____ 11. YOU MAKE SURE THAT THE KIDS HAVE ENOUGH FREE TIME TO DO WHAT THEY WISH.

Wise parents do two things in this regard: 1) they do not allow the kids to become overinvolved in outside activities to the point of physical and emotional exhaustion, and 2) they don't mandate that children always be involved in "meaningful" activities. Plenty of free time is provided to do what a child wants, but that time *does not* include copping out in front of the TV set!

_____ 12. YOU PARTICIPATE IN LOCAL CULTURAL EVENTS AND INFORMAL EDUCATIONAL OPPORTUNITIES AS A FAMILY.

As a parent, you are involved in community activities, and you use them as a way to pleasurably expand your awareness. Plays, visiting artists or dance troupes, and talks by experts are all part of what is regularly available in most sizeable communities or near them. Through such participation, you broaden your knowledge and the children do the same with you as you take advantage of what's available (and often free).

_____ 13. YOU SHOW THE KIDS HOW TO ENJOY AND VALUE EXPERIENCES, NOT PRODUCTS.

Insecure and short-sighted parents make every activity into a competition that must be won; to not win is to risk being labeled a failure. Or, all activities are made into work by rigidly setting goals that must be attained. Such an orientation creates stress in children and interferes with relaxation. Make sure that you model healthy relaxation for your children through nonpressured, fun family experiences.

_____ 14. YOU DO INTERESTING THINGS AND KEEP YOURSELF GROWING.

In other words, there is a growing edge to you. And, as you create new and interesting endeavors for yourself, you take pains to include the kids. There is a creative energy that flows from within you so new activities are relaxing and fun instead of intense and competitive. One result is that life with you is not only interesting, but stimulating for the kids.

_____ 15. YOU SUPPORT AND ENCOURAGE CHILDREN'S CHANGING INTERESTS.

A child's interests typically change from year to year. You understand this and take pains to be supportive in helping a child learn more. And, you don't put down a child's interests because of your own biases. As long as a child is actively involved, you encourage that interest with resource materials, informal field trips, and even meeting people who are knowledgeable in that particular area.

_____ 16. YOU SHOW YOUR CHILDREN HOW TO AMICABLY RESOLVE CONFLICTS.

In all your relationships, especially those with the children, you always make a special effort to respect others' feelings and rights. When there are differences, you make every attempt to resolve them through talking, give and take, compromise, or creative innovation so that everyone's needs are met. And, for yourself and for the kids, you consistently demonstrate positive conflict resolution in your interactions with your spouse.

Learning for a Lifetime

The bottom line is that home-based education is, ironically, as easy as it is important. And, its importance deceives some parents because it costs virtually nothing in terms of dollars and cents. To maximize the tremendous learning potential of the home, what is required is parents who are aware and who are willing to create a family life that is rich in emotional and educational value. The key question that parents must assess is whether their home is providing the kinds of healthy and adaptive learning experiences that will serve the kids well for a lifetime. Or, conversely, whether what is being experienced at home will create later problems.

By way of summary, there are at least four basic learning modalities that occur primarily within the family environment. Parents must fix in their minds that each one is important and that each type of learning *is* occurring whether they realize it or not. The quality of each one of them directly reflects the overall quality of family life and the home-based education that you are providing for your children.

LEARNING MODALITY #1: EXPOSURE TO THE WORLD AROUND. These are basically experiences that broaden a child's perspective. In a world that is steadily becoming smaller, it is increasingly important for a child to experience the world outside the home in positive and stimulating ways under the protective guidance of parents. In this manner, the child comes to understand and accept the world outside the immediate home or community environment and knows how to deal with it confidently.

LEARNING MODALITY #2: INTERACTIONAL EXPERIENCES. This kind of learning accrues from the kinds of interactions directly experienced with parents during the developmental years. What was shared together, the kinds of feedback provided, the nature of discipline, and how it was implemented are all important. From these kinds of experiences, a child learns directly what relationships are all about and how people respond in various kinds of circumstances.

LEARNING MODALITY #3: OBSERVING OTHERS. Related to the above, but equally important, is what a child learns from *watching how parents relate to one another.* In fact, either positively or negatively, the parents' relationship with one another becomes the child's internal frame of reference for constructing relationships later in adulthood. Through observation of parents, important lessons about emotional intimacy, coping with stress, expressing emotions, and conflict management are learned.

LEARNING MODALITY #4: CREATIVE PLAY. Children are naturally creative and inquisitive. And, during the course of their development, they are constantly testing their world and trying new ways of relating to it. By encouraging such creative endeavors (and tolerating the problems and frustrations that result from it), parents can be of immense help in facilitating this kind of unstructured, but very adaptive form of learning.

It goes without saying that aware parents recognize the very significant influence that informal learning at home has on a child's later career success and fulfillment in relationships. It is only the naive who assess their child's progress toward success solely in terms of grades and academic performance. Only when parents accept the importance of home-based learning are they motivated to closely examine family life as they are living it each day and understand what the children are *really* learning from them. And, when parents take a good hard look, some of their discoveries may not be particularly flattering!

The fact is that narrowly training a child only to have an economically successful career without fulfilling relationships and quality life after work is a Pyrrhic victory. That is, it becomes a victory won at excessive cost. In the long run, it's not good for either parents or children. Emotionally undeveloped and with immature perspectives, the kids don't realize what's going on so you must. Someone who knows kids well has noted that "the reason children enjoy the present so much is because they have neither a past nor a future." But you have both and you know the score.

The big question is whether there is a healthy family living at your house these days. By providing a rich family environment for your children right now, you can help insure a fulfilling future for them because they have experienced a healthy past! There is no better possible return on costs. Not only that, it's emotionally fulfilling. It makes life much more interesting. And, it's extremely important, too. When it comes to the kids, for better or for worse, the past of their future is your present. It's up to you. Are you going to give them presents or presence?

Chapter 19

In Defense of Fun: Too Much Achieving Robs Children of Childhood

Everyone wants to have some fun now and then. That's what the good life is all about. Good times together. Letting go. Enjoying life to the hilt. You do just that on a regular basis. Right? Off the top of your head the answer is: "Yes. Of course, I do!" With a little more thought, though, you discover that you've had more fun in the past than now. Years ago, relaxing in good company and getting away from it all to enjoy pleasant activities just for you, just for the fun of it, were high priorities. Now, work has overwhelmed the good times.

From the perspective of maintaining lifestyle balance and being an effective parent, here are three diagnostic questions about leisure to carefully consider. Each one focuses on a key part of the good life that has probably been lost as you've become busier.

DIAGNOSTIC QUESTION #1: THESE DAYS, CAN YOU BECOME SO DEEPLY AND PLEASANTLY INVOLVED IN LEISURE ACTIVITIES THAT YOU COMPLETELY LOSE TRACK OF TIME? For most busy parents, it's no longer possible. Long years of training for success and living as a responsible adult require constant awareness of time. Your schedule now rules your life. What time is it now? Where do I have to be next? How much time do I have left?

DIAGNOSTIC QUESTION #2: AT THIS POINT IN YOUR LIFE, CAN YOU SIT DOWN AND DO ABSOLUTELY NOTHING FOR ONE-HALF HOUR AT A TIME? That means no newspaper, TV, novel, friend to talk to, or sleeping. If you're typical, you can make it for about ten minutes. You steadily become more anxious and seconds later, the guilt hits. Then, without even thinking about it, you get up and find something to do that is defined as "productive."

DIAGNOSTIC QUESTION #3: WHEN WAS THE LAST TIME YOU BECAME REALLY EXCITED IN ANTICIPATION OF A FUN TIME? Usually, it's been quite a while. With your hectic lifestyle these days, you spend virtually all your time trying to get on top of work at work and work at home. There's just no time for pleasurable anticipation. Instead, you work right up to the last minute and then you take some work along with you!

Now, take a look at your kids. They know how to do every one of these three things. And, they do it easily and naturally. Every child can get so deeply involved in play that time consciousness is lost. They can while away time with the greatest of ease without necessarily being "productive" at all in the adult sense. And, children get excited about things daily. The joy of experiencing the fun side of life is still alive and well within them.

The big question is how long these qualities will remain in the kids. Responsible parents, shortly after the kids are born, immerse them in an environment that embodies all the values of a strong work ethic. Mom and Dad begin to directly teach the skills necessary to succeed later in life. As a parent, you become angry when the kids aren't time conscious enough to come home when told. You rail at them constantly for "wasting time" and not being productive. You may even help your child apply achievement-oriented values to play activities and destroy all the pleasure in them as a result. The bottom line is that you are helping your children to lose what you've already lost—the abilty to play and have fun!

These days, there is little doubt that you must be motivated, work hard, undergo long years of training, and apply your intellectual knowledge well to become successful. The problem is that parents, often for highly questionable reasons, begin success training too early and in an entirely unbalanced and heavy-handed way. Driven by a deep fear that their children will not "make it," well-meaning parents push their children so hard virtually from birth onward that they rob their children of childhood.

These frightened and highly success-oriented parents are simply not cognizant of the long-term effects of what they are doing. Clinical evidence is accumulating rapidly that the ability to regularly "let go" to play and have fun is important to health, to the capacity for satisfying relationships, and for emotional well-being, not to mention the fact that much learning takes place during creative free play. As a busy parent, make it a point to preserve this special way of enjoying each day *for you and for the kids.* If you don't know how to play anymore, here are some pointers. After all, families who play together, stay together. And, they're happier, too.

Preparation for Tomorrow

As parents and teachers create an environment in which achieving and success are dominant themes, specific ways of responding are consistently reinforced and highly rewarded. The dominant message is clear and simple: "Work hard today so you can enjoy tomorrow. And, if you don't work for tomorrow, you will fail and never get to enjoy life at all!" This psychological mandate is such an ingrained part of an achievement-oriented society that many successful thirty-, forty-, and fifty-year-old parents are found still compulsively "working for tomorrow" without being able to stop and enjoy the fruits of their labors today.

All conscientious parents must clearly understand the values, attitudes, and skills that are the bedrock of becoming successful in the work world. Within broad limits, these ways of relating are helpful and functional in the marketplace. However, when carried too far, they overwhelm the individual's ability to relax and enjoy life. Here are the seven major components of the success orientation and the downside of each one.

SUCCESS ORIENTATION #1: THE DEVELOPMENT OF ANA-LYTICAL THOUGHT PROCESSES. Critical analysis of information via mental processes is essential to success. Intellectual development begins very early in life and never stops. Induction. Deduction. Extrapolation. Blending new information with known facts. Your ability to think well is the foundation for "making it" because so much of the work you do these days is done in your head.

The Downside: If you can't stop intellectually analyzing everything, then you can't enjoy sensory experiences or the beauty around you. As the saying goes: "Do you stop to smell the roses these days, or do you analyze the fragrance?"

SUCCESS ORIENTATION #2: THE NECESSITY TO ANTICI-PATE AND PLAN. One of society's rules is that to succeed, you are simply not permitted to live fully in the present. You must be constantly anticipating and planning for tomorrow and actively preparing to meet approaching responsibilities. Parents and teachers heavily emphasize this future-orientation beginning very early in a child's life.

The Downside: To the extent that children are taught to psychologically focus on the future, then the validity of the present is denied. Emotionally, the ability to "be in the moment" without worrying about what you must do next is critical to enjoying life.

SUCCESS ORIENTATION #3: THE MANDATE TO COMPETE AND WIN. Competition is as American as the flag, the Fourth of July, and apple pie. In fact, the entire educational system is based on competition and attrition. Those who learn how to compete well within the system gain the rewards of success. And, with well-developed competitive ability comes massive social reinforcement from virtually all sectors of a child's life.

The Downside: The self-esteem of children easily becomes heavily linked to successful competition. If a child has to compete and outdo others at all costs to maintain a sense of adequacy, then that child can no longer play for fun.

SUCCESS ORIENTATION #4: WORKING TOWARD LONG-TERM GOALS. Working toward goals with payoffs far in the future is basic to becoming successful. The individual must learn how to put off fun times now to continue working toward distant goals. The successful individual learns that self-denial, rather than indulging in immediate pleasure, is essential for achievement of long-term goals.

The Downside: Those who are highly oriented toward future goal attainment lose perspective on when they've become successful. Psychologically, they spend their lives waiting to arrive instead of living fully each day.

SUCCESS ORIENTATION #5: SELF-ESTEEM IS EXCESSIVELY LINKED TO EXTERNAL FACTORS. Parents, teachers, the media, and society in general subtly conspire to link a child's self-esteem to quality of achievement. The usual result is psychological performance-dependency. Then, the individual is emotionally driven to constantly achieve in order to maintain a sense of personal adequacy. If such a person has not recently attained a new goal, that person does not feel good.

The Downside: When performance-dependency is present, successful achieving must continue unabated or self-esteem rapidly declines. As a result, the ability to slow down, to relax, and to enjoy leisure activities for their inherent pleasures is lost.

SUCCESS ORIENTATION #6: THE "MORE IS ALWAYS BET-TER" PHILOSOPHY OF LIFE. This heavily reinforced cultural atti-tude says that if you have one, then two is always better. If you have two, then try to get three. Constantly building toward bigger and better things becomes an unremitting and powerful driving force within achievers; they are never satisfied with how much money they have in the bank, the size of their house, their status, or their other symbols of success.

The Downside: With this attitude, the important question is: "When is enough, enough?" The person who can't stop reaching for more not only has difficulty being satisfied with the present, but may also lose the capacity to enjoy what is already possessed.

SUCCESS ORIENTATION #7: THE NECESSITY FOR PROD-UCTS TO JUSTIFY TIME. A basic tenet of the work ethic is that you must constantly be productive and must avoid wasting time at all costs. A corollary is that you must always have products to show for time spent. Individuals with these internalized values usually get a lot done. Why? They are driven to continually work by guilt that rapidly builds every time they slow down.

The Downside: True relaxation requires that moment-by-moment experience be valued above all else. No necessary goals. No products needed. Enjoying such leisure experiences is seriously impaired because of the constant need to produce in order to avoid guilt.

Keeping the Fun in Fun

Virtually from birth onward, children enjoy playing and want to spend time in such activities. Very early, however, the parental mandate to begin training their children to become responsible and competent takes over. This basic conflict of interests creates the natural and ongoing tension between parents and children that is manifest through all the developmental years. As must be already evident, though, problems result when parental and social training for success becomes so strong and pervasive that a child no longer has time to be "just a kid."

As the active form of relaxation, TRUE PLAY is "any activity in which a child or adult becomes deeply and pleasantly involved and that is valued primarily for the process of the experience." FREE PLAY, an extension of this concept, is simply play uncontaminated by the work values and administrative structures characteristic of the adult world. All too often, parents inadvertently destroy the kids' free play by systematically distorting these activities into training exercises on the long road to success.

Free play is not only healthy, but inherent within these activities is tremendous learning. It is sometimes difficult for parents to trust that learning takes place during free play because it is not part of an adult-organized program. Yet, these same parents look back to their own carefree days of childhood with fond memories. Two suggestions for parents are warranted at this point. The first is to make sure that your children have enough time for free play. At least an hour a day is suggested. (**Note:** This time does *not* include watching TV!) Second, to the fullest extent possible, make sure the kids' free play (and yours, too) has all the following pleasure points.

PLEASURE POINT #1: THERE IS ONLY SPONTANEOUS PLANNING. In free play, there are no long-range objectives for the experience, and direction can change from moment to moment. Whatever feels good is what is done. Because there is no pre-planned structure, the moment is enjoyed to the fullest. The spontaneity and the impulsive nature of free play are part of the essential freedom of childhood.

Parent Test: Are you able to enjoy completely unstructured time these days with any planning done on a spontaneous basis depending on what feels good at the moment?

PLEASURE POINT #2: THERE IS DEEP SUBJECTIVE ABSORPTION INTO THE ACTIVITY. The "fun in fun" demonstrated by children during free play is due in large part to their ability to temporarily separate themselves from day-to-day realities. The kids aren't analyzing everything, and there is little or no "objectivity." Children become the characters they are playing and are one with the experience. In the process, they ignore time, problems, and responsibilities for awhile.

Parent Test: Can you presently "let go" in your leisure activities to the point that you are so pleasantly absorbed in the experience that you completely lose track of time?

An Important Aside. At this point, it is important to interject another diagnostic question that reflects a common and insidious problem for all too many parents. If you have confidently concluded that in fact you do "let go" deeply enough in a leisure activity to lose track of time, ask yourself this question as a follow-up: *"Can I let myself become so deeply and pleasantly involved in an activity which I enjoy that I lose track of time without being intoxicated?"*

When this question is asked, a significant number of men and women who thought they could relax and play, if they are honest, discover that they cannot do so these days without the help of chemicals!

The fact is that when the ability to psychologically shift out of a success-oriented way of responding is lost, it is very easy to begin making this same transition using chemicals. A drink . . . or two or three. Prescribed tranquilizers. Street drugs like marijuana and cocaine. The problem is that chemicals work only too well to "turn off" work problems and concerns, thereby relaxing you. However, using drugs in this way creates a prime breeding ground for a major dependency to develop. Then an established drug problem takes on a life of its own with negative consequences that diminish every aspect of life.

Now, while you're still considering this problem, take a moment to review all your leisure activities these days. Can you go fishing for a day without a case of beer along? Are you able to play a round of golf without stopping at the nineteenth hole before, during, and after? Do you have friends over and enjoy pleasant time together without automatically opening the liquor cabinet? If the answers to these questions are no, you have probably lost the ability to "let go" and have a good time without chemical help.

If you see this pattern in your life, it's important that you begin to make efforts to recover the ability to play and enjoy life by making a psychological shift instead of using drugs to do the same. While it's usually not easy or quick, learning to let go naturally once again is eminently worthwhile. Don't forget that the kids are observing you and may pick up the same maladaptive style of coping with stress later. Begin right now to take the chemicals out of your leisure activities and learn to enjoy life the natural way once again.

PLEASURE POINT #3: THE EXPERIENCE IS HIGHLY SENSORY-BASED. That is, emphasis in free play is on experiencing pleasure—period. Fun and pleasant sensations are the name of the game. There is no intellectualizing or achievement-orientation to it. Feeling good during the process is paramount. Although there may be some "building" involved (a fort, a play house), everything is done "just for the fun of it."

Parent Test: In your leisure activities, can you enjoy the experience without the need for an achieved "product" to justify the time spent? Or, to enjoy the moment-to-moment process without waiting until you've achieved a goal to feel good?

PLEASURE POINT #4: THERE IS EXTENSIVE USE OF NAT-URAL MATERIALS. In an increasingly technologically-oriented society, free play consists mostly of simple pleasures. There may be more fun and meaning in a homemade scooter or doll than those purchased at the store. The kids love to make things from materials found around the house (or the neighborhood) and use them for play. And, they will, if parents encourage these endeavors instead of hurrying out to purchase high-tech "store-bought" gadgets.

Parent Test: With your highly complex lifestyle these days, can you still shift gears to enjoy the free and simple joys life has to offer without need for expensive "toys?"

PLEASURE POINT #5: THERE IS ESSENTIAL CREATIVITY IN FREE PLAY. In other words, all children have tremendous creative potential that is consistently expressed during the process of un-structured play. When left to their own devices, the kids will create toys, put together costumes or uniforms, make up games, and construct their own shelters for indoor and outdoor play. Much is learned through this kind of creative expression.

Parent Test: At this point in your life, do you have a leisure outlet that permits you to be creatively expressive?

PLEASURE POINT #6: FREE PLAY IS AN "EGOLESS" ACTIV-ITY. To play without ego-involvement is a particularly strong characteristic of free play and of play in general. When kids play, they are just being themselves. There are no roles, facades, images, or fronts to protect. Little energy is invested in ego-enhancement by besting others through intense competitiveness. Instead, cooperative fun and camaraderie characterize their play.

Parent Test: When you relax these days, can you shed your work role and community image to be completely yourself in a relaxed and easygoing way?

PLEASURE POINT #7: PLAY ACTIVITIES ARE ENJOYED FOR THE MOMENT. In a healthy way, there's truly no future in free play. There's no past, either. When they're playing, the kids exist completely in the present. Someone has wisely commented that the reason children enjoy the present so much is that they have no past and no future to limit them. They shift into "timeless" play easily and often.

Parent Test: Are you able to fully separate from past problems and future expectations to exist fully in the moment for short periods when you relax?

Preserving Play: More Suggestions

In spite of powerful social and educational influences that often undermine time spent in quality play, the importance of this special kind of activity to the health and well-being of the entire family cannot be overstated. Parents must be the primary protectors of this time for the kids. And, they must spend time playing themselves to insure a fulfilling life after work. To back up what you already know about quality play, here are a number of play preservation strategies to use as a framework to protect you and the kids from the destructive emotional consequences of too much success-oriented work.

PLAY PRESERVATION #1: BEWARE OF TOO MANY EXTRA-CURRICULAR "ENRICHMENT" ACTIVITIES. These days, "enrichment" is often a code word for highly competitive achievement oriented activities. Frequently, parents involve their children in so much enrichment that virtually no free time is left. Practically every hour of the day is spent in activities that are highly structured, closely supervised by adults, and excessively goal-focused.

PLAY PRESERVATION #2: TURN OFF THE TELEVISION SET. These days, when the kids aren't at school or doing homework, they are likely to be found in front of the television set. Watching TV is *not* free play. Parents must turn off the TV and send the kids out to play to gain the positive emotional benefits of this quality time. The kids usually can't make this choice for themselves.

PLAY PRESERVATION #3: DO NOT SUBVERT YOUR CHILD'S PLAY INTERESTS. One of the best tenets for preserving quality playtime for the kids is to *let them alone.* Participate only when invited. Offer only an occasional tip or helpful suggestion. Then let the kids take it from there. Resist the urge to direct or take over the activity because you "know better." When you do, then it remains their fun, not your project.

PLAY PRESERVATION #4: WATCH YOUR CHILD'S COACHES CAREFULLY. As a parent, you must make preserving quality play time for the kids a high priority. Part of your vigilance is to remain very aware of the attitudes of various coaches who supervise your child's play. Inappropriate competitive behaviors, negative labeling or put-downs, and hurtful comparisons all show up. It's not good for your child, and it's up to you to stop it.

PLAY PRESERVATION #5: DO NOT ATTEMPT TO VINDICATE YOUR OWN COMPETITIVE FAILINGS VICARIOUSLY THROUGH YOUR CHILDREN. It is said that in the stands of every team sport played by kids are many failed major leaguers (*i.e.*, parents) who berate the coaches, inappropriately push their kids, and rudely name-call. When the game is over, destructive parental quarterbacking continues unabated. As a parent, if you can't be a sport and let your kids be kids, stay away from their games!

PLAY PRESERVATION #6: AVOID GIVING "TOMORROW" MESSAGES. Achievement-oriented parents reinforce in their children the idea that "some day" if they work hard enough, they will be happy and able to enjoy life. The hidden message is that you must be successful *before* you can have fun. Baloney! The high-achieving adult who can't relax belies this message. Instead, consistently communicate that you can work toward success and enjoy life simultaneously.

PLAY PRESERVATION #7: ACTIVELY REINFORCE PLAY AS AN IMPORTANT LIFE SKILL. It's quite easy for successful parents to put a premium on producing, meeting challenges, and succeeding. While these are functional work values, they are inappropriate when applied to play. In short, these values sabotage the ability to really relax and have fun. Parents must help the kids to understand the different skills required for work and play and then selectively reinforce different qualities in each type of activity.

PLAY PRESERVATION #8: AVOID CONTAMINATING YOUR LEISURE ACTIVITIES WITH WORK. Because busy parents have so much work to do, they don't take as much time for leisure as they need. And, when they do get away, they blend leisure with work. Then, while "relaxing," they are so distracted by work-related concerns that it's impossible to really enjoy themselves. Make it a point to model pure and uncontaminated leisure for the kids. You'll feel better, too.

PLAY PRESERVATION #9: TEACH YOUR CHILDREN TO EXPERIENCE BEAUTY THROUGH THEIR SENSES. Beauty is in the eye of the beholder. However, it is much easier to experience beauty if you are taught how to do so. Help your child learn to enjoy beauty by reinforcing feeling, sensing, and experiencing. When a child is taught to intellectually analyze everything, that child misses a deeper level of awareness and pleasure that contributes heavily to emotional completeness.

PLAY PRESERVATION #10: PARTICIPATE IN FUN EXPERIENCES WITH YOUR CHILDREN. One of the delights of parenthood is to share experiences with each child "just for the fun of it." This kind of sharing brings a closeness not otherwise possible. Pleasant memories of fun times together as a family provide inner strength during tough times and a positive bond to parents that lasts a lifetime. Don't let your children leave home without many such experiences with you.

Tomorrow's Child Needs Today

It is a paradox that children who are being trained to survive and function well in tomorrow's world must be able to live in and enjoy the present. Preparing for tomorrow, and denying the validity of today in the process, is a significant part of the liability that comes along with an overdeveloped work ethic. Because of the intensity and complexity of life these days, children must retain the ability to relax. A single generation ago, leisure activities were a bonus for hard work well done. Now, leisure time is nothing less than an absolute health mandate that must be worked into a personal lifestyle at all costs.

The bottom line is simple. As you strive to help your children become healthy achievers, it is necessary to make quality relaxation time an important part of your lifestyle. To do this, perhaps you must first relearn how to enjoy quality leisure time yourself. That means rearranging your priorities so that getting more and more things done doesn't erode leisure time. After all, your emotional and physical health may be affected by neglecting your basic needs right now. Then you must overcome your fears about your children's ultimate success. On the surface, leisure time may seem frivolous or somehow wasteful. In reality, it is an absolutely essential survival skill.

To make quality relaxation time a family priority takes personal strength by parents and in-depth perspective on what real success is all about. A few parents have always lived by a healthy value system, and for them maintaining a work-leisure balance is easy. For most, though, it's necessary to recreate life priorities that have been lost over the years. First, parents must closely examine the fast-paced social milieu in which they and their children now live. Then, from knowledge and insight gained, they must forge a healthy value system that often stands in stark contrast to the emotionally naive social values they are exposed to every day.

The price tag for not creating a healthy and balanced lifestyle for the kids to model may be high in terms of their later adjustment, their basic health, and their quality of life. Problems that could easily have been prevented may not show up until years later. Whether they realize it or not, parents who neglect these important life issues are taking their children on a long and emotionally arduous trip. They're boarding a fast train to the future. The next stop, Tomorrowland Station. Here's what this emotionally hazardous and psychologically needless ride is all about.

The Tomorrowland Express

Clickity-clack! Clickity-clack!
Tomorrowland Express. On the track.
Get on, you kids. You parents, too!
It's ethical. Right. Good for you.

Straight to the future, never bend.
Can't get off til you reach the end.
Analyze, plan, compete, and suppress.
The only ticket for this Express.

Bigger. Better. Now you're cookin'.
Tomorrow's ahead. Keep on lookin'.
Fantasy future. Wait til you're there.
Don't stop now. Don't ever dare.

Pushin' the limits. Not really livin'.
Denyin', denyin' each day that's given.
The future. Tomorrow. Ahead. Someday.
When I get there, then I'll play.

Years now ridin'. Endurin' the pain.
All my life on this hurryin' train.
Been waitin', waitin' to go out and play.
Been hearin', hearin', "another day."

I'm tired, tired and gettin' older.
And scared enough to be bolder, bolder.
Faster! Faster! Who's been drivin'?
Wonderin', wonderin' when it's arrivin'.

Gettin' off now. Do it for me.
Whatever the cost. Need to be free,
From the driver inside, pushin' ahead:
"Don't play! Don't play! Work instead."

Emergency stop! Had enough.
Waitin' inside. Long-ago stuff.
Committin' myself to enjoyin' today.
Makin' the time to go out and play.

Realizin' now. What's been lost.
Precious time. A too-high cost.
Better late than never, never.
Some ride the Express forever, ever.

Years and years, enjoyin' dismissed.
Deep regret. What's been missed.
Know this Express won't be arrivin',
'Til I realize it's me, inside, who's drivin'.

Decision's made. Livin' each day.
Family around me. No better way.
New wonderful feelin's. Not hatin', hatin'
To live my whole life, waitin', waitin'.

                              Bruce A. Baldwin

Epilogue

Doing It Right the First Time

As a parent struggling to do your best to raise healthy, achieving children despite changing realities and daily frustrations, you already know that experience is a hard teacher. There are some tough lessons to be learned during the years that children are in the home and are preparing for their futures. As a wit once remarked, "The problem with experience is that too often you get the test before the lesson!" While you can never know all the answers in advance when raising children, it is eminently possible to prepare well for the tests ahead. Advance preparation for these tests is what BEYOND THE CORNUCOPIA KIDS is all about.

A great myth abounds in middle-class households these days: that is, that the role of parents is to give and to give and to keep on giving to the kids. And, if parents do, then they believe that somehow, some way, these advantaged children will grow up to be just like they are: emotionally mature, responsible individuals with skills that reflect the expectations of the marketplace. It sounds great on the surface. However, on closer examination, there are enough holes in this parental assumption to drive a truck through.

While there is no doubt that parents must give to their children during the crucial developmental years, the key to raising healthy achieving children lies in *what* is being given. The key question is simple. Are you giving your children what they emotionally need to grow toward competent adulthood? Or, are you giving in and giving materially to your children as a response to peer pressure, superficial social values, and the immature needs of the kids? Only you can answer this question. And, it is a question that you must assess continually as your children grow and change.

The bottom line is that preventing the development of emotionally stunted Cornucopia Kids in your family is difficult, but it certainly can be done. Accomplishing this doesn't depend on your social status. Your address. Your career. Your income. Your savings. Your possessions. Your upbringing. Your ethnic or racial background. Or, whether you're a single parent. What it depends on is you. Your values. Your awareness. Your commitment to giving your children what they need emotionally, not what they want. And, the character strength to keep on doing just that for years.

In other words, the key to raising healthy, achieving children lies in the family environment that you create and within which the kids grow and develop. And, the value system that underlies such a family environment cannot be makeshift or random. It must be well thought out. Insights about healthy growth must be consistently translated into practice. Your parenting responses must fit well with the realities that children will experience later in life. And, these values must be thoroughly integrated into every facet of your relationship with your children. Like it or not, your parenting responses reflect your wisdom. And, the kids' experiences within the family and with you do make a difference. They will help or hinder for a lifetime.

But, these positive effects don't have to happen at all. It's seductively easy to give in and shower the kids with material possessions. Someone has commented, with a great deal of truth, that there are basically three kinds of parents in the world. First, there are people who *make* things happen. Second, there are people who *watch* things happen. Finally, there are people who *wonder* what happened! Perhaps you know some parents in this third, distressing category. BEYOND THE CORNUCOPIA KIDS was written to insure that you will *make good things happen* for your children. That you can *watch them grow* in positive ways under your guidance. And, that in the future you won't *sadly wonder why* they turned out the way they did.

Shades of Grey and Judgement Calls

It would be wonderful if all the guidelines and suggestions for effective parenting could be applied in clear-cut ways in every situation. Alas, such is not the case. Nor will it ever be that way. Parents must be reasonably flexible and compassionate in their decision-making. Not all situations are exactly the same. Each child has different needs. All children change with time. And, of course, there are shades of grey and exceptions to every rule. The fact is that no matter how clearly you understand how to raise healthy, achieving children, many situations will require a less than clear-cut decision on your part.

When judgement calls are required (and that is frequently), parents who have some guidelines available find they make more effective decisions. In those sticky six-of-one, half-dozen-of-the-other kinds of situations, here are seven rules of thumb to help sort out your parenting priorities.

RULE OF THUMB #1: WHEN YOU'RE NOT SURE OF YOURSELF, KEEP THE HIDDEN CURRICULUM OF SUCCESS IN MIND. On the surface, the Second Curriculum seems to defy much conventional wisdom about what is important to "making it" these days. While these skills are not regularly graded as in school settings, they become an extremely important foundation for success once formal education is completed. In questionable situations, make it a point to keep these seven skill areas in mind to guide your parental decision making.

RULE OF THUMB #2: WHEN IN DOUBT, BE MORE RESTRICTIVE THAN PERMISSIVE. Much has been written about the increasingly precocious behavior of children. And, what children are consistently exposed to these days, they are emotionally unprepared to handle. Nonetheless, the kids' immaturity or peer pressure pushes them forward anyway. Their long-term perspective just hasn't developed. But, yours has! In the long run, you will almost always come out better as a parent if you err on the side of being a bit too strict rather than too lenient.

RULE OF THUMB #3: WHEN THERE IS A QUESTION, THE RIGHT WAY IS USUALLY NOT THE EASY WAY. This is not only an excellent guideline for parents, but it is also applicable to virtually all of life itself. Taking the easy road usually leads to mistakes, hidden pitfalls, or long-range detrimental effects. Parents who help their children grow to be healthy achievers take care of themselves and put their own relationship high on the priority list. Then they are able to support one another and do what is right for their children despite temporary frustrations, stress, or fatigue.

RULE OF THUMB #4: WHEN YOU'RE UNEASY, LISTEN TO YOUR FEELINGS. Time and again parents who get off the track in their parenting report intuitive feelings of doubt and unease when dealing with their children. In the vast majority of situations, these feelings have a quite valid source that has simply not been clearly conceptualized. When your intuition gives you a signal, first treat that inner sense of unease as valid. Then, despite what you see other parents doing, look inside for the reasons for your reservations and respond accordingly.

RULE OF THUMB #5: WHEN YOU'RE WAVERING, DECIDE ON INNER DEVELOPMENT RATHER THAN EXTERNALLY-BASED GRATIFICATION. One of the major childhood problems these days is basing self-esteem and adequacy on externals. And, it's a problem for many parents as well. Because of the immaturity of children, it is necessary for you as a parent to thwart this unfortunate social trend. It's up to you to make sure that your children feel secure and adequate without possessing all the expensive and transitory "in" things. When you do, your children will have a definite edge over those who need materialistic external supports for self-esteem.

RULE OF THUMB #6: WHEN YOU'RE INSECURE, EXAMINE THE EFFORT-REWARD RELATIONSHIP. Children love to get something for nothing and so do adults. However, that's not the way the real world works. When there's a judgement call to be made, it often helps to examine whether your actions will reinforce the effort-reward relationship in your children. Or, conversely, whether the kids are learning that their actions have no consequences, that what they want can always be obtained through emotional pressure or manipulation, or that parents are always good for freebies.

RULE OF THUMB #7: WHEN IT'S A TOSSUP, LOOK AT YOUR EXPERIENCES WITH THAT CHILD. Children habitually want more than they are developmentally ready for, especially when it comes to privileges. The key here is not your child's age, but your assessment of that child's previously *demonstrated* ability to handle responsibility. Parents who keep giving and giving in to their children in the absence of commitment, responsibility, and trustworthiness are simply reinforcing immaturity. Do yourself and your child a favor. Say yes only when your direct experience with that child reflects an ability to handle the responsibilities involved.

Contemporary "Have" and "Have Not" Children

An astute wag once wryly commented that we are all born with an equal opportunity to become unequal! It goes without saying that in a democracy, each and every individual is guaranteed basic constitutional rights. On the other hand, it is also the nature of a free society to provide each person with an opportunity, but not a guarantee, to fulfill personal potential. In every community there are men and women who have "pulled themselves up by their bootstraps" by virtue of hard work and diligence. They are not necessarily the brightest.

They may not have had the top grades in school. Their parents might not be the most affluent. But, they did have a definite advantage. They learned the ways of the world and the skills required to create the good life for themselves.

Increasingly, however, the quality of parenting along the road to emotional fulfillment and economic success does make a difference. There are parents who, whatever their status in life, see beyond the superficial and teach their children the basics. And, there are far too many parents who naively "go with the flow" of what everyone else is doing, assuming that that flow is good. Thus, in this country, independent of socioeconomic status, children are developing into "have" and "have nots." The difference lies in the depth of parental understanding and the ability to parent in ways that promote learning the Hidden Curriculum of Success. In our society, these are the "have" children who often have more going for them than their more materially indulged "have not" peers.

Now that you're finished with this book, you know all about Cornucopia Kids and why they develop the way they do. And, you also are knowledgeable about how to raise healthy, achieving children. You realize just why giving too much to children may be giving too little. Again, it's up to you as a parent to make the choice to give your chidren what they need emotionally, not what they want materially. And, it's important that you make that choice and stick with it. The last word is simple. *In contrast to most life tasks, when you parent you must do it right the first time. There is no time to do it over!*

GLOSSARY

ASSERTIVENESS: The ability to openly but tactfully communicate feelings, positions or expectations to others and follow through with them in ways that protect personal integrity and engender respect by others.

CORNUCOPIA COCOON: The lax and indulgent home environment created by misguided parents that fails to teach the expectations of the marketplace and the requirements for mature adult functioning.

CORNUCOPIA KID: A child with the expectation, based on years of experience in the home, that the good life will always be available for the asking without the need to develop personal accountability or achievement motivation.

ETIQUETTE: Social responses reflecting the rituals and the ceremonial aspects of human interaction. Advanced manners in which the emphasis is on form over function. See Manners.

FIRST CURRICULUM: The formal education of a child taught primarily in school settings with emphasis on intellectual development through structured coursework.

FIVE C'S OF DISCIPLINE: Consistent Caring Communication about Choices and Consequences. See Parental Discipline.

FOUR I'S OF ADOLESCENCE: Idealism, Intensity, Immediacy and Impulsivity.

FREE PLAY: True play activities that are uncontaminated by the work values and administrative structures characteristic of the adult world.

GOODNESS OF FIT: The agreement between the values being taught in the home with the expectations of marketplace and the requirements for mature adult functioning.

HIDDEN CURRICULUM OF SUCCESS: A constellation of seven basic skill areas, critical to success late in life, taught by parents to children primarily through ungraded experiences in the family environment. Must complement the First Curriculum taught in school.

HOTHOUSING: A horticultural term relating to forced blooming of flowers by artificially altering growing conditions to hasten or "force" maturation. In parenting, refers to forcing precocious achievement in children prior to developmental readiness.

MANIPULATION: See Psychological Game.

MANNERS: Basic skills that help to order human interaction, protect health, convey respect for others' rights and that reflect sensitivity to the feelings of other people. In contrast with etiquette, emphasis is on function over form.

MANNERS MANDATE: The necessity for parents to teach good manners as the process of helping a child learn accepted social responses that will determine the quality of that child's relationships for a lifetime.

PARENTAL DISCIPLINE: The process of creating external boundaries for a child's behavior and positively and negatively reinforcing compliance with them to create the capacity to make similar choices as an adult.

PSYCHOLOGICAL GAME: An unhealthy interaction in which one individual uses an emotional vulnerability in another person to arouse emotions and thereby apply emotional pressure to facilitate meeting personal needs in an inappropriate manner.

SECOND CURRICULUM: A synonym for the Hidden Curriculum of Success that must be taught by parents.

SELF-DISCIPLINE: The ability of a child (or adult) to make responsible choices based on internalized values and personal commitments despite easier or more pleasurable alternatives.

SOCIALIZATION: The process of teaching a child the values and behaviors that are necessary for adaptive social living in a given culture. Primarily learned through interactions with parents.

TRUE PLAY: Any activity in which a child or adult becomes deeply and pleasantly involved and that is valued primarily for the process of the experience. A synonym for active relaxation.

WORK: Personal effort directed toward achieving a specific goal during which focus is dominated by the rewards, tangible and intangible, expected at successful task completion.

GAME PLAN

Your Name for the Game:
Describe the Problem Situation:

Analysis

Step 1: Describe the Provocative Behavior of the Player.

Step 2: Define the Emotions Aroused in the Pawn.

Step 3: Outline the Responses Expected by the Player.

Step 4: Specify the Payoffs for Player if Successful in Eliciting Expected Responses.
    A. Tangible Benefit(s)

    B. Emotional Reward(s) Ranked by Importance

        _____ Nurturance   _____ Attention

        _____ Revenge   _____ Control

Intervention

Step 5: State the Nature of Your Emotional Vulnerability.

Step 6: Define Healthier Responses to be Made in the Problem Situation.

    a.

    b.

    c.

    d.

    e.

    f.

Appendix 1: Outline for Analysis of a Game Plan

INDEX

Would Another Copy of
BEYOND THE CORNUCOPIA KIDS
Be Helpful?

Parenting for success is now more difficult than ever. Perhaps another copy of this insightful new book would be helpful to you or to others interested in raising healthy achieving children.

Consider these uses for BEYOND THE CORNUCOPIA KIDS:

▶ For YOUR ADULT CHILDREN to use as a guide now that they have their own families.

▶ To GIVE TO FRIENDS who are experiencing problems in parenting their children.

▶ For use as a STUDY GUIDE in parenting discussion groups and Sunday School classes.

▶ To suggest as a LIBRARY RESOURCE BOOK on effective parenting.

▶ For use by professionals as RECOMMENDED READING to parents attempting to resolve parenting problems.

▶ As an EDUCATIONAL RESOURCE for teachers and educators who are working with your children.

▶ To use as the BASIS FOR FUNDRAISERS by school organizations and community groups.

▶ To use as BACKGROUND READING for seminars on positive parenting.

▶ As a THOUGHTFUL GIFT to someone you care about—anytime!

NOTE: Substantial discounts are available for bulk orders of more than five books and for fundraisers. CASSETTE TAPES on many of the topics contained in this book are also available. Call or write DIRECTION DYNAMICS for details.

DETACH HERE AND MAIL

YES, please send me _____ additional copies of BEYOND THE CORNUCOPIA KIDS at $9.95 each (plus $1.75 postage). NC Residents please add $0.50 state sales tax for each book purchased. My check or money order is enclosed, made out to DIRECTION DYNAMICS.

MAIL COUPON TO: SEND MY BOOK(S) IMMEDIATELY TO:

                                  Name: _____

DIRECTION DYNAMICS   Address: _____

309 Honeycutt Drive   _____

Wilmington, North Carolina 28412 City: _____ State: _____

Telephone: (919) 799-6544   Zip Code: _____

                          Telephone: _____